BEYOND LEGITIMATION

Beyond Legitimation

Essays on the Problem of Religious Knowledge

Donald Wiebe
Professor of Divinity
Trinity College, Toronto

St. Martin's Press

First published in Great Britain 1994 by
THE MACMILLAN PRESS LTD
Houndmills, Basingstoke, Hampshire RG21 2XS
and London
Companies and representatives
throughout the world

This book is published in Macmillan's *Library of Philosophy and Religion*
General Editor: John Hick

A catalogue record for this book is available
from the British Library.

ISBN 0–333–61490–9

Printed in Great Britain by
Antony Rowe Ltd
Chippenham, Wiltshire

First published in the United States of America 1994 by
Scholarly and Reference Division,
ST. MARTIN'S PRESS, INC.,
175 Fifth Avenue,
New York, N.Y. 10010

ISBN 0–312–12084–2

Library of Congress Cataloging-in-Publication Data
Wiebe, Donald, 1943–
Beyond legitimation : essays on the problem of religious knowledge
/ Donald Wiebe.
p. cm.
Essays originally published 1973–1993.
Includes index.
ISBN 0–312–12084–2
1. Knowledge, Theory of (Religion). 2. Religion and science.
I. Title.
BL51.W3752   1994
210′.1—dc20
                                                94–8864
                                                CIP

Contents

Acknowledgements

The essays and papers in this volume have already appeared in various scholarly journals. Only minor changes have been made in reproducing them here. The changes involved bringing some uniformity of style to endnotes and citations, the corrections of some infelicities of expression, and the revision of exclusivist language in the earlier essays. I am much indebted to Mr Russell McCutcheon for his work on these tasks and for getting the manuscript into near final form. I would also like to thank Ms Muna Salloum for her organizational skill which benefited me enormously in bringing this project to completion, and Ms Anne Rafique, the publisher's editor, for advice and assistance which has saved me from a few serious blunders and so has helped make this a better book.

I thank the editors and publishers for their kind permission to reprint the following articles and essays which originally appeared in their journals and books:

'"Comprehensively Critical Rationalism" and Commitment', *Philosophical Studies*, 21 (1973): 186–201.
'Is Religious Belief Problematic?' *Christian Scholar's Review*, 7 (1977): 22–35.
'The Cognitive Status of Religious Belief', *Sophia*, 23 (1984): 4–21.
'Explanation and Theological Method', *Zygon*, 11 (1976): 35–49.
'Science and Religion: Is Compatibility Possible?' *Journal of the American Scientific Affiliation*, 30 (1978): 169–76.
'Religion Transcending Science Transcending Religion...', *The Dalhousie Review*, 65 (1985): 196–202.
'Is Science Really an Implicit Religion?', *Studies in Religion*, 18 (1989): 171–83.
'Religion, Science, and the Transformation of "Knowledge"', *Sophia*, 31 (1993): 36–49
'Has Philosophy of Religion a Place in the Agenda of Theology?' *Toronto Journal of Theology*, 5 (1989): 9–15.
'Postulations for Safeguarding Preconceptions', *Religion*, 18 (1988): 11–19.
'Philosophical Reflections on Twentieth Century Mennonite Thought', H. Loewen (ed.), *Mennonite Images: Historical, Cultural,*

and Literary Essays Dealing with Mennonite Issues, (Winnipeg: Hyperion Press, 1980): 149–64.

'Comprehensiveness as the Integrity of Anglican Theology', *St Luke's Journal of Theology*, 28 (1984): 23–38.

'The Ambiguous Revolution: Kant on the Nature of Faith', *Scottish Journal of Theology*, 3 (1980): 515–32.

'The Centripetal Theology of *The Great Code*', *Toronto Journal of Theology*, 1 (1985): 122–7.

'An Unholy Alliance? The Creationists' Quest for Scientific Legitimation', *Toronto Journal of Theology*, 4 (1988): 162–77.

Preface

The essays gathered here contribute to the making of a book I had never envisaged writing. In fact, the conclusions to which one is directed by the essays in Parts II and III are precisely those I had always thought I should eventually disprove. From my earliest theological training I had committed myself to trying to bring some resolution to the 'faith versus reason' problem in the history of Christian thought. It had always seemed to me, from my then 'faith perspective', that the perpetual tension between the two was entirely unnecessary. And yet the constant debate and conflict between science and religion from Copernicus and Galileo to Darwin and E. O. Wilson suggested quite the contrary. I was convinced, however, that resolution of the science/theology controversy would clearly reveal an essential complementarity between faith and reason. My research as a graduate student, therefore, was almost wholly comprised of an investigation into the nature of the relationship of modern Western science to theology in hopes of answering the question 'Can theology survive the impact of modern science?' in the affirmative. Having broached the question in my MA thesis, I attempted in my doctoral dissertation to provide for religion more generally what Ninian Smart appropriately referred to in his work as a compatibility system – that is, a way of establishing, on intellectually (scientifically) acceptable grounds, a structural identity between religion and modern science that would justify religion's claims to cognitive significance.

Despite several years of work on this project I was unable to construct the coherent and persuasive compatibility system I had envisaged. I did not, however, give up the project. I suggested, rather, that sure conclusions were not to be expected in projects of this kind. As I stated it then: 'In an enterprise of this sort the work undertaken is not so much completed as temporarily suspended, for the dissolution of long-standing myths is never likely to be the result of one quick, direct assault, but rather the product of a steady erosion, over a long period of time, of the uncritical foundations upon which they rest. And the assumption of an inherent conflict between science and religion which has been under scrutiny in the preceding pages is just such a long-standing myth'. Consequently, I

continued work on this problem for several years more, producing
a series of articles that I expected would eventually establish the
conclusion I had always assumed on religious (in this case,
Christian) grounds to be necessary – although of the variety of
necessity involved here I was never too sure. Although I appeared
to have made some progress on the project, establishing some iso-
morphisms as it were, between scientific and theological structures
of thought both in respect of doctrines and methods, the case on
behalf of compatibility on the whole always seemed to fall short.
Where substantive or doctrinal agreements between science and
religion were achieved, methodological procedures in arriving at
them diverged drastically and where methodological and structural similarities could be shown to exist between theology and
science the substantive claims of the former were extremely
improbable (that is, lacked plausibility), compared to the claims
made in the sciences.

Without appreciable gains, it seemed to me that the very project
itself might be flawed and that critical scrutiny of the assumptions
upon which the formulation of the original problematic were based
would be in order. This is not to say that I suddenly came to see that
everything I had written and published up to this point was wrong.
Nor did I simply assume that the lack of any startling progress in
this undertaking constituted irrefutable evidence for the falsehood
of the assumption of a faith/reason complementarity on which my
work had been predicated. However, it did seem to me prudent, in
light of the results of my work, or perhaps better, the lack of significant results, to consider that a distinct possibility. I became persuaded that persistently negative, or at best meagre, results required
me to put to critical scrutiny the assumptions upon which I had
until then been operating. This, however, not out of anxiety that I
should somehow find that my being a Christian and wishing still to
remain intellectually respectable in the eyes of the academic community had skewed my scholarship and affected my reasoning and
understanding. The possibility of such ideological influence on my
thought had always been an aspect of the 'critical apparatus' with
which I had worked, as it is for most philosophers of religion and
theologians. It is simply that, as in all intellectual exercises of this
kind, with repeated disappointment in resolving the 'problem'
under scrutiny, it seemed not only possible but probable that some
error lay in the very formulation of the problem itself or with the
assumptions on which that formulation rested.

My first step in this direction was to put to the question my perception of the assumption of an inherent conflict between science and religion as mythical rather than hypothetical. Furthermore, upon reflection it appeared to me that a rather significant, but as yet unrecognized, assumption underlay all my attempts to construct a compatibility system that would genuinely – on the cognitive/epistemic level – harmonize science and religion: I was, that is, identifying theology with religion. To put the matter a little less startlingly, I had been assuming that 'theology' and 'religious thought' were essentially indistinguishable and, therefore, that a harmony between science and theology implied a harmony of science and religion. Though the assumption was not surprising, I was not altogether sure that it carried the force of a self-validating truth. That 'theology' and 'religious thought' deal, so to speak, with the same subject matter did not seem more than superficially adequate grounds for the identity claim, for on such an account the philosophy of religion more generally would also have to be taken to be indistinguishable from religion; to be, that is, religious. The latter I was unwilling to assume, even though many philosophers do indeed approach religion in a fashion that makes of their work an essentially religious activity. Not all philosophers of religion operate in such a fashion, however, and it is obviously not essential to the task to do so. Moreover, on further reflection it seemed to me that some theologizing, at least in the history of Christian thought, was, and still is, considered to be detrimental to the faith and an undermining of the Christian religion. The intellectual ferment of the twelfth century, and especially the conflict between Abelard and Bernard of Clairvaux, constitutes a case in point. The conflict there appears to be a good deal more than a simple difference of belief, for the difference in doctrine and religious opinion is generated by a difference of intellectual procedure – of method – which suggested to me the possibility of the existence of rather distinct and opposing modes of thought being employed by the protagonists. In *The Irony of Theology and the Nature of Religious Thought* I put these assumptions to the test, not by focusing directly on the question of the compatibility of science and religion but rather by attending to the 'role' and 'relation' of theology in or to religious thought. By clarifying those matters I was able to show that the assumptions on which the construction of compatibility systems has proceeded are unwarranted and, consequently, that the quest for the perfect compatibility system, philosophically speaking, may be a wasted effort.

Occasional papers for a variety of conferences, colloquia and publications, furthermore, allowed me to explore various aspects of the science/religion/theology relationship from this alternative perspective. And it is the collection of these papers, together with those from the earlier period of compatibility system-building that comprise this book.

I have divided the essays into three sections or parts. The first includes those articles that either argued for the possibility of a compatibility system or developed one or more themes of critical significance to the construction of such a system, such as the structure and cognitive status of religious belief, the place of explanation in theological thought, and the complex interrelationships amongst reason, commitment and belief. Michael Polanyi's *Personal Knowledge: Towards a Post-Critical Philosophy* and Thomas Kuhn's *The Structure of Scientific Revolutions* played a dominant role in the argument offered in these essays. Further critical thought on the subjectivist impulse in the thought of Polanyi and Kuhn, however, revealed weaknesses not at first seen, and the meagre results achieved in these essays suggested that my early confidence in the possibility of revealing an underlying compatibility between scientific and religious belief might benefit from a critical review.

The essays in Part II were written in a deliberate search for an alternative framework to the compatibility system within which a more plausible account of the relation of science to religion might be rendered. This seemed to me a more appropriate response to my misgivings about the compatibility hypothesis than piecemeal criticisms of the weaknesses of my own earlier efforts at building a compatibility system. Having proceeded on the basis of an unwarranted assumption of the inherent identity of theology and religion it seemed not inappropriate now to see what proceeding without that assumption might produce. And what the essays in this section make clear, to put the matter bluntly, is not only that religion is not scientific in structure or intent, but also that science is not simply a different form or kind of religion. Religious and scientific modes of thought, that is, are shown to be so divergent as to be mutually exclusive undertakings.

The essays in Part III illustrate clearly the tensions between scientific and religious thought revealed in the essays in the preceding parts. The first two focus on specific and concrete concerns within particular religious communities while the last three are somewhat more general and abstract.

I am well aware that the overall thrust of the essays in this volume do not show conclusively the futility of the compatibility project. Nevertheless, in juxtaposing analyses of the science/religion relation in two paradigmatic explanatory frameworks I have been able, I think, to show that the compatibility claims made on behalf of religion's relation to science are not persuasive; I have shown, that is, that the proposed compatibility arguments do not provide the scientific legitimation for religious belief which is sought. Furthermore I have provided an alternative approach to accounting for religious belief (knowledge) claims that permits a more accurate understanding of particular historical religious traditions than does the more abstract intellectualist approach of the philosophers concerned with 'justifying' religious beliefs in light of contemporary scientific belief. Such an approach does not automatically entail the falsity of religious belief claims nor exclude an interest in the question of their truth or falsity. It does, however, show quite clearly that such beliefs are beyond cognitive legitimation in the usual sense of that notion and therefore that the religious believer, cognitively speaking, lives a kind of schizophrenic existence.

Part I
Compatibility Systems and the Legitimation of Religious Belief

1

Comprehensively Critical Rationalism and Commitment

The theologian's claim to cognitive significance for his or her religious beliefs is today under sustained attack from philosophical quarters as an outrage against not only reason, but morality as well. Reason, it is claimed, can provide us with an adequate account of knowledge and its growth – an account which needs no recourse to concepts such as 'faith', 'belief', or 'commitment'. Religious beliefs, however, as everyone knows and the theologian is quite ready to admit, are often espoused in direct contravention of such 'rules of reason' – they follow rather from religious experience; from 'the immediate utterances of faith'. Faith and reason therefore are assumed to be incompatible. Consequently the theologian is forced either to deny cognitive significance to faith (belief statements) or give up the claim to intellectual integrity. To affirm both is therefore to deny the possibility of a 'morality of knowledge' – a system of rational principles able to account adequately for our knowledge. And such a denial, it is warned, opens 'the gateways to intellectual and moral irresponsibility'.[1]

This challenge to theology's claim to epistemological significance is not exactly new. It is but a variant of a problem as old as philosophy itself. Unlike its earlier forms, however, this new 'dogma of the autonomy of reason' has a powerful persuasive ally in modern scientific method brandished as the paradigm of all rational procedure. With the success of the scientific revolution in its revolt against the Church (following the traditional account of Galileo's struggle, that is) and the continued success of scientific method, it appears that reason's claim to autonomy will at long last be made good. Hence the counsel of philosophers that we regain our nerve and 'counterpose the public and self-critical absolute of reflective intelligence or scientific method in its most comprehensive sense' to the 'tom-tom of theology and the bagpipes of transcendental metaphysics'.[2]

This paper tries to contest the opinions of such militant rationalists. The point of their challenge is simple enough: either reason (i.e., 'reasoning' or what Tillich calls 'technical reason') is limited or it is not; if it is unlimited and fully autonomous then there is no need of, nor room for, faith (theology) in the cognitive endeavours of humans; if it is limited, however, then there exists, by implication, a need for powers that go 'beyond' our reasoning powers. My defence of the theologian's claim hangs on the outcome of my analysis of W. W. Bartley's theory of rationality as set out in his *The Retreat to Commitment*. I choose to discuss Bartley's characterization of rationality because it presents, I think, the most adequate and most comprehensive characterization of the 'dogma of the autonomy of reason' using scientific method as its paradigm of rational procedure. Moreover Bartley especially sets out to rob the theologians of what he calls their rational excuse for irrational commitment – to deny them their claim to both religious identity and rational integrity (identity). My critique of Bartley rests largely on the analysis of scientific method as presented by Michael Polanyi in his *Personal Knowledge*. Before proceeding to my discussion of Bartley, therefore, I shall briefly outline Polanyi's characterization of scientific method.

The prestige accorded science as the paradigm of a rationality without limits is, according to Polanyi, wholly undeserved. It is so accorded, he claims, because it is thought to provide – and guarantee – impersonal, objective (and hence reliable) knowledge. This 'dogma of objectivism', as it might be referred to, the doctrine that impersonal objective knowledge is humanly possible, I take to be the central doctrine of the 'dogma of the autonomy of reason'. A contrast, it is assumed, exists between the objective (reliable) 'knowledge' of scientific procedures and the subjective (not wholly reliable) 'beliefs' produced by non-scientific disciplines. Polanyi denies that such a contrast exists – science too involves personal judgement so that:

> any account of science which does not explicitly describe it as something we believe in, is essentially incomplete and a false pretension, [for] it amounts to a claim that science is essentially different from and superior to all human beliefs which are not scientific statements, and this is untrue.[3]

Science, like theology, cannot escape its fiduciary character, for 'all truth is but the external pole of belief, and to destroy all belief would be to deny all truth'.[4] This is not to deny the significance of critical doubt but rather to acknowledge that such doubt is episte-mologically barren unless it is balanced with acritical belief and commitment. The aim of epistemology in general therefore must be 'to re-equip humans with the faculty [of faith and commitment] which centuries of critical thought have taught them to distrust'.[5] Thus religious belief and scientific knowledge (non-religious beliefs) differ very little:

> Though religious beliefs are often formulated more dogmatically than other beliefs, this is not essential. The extensive dogmatic framework of Christianity arose from ingenious efforts, sustained through many centuries, to axiomatize the faith already practised by Christians. In view of the high imaginative and emotional powers by which Christian beliefs control the whole person and relate him to the universe, the specification of these beliefs is much more colorful than are the axioms of arithmetic or the pre-mises of natural science. But they belong to the class of statements performing kindred fiduciary functions.[6]

There is much in this brief characterization of science which is 'hard to swallow' to say the least. Any justification of Polanyi's remarks must, however, await analysis and discussion of Bartley's treatment of rationality, based on an objectivist view of science.

An epistemology which can account for our knowledge and its growth only by reference to an element of belief and commitment on the part of the knower Bartley considers a conscious flight into irrationalism; a desperate and illegitimate attempt to save 'theologi-cal truth' (knowledge) from eclipse by 'scientific truth' (knowledge). The bid by the theologian for both religious identity and rational integrity in spite of this element of irrationality, was in the past legit-imately rooted in the then philosophical problem of 'the limits of rationality' or 'dilemma of ultimate commitments'.[7] The theologian, that is, was provided a 'rational excuse for irrational commitments'[8] for reason itself was unable to avoid ultimate commitments. Bartley, claiming that this is the only serious argument for Christian com-mitment, readily admits that 'if correct, the argument about the limits of rationality can then provide a Protestant with rational excuse for his irrational commitment to Christ and a secure refuge from any criticism of this commitment'.[9] Thus 'when the conscious irrationalist talks of "the leap of faith" he sincerely believes he is referring to a universal human condition'[10] and understandingly makes use of the *tu quoque* argument in response to charges of irrationalism in the theological enterprise by his rationalist opponents. It is the ground supporting the theologian's use of the *tu quoque* that Bartley sets out to erode: 'If I succeed in refuting the *tu quoque* arguments and solving the problem in which it is rooted, then [their] excuse will be invalid for future irrational commitment'.[11] Bartley therefore proposes an alternative characterization of rational procedure as the solution to the dilemma and the dissolution of the theological enterprise. I shall therefore proceed to an analysis and critique of his proposal that we adopt 'Comprehensively Critical Rationalism' (subsequently referred to as CCR).

Bartley bases his new theory of rationality (CCR) on 'Popper's observation that traditional philosophy is authoritarian or justificational in structures and [his] own observation that these philosophies have fused the ideas of justification and criticism'.[12] He claims that Popper was the first to separate explicitly the notion of justification from the notion of criticism and to maintain that the full character of rationality is contained in the notion of 'criticizability' alone: that is, that which can be held rationally is that which can and is always held open to criticism and hence possible falsification. Emphasizing the difference between this characterization of rationality and its predecessors he writes:

> It differs from Comprehensive Rationalism in having altogether abandoned the ideal of comprehensive justification. And it also differs from Critical Rationalism, wherein a rationalist accepted that his position was rationally unjustifiable but went on to justify it irrationally by his personal and social amoral commitments to standards and practices that were not themselves open to assessment or criticism since ... criticism and rational justification are fused. Within a justificational approach, such a move might seem unavoidable. We cannot go on justifying our beliefs forever since the question of the correctness of the conclusion shifts back to the question of the correctness of the premises; and if the premises are never established or justified, neither is the conclusion. Since we want to justify and cannot do so rationally, irrational justification or commitment seems the only resort. So, if rationality lies in justification, it is severely limited by the necessity for commitment.

But if rationality lies in criticism, and if we subject everything to criticism and continued tests, including the rationalist way of life itself, then rationality is unlimited. If all justification – rational as well as irrational – is really abandoned, there is indeed no reason to justify irrationally a position that is rationally unjustifiable. The position may be held rationally without needing justification at all – *provided that it can be and is held open to criticism and survives severe testing*.[13]

The sole task of such rational procedure therefore is simply 'to get rid of error wherever and however it appears'.[14] CCR consequently, claims Bartley, is both internally consistent and achieves a maximization of rationality. He concludes that:

the case for arbitrary ultimate commitments rested entirely on the claim that rationality was so limited logically that such commitment is inescapable, [but that] there are no such logical limitations for rationality in the proposed nonjustificational, critical approach.[15]

Although one might argue that CCR can be accepted as a logically adequate characterization of abstract rationality,[16] one is nevertheless forced to deny, I think, that it can provide us with a rational account of our knowledge. I shall argue that even if it is logically adequate, it is epistemologically inadequate. It can neither account for the existence of our knowledge nor its growth. CCR, being a generalization of Popper's critical policy in science, inherits the inadequacies of Popper's attempts to account for our knowledge in terms of 'conjectures and refutations'. This inadequacy, I shall attempt to show, can be overcome only by the adoption of a fiduciary element into the characterization of rational procedure – even the rational procedure of scientific method. And such a qualification once again permits the theologian to make use of the *tu quoque* and hence maintain her/his claim to rational integrity.

Popper's account of the growth of our scientific knowledge in terms of 'conjectures and refutations', I maintain, accounts neither for the transition the scientist makes from observation to theory (i.e. for the very fact that we even have knowledge), nor for the transition of scientific allegiance from one theory to another (i.e. for the growth of our knowledge). I shall deal with each of these transitions separately.

Popper maintains that the problem of the first transition, that from observation to theory, does not in fact even exist. He regards the problem of how a scientist discovers theories as being a purely psychological and not a logical or epistemological one. He is interested, so he claims, not so much in the fact that we do have theories as he is in the logical problem of how we get *good* theories. This can only be done by criticizing earlier theories in order to eliminate (falsify) the bad and inventing new ones to replace them (i.e. refutation followed by a new conjecture). One might object that in taking on such a task Popper involves himself in an infinite regress but he avoids that criticism by positing the existence of some primordial, innate hypothesis which is 'inborn knowledge'[17] – knowledge, however, which is not *a priori* valid. This concept of 'inborn knowledge' not only provides the dogmatic basis he requires for his philosophy[18] – it also, conveniently, permits Popper to deny that science proceeds from our experience of reality to theories of reality. The transition we must account for instead is that from a problem-situation in which we find ourselves, to a theory as its solution. And that is done, very simply, through a procedure of conjecturing and refuting possible solutions.

This I maintain is simply an evasion of the problem and not a solution. Popper's 'innate knowledge' hypothesis is both *ad hoc* and obscurantist in its effects. First, the hypothesis can be neither proved nor disproved because there is no way of testing it. It is invoked, it would appear, simply to escape an infinite regress in which Popper embroils himself by denying the existence of any transition from observation (experience) to theory. Moreover, it arbitrarily blocks any further research into the question of the exact nature of the relation of our bodily experience of reality and our theories that we develop to explain reality – assuming, as I believe he does, that the inductivist failure to establish the existence of a definite relationship between the two demonstrates the non-existence of any such relation.[19] Its function therefore appears to be merely that of avoiding criticism and preventing any further discussion as to the logical bearing of the discovery of our ideas on their justification.[20] His claim, therefore, that the relation of observation to theory is that of posing problems, merely shifts the problem without solving it. The difficulties of the observation/theory query are not so easily dissolved, for one must now proceed to a discussion of the relationship of the problem-situation to observation. The nature of that transition from observation to the problem-situation also needs clarification, for, as Polanyi puts it, the very recognition of 'a problem which can be solved and is worth solving is in fact a discovery in its own right'[21] just as is the 'discovery' of a solution (a theory or hypothesis).

With respect to the second transition, that of the scientist's allegiance from one hypothesis to another, Popper fares no better. Popper denies, and correctly so I think, that this transition is made on the basis of the verification of a once tentatively held theory or hypothesis – or from a theory not as well verified to a theory more thoroughly verified. He does not, however, with that rejection deny that the transition from one hypothesis to another is a logical procedure. Quite to the contrary, he claims that 'we must indeed reject the view that a belief in science is as irrational as a belief in primitive magical practices – that both are a matter of accepting a "total ideology," a convention, or a tradition based on faith'.[22] A logical transition is still possible in spite of the failure of verification to effect it. The alternative logical procedure suggested by Popper is a logic of refutation which is radically and fundamentally different from the logic of confirmation – the latter being inductive and so inherently incapable of providing logically valid generalizations from observation to theory, whereas the former is deductive, making the falsification of theories deductively valid by the classical logic of *modus tollens*.[23]

However, even if one does acknowledge that a distinction between the logic of confirmation and the logic of refutation does exist, one need not acknowledge, in spite of Popper's repeated warnings that a minimization of the distinction can only lead to confusion, that it has the fundamental significance he attaches to it. In at least one important respect the two logics are fundamentally the same – neither of them are, so to speak, 'logically airtight'. Just as absolute verification is not possible, so absolute falsification is not possible for the simple reason that the basic statement used to falsify the hypothesis in question is itself an hypothesis which may at some time in the future itself be falsified. He admits, therefore, that 'the empirical basis of science has nothing "absolute" about it; that science does not rest upon rock bottom'.[24]

Recognizing the justice of this criticism, he nevertheless claims:

I need not therefore withdraw my proposal to adopt falsifiability as a criterion of demarcation. For I am going to propose that the *empirical method* shall be characterized as a method that excludes precisely those ways of evading falsification which my critics rightly insist are logically admissable.[25]

Yet agreement on such methodological rules or principles has not been forthcoming. Since neither verification nor falsification can be absolute there may always be some 'ground' (for Polanyi 'grounds' that are not themselves formulable and criticizable) for the adoption of an otherwise 'falsified' theory or the rejection of an otherwise 'verified' theory. Thus Darwin no more gave up his theory of evolution in spite of the intersubjectively accepted basic statements of the physicists which appeared to contradict flatly his thesis, than the well-established, 'well-verified' system of Newtonian physics remained immune to criticism, and ultimately, rejection. Therefore, if falsification is never final, then the decision not to treat as false an hypothesis which has been 'falsified' (i.e. refuted by an intersubjectively accepted basic statement) is not necessarily irrational. Consequently the transition of the scientist's allegiance from one theory to another is no more a progressive step-by-logical-step progression for Popper and his nonjustificational epistemology than it is for the positivistic verificationists (justificationists). The transition in either instance involves a personal appraisal and personal judgement on the part of the knower. Shifts of allegiance from one theory to another therefore, cannot be accounted for in strictly mechanical or logical terms. (This is not to deny that science very often does proceed in accordance with strict rules. I merely wish to highlight here the distinction, made by Kuhn in his *The Structure of Scientific Revolutions*, between normal science and extraordinary science. To deny the existence and significance of extraordinary science, in which rules are contravened rather than observed, is to deny the heart of scientific progress – the growth of our knowledge.)

Bartley's Comprehensively Critical Rationalism inherits these criticisms. Like Popper, Bartley ignores the problems involved in the nature of the first transition by adoption of Popper's 'innate knowledge' hypothesis. Concerning the second transition however Bartley deviates just a little from Popper. For Popper the evidence gained while trying to refute an hypothesis may afford a good critical reason for accepting it, although only tentatively so.[26] Not so for Bartley. If, for example, survival of criticism is regarded as a criterion of acceptance, its inadequacy becomes immediately obvious; for by itself such a principle would imply that the scientist ought to accept incompatible theories because they have all survived criticism so far. Moreover such 'survival of criticism' itself could not provide any sort of absolute justification any more than could a programme of verification. (Nor is any criticism itself final and closed to further criticism and possible rejection.) Bartley separates criticism from justification. Nevertheless this does not, so far as I can see, provide any alternative account of how it is that we come to accept certain theories and hypotheses in preferences to others. He appears therefore simply to evade that whole issue and fails, by default, to give an adequate account of the growth of our knowledge.

Bartley's conception of rationality, it would seem, could appropriately be labelled 'rationalism with a vengeance'. Although inadequate of itself to account for knowledge, it refuses to recognize the necessary fiduciary component in all our knowledge for fear of losing itself in a sweeping fideist account of knowledge. Thus it pretends to autonomy and blinds itself to its own real but unrecognized fiduciary character in what, if I were to play psychoanalyst, I might suggest is a neurotic attempt to suppress the legitimate role of faith in all our cognitive endeavours.

If we do in fact come by our knowledge in a rational manner – understood as a logical step-by-step procedure, and if our knowledge grows in a similar fashion – then neither Popper nor Bartley has revealed to us the nature of that rational procedure. This does not prove that such a rational procedure does not exist. Nevertheless there does seem to be adequate evidence to suggest that the contrary is the case. Kuhn in *The Structure of Scientific Revolutions* points out that as a matter of historical fact, many of the major advances made in scientific disciplines were made not in a logical step-by-step manner but rather in direct contravention of such procedures that had been set up as normative for the discipline. Koestler's remark regarding Aristarchus' rediscovery of the heliocentric theory of the universe some fifteen centuries after its original proposal is apropos: 'We are faced here with one of the most astonishing examples of the devious, and crooked ways of the "Progress of Science".'[27]

If in the face of such evidence our scientific knowledge is still to be conceived as having been achieved in a rational manner, one must then deny the necessity of such logical procedures. Michael Polanyi does this. He claims a broader realm for rationality than strict logical certainty and goes on to state that the 'basis' of both transitions exists in a fiduciary commitment on the part of the scientist. To deny this fiduciary character of knowledge and rational procedure only continues the muddled thinking present in our epistemologies and the inadequacies of our theories of rationality:

whichever way we turn we cannot avoid being faced with the fact that the validity of scientific statements is not compellingly inherent in the evidence to which they refer. Those who believe in science must admit, therefore, that they are placing on the evidence of their senses an interpretation for which they must themselves take a distinct measure of responsibility. In accepting science as a whole and in subscribing to any particular statements of science, they are relying to a certain extent on personal convictions of their own.[28]

It would appear therefore that the deficiencies of Popper's and Bartley's accounts of our knowledge and its growth can be made well only if they qualify their characterizations of rationality in a 'fiduciary' direction. This does not deny the gains that critical philosophy has made. It rather complements the critical approach, rescuing 'what is best in critical philosophy by providing a Critique of Critical Reason'.[29] Polanyi succinctly expresses this dialectical – critical/acritical – nature of all our knowledge in explaining the aim of his own epistemological work as the attempt to provide ourselves with a framework which permits us 'to hold firmly to what we believe to be true, even though we know that it might conceivably be false'.[30] This dialectic I believe will become more apparent after an analysis and critique of Bartley's concept of the theological enterprise.

The implication that the adoption of CCR necessarily involves a rejection of the cognitive claims of all those disciplines recognizing a fiduciary component as a necessary element of our knowledge is to be found in Bartley's rejection of theology as irrational. An analysis of his argument however, shows it to be unsound. It appears to me that the analysis reveals not only that CCR need not preclude commitment from its account of rational procedure, but rather that no description of rational procedure which excludes such commitment is complete (i.e. epistemologically adequate).

Bartley concludes in the epilogue to *The Retreat to Commitment*:

> ... if my argument is sound, there can no longer be a general rational excuse for ultimate irrational commitments and those who continue to make them will *really* be irrationalists, in the sense that they will not be able to retain their Protestant theological identity with the intellectual integrity which the argument about the limits of rationality afforded them, as long as it went unrefuted.[31]

As the statement stands we can, I think, fully agree with Bartley. However, it seems to me that there is a tacit assumption included in the argument which is unwarranted. Bartley assumes that all commitments, and religious commitment in particular, constitute a conscious flight into irrationalism. He assumes that religious identity can only be maintained by an *ultimate* commitment where 'ultimate' means not being open to any further assessment or criticism and hence being, in principle, unfalsifiable. And this ultimate principle for the Protestant is to be found in the principle of 'Jesus is Lord.' He maintains that this characterizes 'a naively self-conscious Christian Protestantism resolved to hold fast to Jesus no matter now irrational a policy that may turn out to be'.[32] Even if such an uncritical position with respect to the identifying principle may indeed be held by leading theologians such as Karl Barth, as Bartley suggests, such a position is not itself a necessary requirement for Christian identity. Indeed it reveals, I think, a flagrant failure on Bartley's part to distinguish between at least two possible uses of the phrase 'ultimate commitment'. The first use refers to a commitment that is basically irrational in that it is adopted uncritically and never opened up again to further criticism or reassessment, for this would open it to possible rejection. I shall designate this the pejorative use of the phrase. It is this understanding which Bartley has of all commitment. The other use concerns a commitment which is 'ultimate' in the sense that it predominates and guides all subsequent decisions made by the person who holds it. Such a commitment, to be sure, is neither lightly made nor rejected, but neither need it be made 'ultimate' in the pejorative sense – provided one is willing to accept the distinction between apparent falsification and actual falsification (absolute). Basil Mitchell for example claims of the Christian theologian's commitments that though open to falsification they are very difficult to falsify absolutely. Thus such commitments are more than 'provisional hypotheses to be discarded if experience tells against them' and other than 'vacuous formulae (expressing, perhaps, a desire for reassurance) to which experience makes no difference and makes no difference to life'.[33] The principle of the theologian may be said to be ultimate in the sense that rejecting it results in a loss of Christian identity; it need not be ultimate in the sense that it is not open to criticism and, in particular, potentially fatal criticism.[34] Thus, while convinced that the principle holds and is true, one maintains identity as a Christian, and yet maintains rational integrity in holding that (formulated) conviction open to possible rejection. Christians, that is, hold firmly to what they believe to be true, realizing full well all the while that it is conceivable that they could be wrong. It must be remembered, however, that even though the commitment is open to criticism and possible rejection, the criticism of itself cannot logically force such a rejection. Bartley illegitimately appears to suggest something like this in his argument against the theologians:

> Some of the dramatic argumentative themes just discussed, which are characteristic features of the writings of such theologians as Tillich, Niebuhr, Brunner and Bultmann – ideas of sin and symbol, broken myth, and biblical *Weltanschauung* – are so intriguing and familiar that many people have come to regard them as the most important feature of contemporary Protestantism. This is a mistake: as perhaps only Barth has adequately appreciated, such arguments are quite unimportant.
>
> They are unimportant not because, as Barth might say, they are irreverent, but because they are not taken seriously. Although they are billed as arguments in support of the Christian position, they are not treated as such: when some of these arguments are toppled, the theological edifice they are supposedly buttressing does not even lean. And the fact that a man sees no reason to abandon a position when an argument he puts forward to support it is refuted indicates that his position, far from *depending* on the argument, was held independently of it. He may use the argument as a tool to convert others or to exorcise his own doubts; such arguments are the neon lights, not the foundations of the theological edifice.[35]

But this, as Kuhn in another context suggests, is the function of all argument, whether used in theology or science:

> to say that resistance is inevitable and legitimate, that paradigm change cannot be justified by proof, is not to say that no arguments are relevant or that scientists cannot be persuaded to change their minds.[36]

Thus, contrary to Bartley's claim, the Christian's commitment need not be 'ultimate' in the pejorative sense of the term, and hence need not be irrational in order to provide the devotee with a religious identity. It can be readily agreed upon by the theologian that Bartley is quite right when he claims that a Christian may abandon any statement about the content of the Christian message – on the ground that it is an inadequate statement of what the message really is[37] but that he may not *as a Christian* abandon the Christian identity ... which is submission to the Word of God whatever its content may turn out to be,[38]

for this is trivially obvious and acceptable. Surely no one can, *as a Christian*, abandon that principle which confers identity upon one as a Christian; but the same is trivially true for the rationalist who cannot reject the principle 'criticism is itself open to criticism' (which confers rationalist identity upon its possessor) without at the same time losing the identity which it confers upon its possessor. Bartley apparently thinks that there is a fundamental asymmetry between the adoption of the Protestant principle and the adoption of the Rationalist principle. I suggest, quite to the contrary, that the asymmetry exists only in so far as he *decrees* that the adoption of the Protestant principle must of necessity be ultimate (in the pejorative sense) in order to confer religious identity, and is consequently irrational, whereas the adoption of the Rationalist principle need only be tentative and hence rational, to fill exactly the same function. This is not a necessary condition for Christian identity:

> Though religious beliefs are often formulated more dogmatically than other beliefs, this is not essential.... The specification of these beliefs is much more colorful than are the axioms of arithmetic or the premisses of natural science. But they belong to the same class of statements performing kindred fiduciary functions.[39]

Therefore, I suggest that the theologian once again can make effective use of the *tu quoque* argument against the rationalist challenge. The rationalist who, for example, proceeds to criticize Christians by pointing out that if their identifying principle is open to criticism they stand in danger of forfeiting their identity as Christians – implying thereby that the Christian's identifying principle needs to be one involving an ultimate commitment (in the pejorative sense) – leaves the rationalist position wide open to the *tu quoque*. And this *tu quoque* unlike its predecessor does not preclude the use of criticism even with respect to one's own identifying principle, so that both philosophers and theologians may and still do defend their positions – as do scientists – and not merely preach them.

CCR, therefore, if taken as fully characterizing rationality, makes all our knowledge irrational. However, a little modification might easily make it a viable alternative; if CCR, that is, were to adopt 'commitment' as an integral part of the rational procedure, despite its initial appearance of inconsistency with the criticizability thesis. It appears to me that Bartley is aware of this lacuna but makes little issue of it:

> The claims that a rationalist need not commit himself even to argument is not that he will not or should not have strong convictions on which he is prepared to act. We can assume or be *convinced* of the truth of something without being committed to its truth. As concerned here, a rationalist can, while eschewing intellectual commitments, retain both the courage of his convictions and the courage to go on attacking his convictions − the courage to think and to go on thinking.[40]

To be sure, rationalists need not ultimately be committed even to argument, but just as surely they must be convinced that argument 'works', or else forfeit identity as a rationalist. Similarly Protestant theologians need not ultimately be committed to the 'Jesus is Lord' principle in order to maintain a Christian identity, although they too must be 'convinced' of it in the sense of seeing it as a solution to certain problems facing humanity. If such 'conviction' does not bar the rationalist from the courage 'to think and to go on thinking', neither does it prevent the theologian from proceeding in a similar manner. Bartley's supposed distinction here between 'conviction' and 'commitment,' as indicative of a fundamental distinction between fiduciary and non-fiduciary cognitive endeavours, therefore is contrived. Bartley's talk of 'conviction', that is, is simply a disguised reintroduction of 'commitment' into the characterization of rational procedure.

It is therefore, to an acritical philosophy of knowledge, a philosophy that sees commitment as a precondition of rationality, that we must turn in order to find a solution to the problem of epistemology left unsolved by traditional critical theories of knowledge. All accounts of our knowledge ignoring the necessary fiduciary component of it are found wanting. Knowledge, as Polanyi claims, is 'personal' and can never be adequately accounted for in strictly impersonal, strictly logical terms. I suggest therefore, with no pretence to having demonstrated the fact, that an analysis of those theories of rationality designed to provide us with a 'morality of knowledge', that will include scientific knowledge but exclude what is called religious knowledge, are either too strong and so exclude not only the possibility of religious knowledge but of scientific knowledge as well; or too weak, in that by adopting a viable account of the growth of our knowledge religious belief is permitted to slip in as 'justified' – i.e. as knowledge – as well. Thus, even while assuming a theory of rationality unable to account adequately for our scientific knowledge and its growth to be an adequate theory of rationality, the cognitive claims of the theologian are unscathed.

This adoption of a dialectical – critical/acritical – approach to knowledge and dialectical description of rational procedure may appear to be a logical muddle nervously excogitated as a last desperate attempt to save the theological enterprise from oblivion. It appears contradictory, however, only on the basis of the assumption of traditional critical rationalism – that is, that impersonal, objective knowledge (in contrast to personally held beliefs) is attainable. This assumption has not been borne out by the theories of rationality developed upon it. I have claimed therefore that the objective model of knowledge is untenable, and have suggested Polanyi's concept of 'personal knowledge' as an alternative – an acritical philosophy that overcomes the inadequacies of its critical predecessors:

[My] view involves a decisive change in our ideal of knowledge. The participation of the knower in shaping his knowledge, which had hitherto been tolerated only as a flaw – a shortcoming to be eliminated from perfect knowledge – is now recognized as the true guide and master of our cognitive powers. We acknowledge now that our powers of knowing operate widely without causing us to utter any explicit statements; and that even when they do issue in an utterance, this is used merely as an instrument for enlarging the range of the tacit powers that originated it.... We learn to accept as our ideal a knowledge that is manifestly personal.[41]

Polanyi therefore insists that:

the function of philosophic reflection consists in bringing to light, and affirming as my own, the beliefs implied in such of my thoughts and practices as I believe to be valid; that I must aim at discovering what I truly believe in and at formulating the convictions I find myself holding ... thus the process of examining any topic is both an exploration of the topic, and an exegesis of our fundamental beliefs in the light of which we approached it: a dialectical combination of exploration and exegesis.[42]

Critical doubt therefore, I maintain with Polanyi, is barren and must be balanced with acritical belief and commitment if we are to account for our knowledge. The holding of beliefs, religious or otherwise, is no longer a problem to be explained but a fact to be described. And this, suggests Polanyi, points to the religious-theological dimension of all human cognitive work. The task of the scholar in the academic community is, as much as is the task of the theologian within the community of faith, a matter of clarifying personal beliefs so as to establish a framework within which reason can function responsibly.

> Science or scholarship can never be more than an affirmation of the things we believe in. These beliefs will, by their very nature, be of a normative character, claiming universal validity; they must also be responsible beliefs; but eventually they are ultimate commitments issued under the seal of our personal judgment. To all further scruples, we must at some point finally reply: "For I believe so."
>
> We are living in the midst of a period requiring great readjustments. One of these is to learn once more to hold beliefs, our own beliefs. The task is formidable, for we have been taught for centuries to hold as a belief only the residue which no doubt can conceivably assail. There is no such residue left today, and that is why the ability *to believe with open eyes*, must once more be systematically reacquired.[43]

Polanyi's work in epistemology I suggest therefore heralds a late-twentieth century renaissance for theology in particular; the dawning of a post-critical age of Western civilization wherein we can once again respond, not to our Graeco-Roman heritage alone, but also to our Judaeo-Christian heritage.

2

Is Religious Belief Problematic?

A discussion of religious belief, as a discussion of belief in general, must indicate clearly and precisely the object and intention of the analysis to be undertaken. Care needs to be exercised, for example, in distinguishing kinds of belief – behavioural beliefs from rational beliefs, conscious from unconscious beliefs, 'belief that' from 'belief in,' and so on – if confusion is to be avoided.[1] Similarly it must be made clear whether the analysis is to concern itself with 'the logic of belief' or 'the psychology of belief', with the justification, confirmation and acceptability of beliefs or with their genesis and 'social legitimation'. Bearing in mind that these distinctions are largely 'analytical' and that one cannot rigidly separate the different 'aspects' of belief in any simple fashion, I shall nevertheless restrict attention in this chapter to the question of belief as a conscious mental state. I shall be concerned only, or primarily, with 'belief that' – with belief as the conscious acceptance of a statement or proposition about some state or states of affairs in 'the world', so to speak, whether past, present or future. 'Believing' in this sense is a cognitive state of mind, although this is not meant to imply that there are no emotional and expressive overtones connected with such beliefs, or that such overtones are of no importance. And it seems to me that religion also understands 'religious belief' to imply a 'cognitive act' or to involve reference to a 'cognitive state of mind'. H. H. Farmer is quite right to claim, I think, that 'once persuade the religious man that the reality with which he supposes himself to be dealing is not 'there' in the sense in which he supposes it to be 'there' and his religion vanishes away'.[2] Stressing the theoretical character of religious belief, however, need not imply that religion is nothing but such an intellectual act. Religion is, to be sure, more than intellectual assent to belief claims (propositions, statements, etc.), since it involves the

17

adoption of a particular style of life and a commitment to a peculiar set of moral ideals, as well as participation in ritual and liturgy, and so on. But it also concerns itself with an external reality. As Boyce Gibson puts it, 'Religion has an intellectual as well as a moral component. It is not a way of life imposed upon a state of affairs, it is a way of life with a conviction about a state of affairs built into it.'[3] Religious belief, therefore, is not merely symbolic and/or expressive but also theoretical and cognitive. That religious belief has a cognitive status, however, does not preclude its acceptability. The question to be considered in this chapter, then, is 'Is religious belief as theoretical problematic?'; 'Is religious belief 'cognitively significant' – worthy of inclusion in our "system of knowledge" of the world?'

There is, of course, an obvious sense in which religious belief as theoretical is problematic in modern society. Sociologists point out, for example, that religious believers today form a 'cognitive minority' and so feel the same pressures and tensions that other minorities experience.[4] But such problems are of a practical character affecting the psychological, and perhaps social stability of the believer. Such problems are not my concern here, except in so far as they stem from the adoption of a 'variant (deviant?) form of rationalism', for they are of an external and practical order and not intrinsic to religious belief itself. My concern here, therefore, will be focused on the rationality of religious belief understood theoretically.

Asked in this way, the question 'Is religious belief problematic?' it is argued, requires a positive response. It seems, that is, that the 'cognitive majority' within which even the religious believer is forced to live, has discovered, so to speak, a 'morality of knowledge'[5] that religious believers either ignore or contravene in the adoption of their system of religious beliefs. Their religious beliefs may be meaningful and suggest some criteria for determining their truth or falsity, but not conclusively so – not with the same 'certainty' to be found in the sciences. Consequently religious believers who claim cognitive significance for their beliefs espouse a dual epistemic standard. It seems, therefore, that they both affirm (in secular matters) and deny (in spiritual or religious matters) the canons of rationality discovered and so involve themselves in self-contradiction and, hence, irrationality. The religious believer, therefore, is forced, so it is claimed, to choose between 'religious identity' and 'rational integrity'.[6]

In a sense, this conflict between the 'cognitive minority' and the 'larger academic world' is a re-emergence of the old science/religion controversy of the last century and early decades of the present century. However, whereas the controversy then concerned only issues of substance such as 'creationism *vs* Darwinism', at least largely so, the present debate involves both the content of belief and the way religious believers gain and hold their beliefs. There is a good deal of recent philosophical discussion that claims there is a radical methodological incompatibility between religion and science – so much so, that the claim to cognitive significance for religious beliefs contributes to the 'corrosion' of the only 'machinery' we have of coming to sound judgements in matters empirical and theoretical.[7] Such action, so it is exclaimed (argued?), calls 'into question the very conception of scientific thought as a responsible enterprise of reasonable men'.[8] Religious believers, then, are in a cognitive minority, not only in terms of *what* they believe but also, and more importantly, in terms of *how* and *why* they believe. Religion, unlike science, espouses a 'second' epistemology which requires reference to belief and commitment in order to account for or 'rationalize' its belief system and that is considered a conscious flight into irrationalism. To suggest then that religious belief is cognitively significant, the philosopher claims, can but 'open the gateways to intellectual and moral irresponsibility'.[9]

A common response to this indictment on the part of theologians and philosophers of religion has been, simply, to deny the cognitive import of religious beliefs and to emphasize exclusively their moral/practical 'meaning'.[10] And that the problem is circumvented in such a tack cannot be denied. But it seems to me that the position embroils one in even greater difficulties. Taken as a description of how religious believers understand their faith it is simply false, for the majority of believers, as I have suggested above, take their credal affirmations to *refer* to a Reality, that is, in some sense, 'out there' and external to oneself, analogous to the way the 'world' is 'out there' and external to oneself. And taken as a prescription as to what religion *ought* to be (or as an essentialist definition as to what *true* religion *really is*) it is inadequate since moral prescriptions and recommendations do not occur *in vacuo* but rather presuppose or assume a particular kind of world in which these specific recommendations rather than others make 'sense'. Unless such assumptions are involved, that is, the prescriptions and recommendations are wholly arbitrary and hence irrational. A 'stance' that can recommend action without reason hardly escapes the indictment of irrationality and irresponsibility.[11] The noncognitivist interpretation of religious belief, therefore, is not only inadequate, but wrong.[12] Its

inadequacy, however, does not entail the truth of the original indictment. A cognitivist interpretation of religious belief that escapes the
charge of irresponsibility, I shall argue, is entirely possible once the
natures of knowledge and belief are properly understood.

II

It is true that science seems to have gained a 'convergence of opinion' on matters epistemological that religion has always failed to
achieve. It seems, as well, to have gained a rational understanding
and control of the universe far superior in these matters because it
provides an 'ethic' or 'morality of knowledge' – a way of distinguishing, in other words, knowledge from mere belief – an 'ethic'
not shared by the religious community. I have no intention of denying that such a 'morality of knowledge' exists. I shall argue, however, that such a 'morality' is not exclusive to the scientific
community and point out further that how that morality of scientific
knowledge is to be described is a matter of heated controversy and
debate. The root of the problem of interpretation in this matter, I
suggest, is the common but uncritical assumption that there exists a
radical distinction between knowledge and belief. To focus critical
attention on precisely that assumption is, therefore, the chief intention of this chapter. Remarks about the rationality of religious belief-
claims here, consequently, will be more general and of a more
programmatic nature.[13]

III

This generally assumed contrast between knowledge and (mere)
belief – and hence between 'scientific knowledge' and 'religious
belief' – no doubt finds its origin (in the West, at least), in the Par-
menidean distinction between *aletheia* and *doxa* adopted by Plato to
distinguish the absolute and immutable knowledge of the Forms
(*episteme*) from the 'knowledge-belief' (*doxa*) of the (constantly
changing) empirical world. This platonic ideal of knowledge that
precludes all corrigibility has dominated Western thought, and I suggest, still subfuses the present concern for 'objective knowledge'

based on rules of logic and evidence which can be easily distinguished from beliefs which, although based in part on evidence, rely heavily on imagination, persuasion and rhetoric.[14] 'Objective knowledge', it is supposed, is gained impersonally by following rules that exist outside one's mind, so to speak, whereas beliefs are much more idiosyncratic and personal; evidence and rules logically *entail* (and hence 'guarantee') knowledge whereas beliefs are, at best, *suggested* by the evidence. If it can be shown, however, that 'knowledge' in the sense of incorrigible statements or propositions does not exist, then belief and knowledge will no longer need to be seen as contrasting or exclusive terms and a morality of knowledge that attempts to delineate a rule whereby 'scientific knowledge' and 'religious belief' can be easily distinguished will be seen to be fundamentally misdirected.

Belief as a conscious mental state is expressible in statements and propositions and can, for my purposes here, be equated with its expression in fact-stating propositions. Such propositions, however, must be carefully distinguished from both sense-statements (i.e. first-person present tense utterances about one's own sensations) and tautologies (logical and, possibly, mathematical formulae) which really tell us nothing about the world external to ourselves and are, in principle, incorrigible. The former are purely psychological and the latter purely logical making them closed to further assessment.[15] It also, however, makes them empirically vacuous. Fact-stating (or *apparently* fact-stating) propositions, on the other hand, are of various sorts: they may be singular empirical statements informing one as to the existence of some entity or other (for example 'There is a Loch Ness monster'); general or theoretical empirical statements (such as 'All swans are white'); and metaphysical statements (which seem also to be either singular – 'God exists'; or theoretical – 'All that appears is *maya*'). Such fact-stating propositions, I want to suggest here, are all corrigible. That general empirical statements are so is clear since universal law-like statements are falsifiable by the occurrence of one counter-instance to the generalization.[16] It is obvious that such generalizations may have a great deal of evidence in their support and yet still be false, for no (finite) series of particular empirical statements *entails* the generalization. Scientific knowledge, then, composed largely of such theoretical statements, obviously lacks the *certainty* of the sense-statements and tautologies – and inversely so to the richness of their empirical content.[17]

That general metaphysical statements are similarly open to falsification is not so obvious.[18] It is difficult, for example, to know which statement, in fact, one ought to dub 'metaphysical'. According to Popper, for instance, all particular propositions are metaphysical since particular statements are unfalsifiable.[19] (They are only verifiable, and their verification, as will soon become apparent, is largely a matter of convention.) Declining acceptance of that definition as counter-intuitive I suggest rather that statements involving concepts with reference to non- or trans-empirical entities be read as metaphysical. Even this definition, however, requires some amendment, for on this reading some theoretical physical statements involving reference to micro-entities which are in principle unobservable appear metaphysical and it would, I think, be inappropriate to class more obviously metaphysical statements referring to God, Brahman, Nirvana, etc., with scientific statements in theoretical physics. The distinction between the two then seems to be one of content rather than structure. Consequently, if the latter are open to falsification then so must be the former, even though falsification there may be a more difficult undertaking. There is no ground for objection to their falsifiability in principle since even wholly trans-empirical terms and concepts and the statements that embody them may involve empirical entailments and incompatibilities that are embodied in statements more directly open to verification/falsification procedures.[20]

Problems arise, however, when it comes to particular empirical statements (and, *mutatis mutandis* particular metaphysical statements). It is not possible to argue the claim in detail here, that not even in singular empirical statements do we have incorrigible *knowledge* as over against mere *belief*, but the essential point can be made briefly. First, it must be seen that it is not possible to equate 'seeing' with 'knowing.' Observation, that is, is not pure sensation but is, rather, 'theory-laden' and so a function of the mind as well as eye. Seeing is always an interpretive undertaking. As Hanson put it, 'there is more to seeing than meets the eyeball'.[21] Popper refers to this as the 'transcendence' inherent in all description.[22] And Lakatos rejects this 'naturalistic doctrine of observation', pointing out that there is no natural borderline between theoretical and observational propositions.[23] Lakatos furthermore, quite rightly, points out that one cannot prove a factual proposition from experience. Propositions can only be derived from propositions and those propositions are in turn derived from descriptions of our experience – which, as has just been pointed out, are theory-laden.[24] All this seems to suggest then that there is no more certainty to be connected with singular or particular empirical propositions than applies to general or theoretical empirical propositions. One is forced, upon analysis of the nature of these claims, then, to conclude that there is no 'strong sense' of 'know' when it comes to observation statements, any more than there is a 'strong sense' of 'know' with regard to general theoretical claims. The certainty of which Norman Malcolm (for example) speaks, therefore, is a psychological certainty only, for singular empirical statements are not really different in kind, but only different in degree, from general empirical statements.[25]

If all factual knowledge-claims then are corrigible, it seems to me that one can rightly conclude that the generally accepted assumption of the distinction between knowledge and belief is not, in fact, acceptable. To speak of 'scientific knowledge' and 'religious belief' is therefore hardly fair. One must rather speak of 'scientific beliefs' and 'religious beliefs'. Scientific claims are no less corrigible in principle than are religious claims. Whether scientific claims have greater evidence in their support than do religious claims is then a matter for debate and not prescription. Further there can be no morality of knowledge that *guarantees* scientific beliefs, or any other beliefs. So the holding of religious beliefs is no longer problematic methodologically since there is no logical step-by-step procedure for the validation of any beliefs – scientific, religious, or otherwise. Whether the acceptance or rejection of a particular set of religious beliefs is intellectually irresponsible is a matter for investigation that must concern itself not only with the general principles of judgement but also with the principles of judgement appropriate to the set of religious propositions as a peculiar and specific domain of knowledge, as I shall point out below. It must, that is, closely sift and examine the evidence adduced and assess the value of the arguments proffered.[26]

IV

Such a reductive analysis of knowledge is not wholly free of problems and it must be admitted that it has its opponents. The problems, however, are not, I think, critical.

J. Pieper in *Belief and Faith* insists that 'belief cannot establish its own legitimacy. [He claims rather that] it can only derive legitimacy from someone who knows the subject matter of his own accord... [for] if *everything* is belief, then belief is eliminated'.[27] It is difficult to see, however, why such knowledge (*episteme*?), even if possible, is necessary – unless, of course, one assumes that beliefs must have some unshakable foundation. Surely if belief means 'believing someone' – 'regarding something as true on the basis of the word of another' – then a belief can be proper even though the other does not 'know' but only believes himself 'to know'. Beliefs can then be based on *supposed* knowledge – that is, on other beliefs.

Even if 'knowledge' is in fact definable in terms of belief it will still be necessary, as H. H. Price points out in his Gifford lectures, 'to distinguish between the sort of belief which amounts to knowledge and the sort which does not'.[28] As he goes on to point out, 'we still contrast knowledge with "mere" belief, and the belief which does not amount to knowledge is still regarded as an inferior substitute for the belief which does'.[29] It is obvious, however, that that distinction cannot be based simply on the attendance of 'complete conviction,' for that reveals merely a psychological (subjective) certainty. One must always, that is, distinguish between knowledge and the claim to knowledge.

The only mark that could distinguish the belief that is knowledge from the belief that is not, is *evidence*. And Price does talk of 'conclusive evidence' but fails to spell out what he means by 'conclusive'.[30] He admits that it is not deductive conclusiveness, and in another context, suggests that it is 'inductively conclusive'.[31] Yet the 'conclusivity' here is not equivalent to the incorrigibility claim of Malcolm. Price simply says, therefore, that 'conclusive evidence' is that which 'settles' the issue.[32] But 'settles' here is ambiguous in the extreme.

I do not deny that what Price calls for here is legitimate. But there is a way of satisfying his request that still keeps within the bounds of the reductive analysis of knowing that I have proposed above. Following Austin, it is quite possible, I think, to take 'I know', as a performative rather than as a descriptive utterance.[33] To say, 'I know,' that is, is not to describe a mental event or feat superior to that of believing but rather to perform an act – namely, the act of 'giving one's word' to someone, that in the light of one's present knowledge, 'that *p*' is true. The phrase 'I know' has a guarantee-giving character about it and is, therefore, much like promising.[34] To know, then, is a personal and a responsible act always open to correction, change and development and not an impersonal, wholly rule-governed and mechanical 'procedure.'

It is important, in the light of this analysis of knowledge and belief to re-emphasize that I accept the assumption that the sciences provide us with a paradigm for 'knowing'.[35] But what I wish to point out now is that there is no firm agreement as to which of the sciences is the paradigm science and that the right description as to how scientific knowledge is achieved (i.e. of the 'morality of scientific knowledge') is still a matter of heated controversy. If one considers the two basic criteria generally adopted by philosophers concerned with the question of the acceptability of beliefs, namely 'objectivity' and 'justifiability', one can, I think, fairly easily delineate the major 'moralities of scientific knowledge' proposed. Traditionally these two criteria of acceptability have been fused; that is, justified true beliefs were automatically objective in the sense that the proposition concerned was intersubjectively testable. In the early decades of the present century, however, the possibility of accepting one of the criteria while rejecting the other in discussing the acceptability of knowledge-claims (propositions) has been explored in interesting fashion. This splitting up of the formerly two-fold criterion of 'knowledge' gives rise then to four possible alternatives that may be displayed in diagrammatic form as follows (with apologies for the awkwardness of the designations):

| JUSTIFICATION | OBJECTIVITY | |
	YES	NO
YES	Justificationary objectivism	Justificationary non-objectivism
NO	Non-justificationary objectivism	Non-justificationary non-objectivism

Three of the four hypothetical possibilities have been seriously considered and persuasively argued as providing us with an adequate account of our knowledge and its growth (non-justificationary non-objectivism being excluded on logical grounds). The first, justificationary objectivism, attempts to account for our scientific knowledge in terms of talk of justified true beliefs. Such beliefs, in order to be justified must, it is claimed, be open to intersubjective scrutiny and hence must display an objective character – that is subject to independent and impartial (depersonalized) criteria of truth. Non-justificationary objectivism considers scientific knowledge to consist of mere conjectures as to the nature of reality which are open to (absolute) criticism and replacement. Scientific knowledge is distinct from mere belief, then, not in that it is justifiable as other beliefs are not, but in that it, unlike metaphysical and religious beliefs, is open to criticism. 'Falsifiability' is the criterion for distinguishing science or knowledge from non-science or extrascientific beliefs. Justificationary nonobjectivism involves the claim that all knowledge including scientific knowledge, is inherently 'personal' and so cannot be fully formulated, fully justified, or wholly critical. The growth of knowledge it claims is not, consequently, subject to the fully explicit rules of acceptability of either of the objectivist views. It denies, without, however, espousing an outright subjectivism, the existence of a wholly explicit, fully formulable evaluative standard whereby truth (knowledge, right belief, etc.) is to be distinguished from falsehood and error.

It is obvious that space does not permit analysis of the various proposals within this chapter.[36] I suggest nevertheless, that if the reductive analysis of belief outlined (all too briefly) in this chapter is in any degree acceptable, a fiduciary account of science will be required – that is, a justificationary non-objectivist interpretation of science will be required. The objectivist approaches in interpretation here, that is, can be shown to be inadequate in their accounts of how scientists proceed and how science has developed over the centuries. This case has been made in admirable – even if not wholly conclusive – fashion by Polanyi and Kuhn and has been supported by the analysis of the nature of science by others such as E. Harris, Paul Feyerabend, Ronald Nash, et al.[37] The question concerning which of the various proposals as to the meaning of 'the morality of scientific knowledge' is the most adequate is still of much debate. There is as yet no convergence of opinion on the matter of the morality of (scientific) knowledge.

V

If, as it has been plausibly argued,[38] one can adopt a pluralist approach to truth, and talk, therefore, of 'domains of truth' rather than simply *the* Truth, it follows that one must also talk of 'moralities of knowledge'. A domain of truth involves a set of propositions characterized, in part, by the fact that some of the principles of judgement appropriate to them apply *only* to them. In biology, for example, there are principles of judgement exclusive to biology and which, though they do not contradict the principles of judgement exclusive to physics (and in some sense even rest upon them), they nevertheless go *beyond* them. (Hence the distinction between organismic and molecular biology, for example). Consequently what constitutes 'biological knowledge' presumes a 'morality of knowledge' different to that presupposed by 'physical knowledge'. The same can be said of historical knowledge[39] and could be argued for moral knowledge and religious knowledge.[40] That a greater convergence of opinion is achieved in physical knowledge, then, is not *ipso facto* an argument against 'religious knowledge'; for by that same token 'physical knowledge' would seem to involve a denial of biological or historical knowledge. That *all* knowledge can and will eventually be reduced to physics (physical knowledge) is at best a 'research programme' and not itself indubitable knowledge. That such physical knowledge brings about a greater convergence of opinion amongst practitioners in the field may be due not so much to a more rigorous epistemic ethic but rather to the nature of the subject matter under scrutiny.[41] Physics, that is, deals with a primitive and therefore a relatively simple, level of reality. Matter, lacking the intentionality of sentient, rational creatures, is more easily scrutinized and more easily subjected to quantificational analysis leading us to expect a greater convergence of opinion in these matters. Claims in physics, therefore, are not, on that account, more acceptable as claims to knowledge than less conclusive statements in history. The difference in conclusiveness rests not in the peculiarity of the ethic adopted but rather in the nature of the reality under scrutiny.

To insist on a pluralist approach to truth involving a plurality of 'moralities' of knowledge is not to espouse an outright relativism. To claim that there are 'rules' of judgement peculiar to certain spheres of inquiry is not to deny the existence of general conditions in all 'domains of truth'. General rules such as 'the identity of indiscernibles', or 'the law of non-contradiction' are of critical significance in all domains of truth so that one can well draw analogies between the different domains. To claim that religious belief involves an abrogation of these more general principles of judgement seems to me a difficult case to make out.[42]

VI

The central problematic of this chapter is, it will be recalled, 'Is religious belief as theoretical problematic?' I have argued throughout

that there is no obvious sense in which it is methodologically problematic. The structure of scientific belief-claims parallels closely that
of religious belief-claims. And like the former, religious belief-claims
are corrigible and hence open to rejection. Scientific claims then are
no more inherently acceptable than are religious claims for both rest
on evidence which in the very nature of the case must be less than
conclusive. Furthermore, the fact of a greater convergence of opinion in science than in religion, as I have suggested, might well be
accounted for in terms of the degree of complexity of the subject
matter under scrutiny – and perhaps even more plausibly so – and
not in terms of a more rigorous morality of knowledge which is
ignored by the religious and undermined by the acceptance of religious belief-claims. Whether or not a particular religious belief-
claim is acceptable or not is not easily settled for such claims are
often 'peculiar' – not straightforward as are most empirical or theoretical scientific claims – and require not 'proof' but what Basil
Mitchell has called a 'cumulative argument'. As Wisdom has put it,
argument in this realm of discourse is less like the links of a chain
and more like the legs of a chair.[43] Argument in religion, that is, can
bring about a convergence of opinion (but that it is not epistemically
coercive is readily admitted and can be accounted for, as I have suggested above by its complex and 'mysterious' nature as well as in
terms of moral arguments against 'brute epistemic force on the part
of God').[44]

If religious belief as theoretical and, therefore, as falsifiable in
principle, is not a problem methodologically (epistemically) it may
nevertheless be claimed to be a problem *religiously*. It might be
argued, that is, that religious faith involves a certitude that beliefs of
such a theoretical nature lack.[45] I see no reason, however, why faith
requires theoretical certainty, for faith as *fiducia* or trust surely seems
to suggest exactly the opposite. I shall not attempt to argue this
point here for limitations of space. My only claim here – and it is an
important one even though simple – is that religious belief-claims
are not logically or structurally different from any other belief-
claims – of common-sense, science, etc. There is no sound argument
to show, I conclude, that religious belief-claims are methodologically problematic and hence in outright conflict with belief-claims in
other realms of discourse.

3
The Cognitive Status of Religious Belief

I

It will have surprised many, I suspect, to have seen Malcolm L. Diamond's article on 'Wisdom's Gods.'[1] This is not the kind of topic one expects to be discussed in the philosophical theology of the eighties. And it is obvious that Diamond anticipated the possibilities of such a response for he attempts to persuade the reader that he has found a 'fresh perspective' on Wisdom's work that makes this 'rehash' not only acceptable but necessary and important in the fight against positivism.[2] That fresh perspective derives from Diamond's apparently recent 'insight/discovery' that Wisdom's 'Gods' concerns the question of the cognitive status of 'God-talk' and that cognitivity is a positivist issue.[3]

According to Diamond, Wisdom, like Wittgenstein, had no use for positivist philosophy, particularly as it concerns religious matters, but unlike Wittgenstein, was not 'thorough-going' in his rejection of positivism.[4] Wittgenstein, claims Diamond, 'eliminates the gap that positivists set between what they regarded as the cognitive and non-cognitive domains',[5] whereas Wisdom in his concern with the cognitivity of religious discourse did not. In this difference, according to Diamond, is to be found the 'vestigial' positivism of Wisdom which, he continues, 'shows that he failed, at least fully, to internalize Wittgenstein's paradigm shift.'[6] Wisdom, like Thomas Kuhn, he maintains, ought to have carried this Wittgensteinian truth into the philosophy of science if he wished to evade the ravages of positivism in the philosophy of religion.[7]

Diamond's continuing concern with positivism in the philosophy of religion is, I think, a salutary one. His critique of positivism here, however, is unpersuasive and his interpretation of Wisdom neither fresh nor convincing. D. Z. Phillips who, like Diamond, is in sympathy with much of Wisdom's philosophical programme, raises essentially the same criticism now lodged by Diamond.[8] In an article with the self-same title, Phillips argued that for Wisdom, and mistakenly so, religious beliefs are hypotheses of at least a quasi-scientific sort even if not outrightly 'experimental'. Although the strategy in the argument differs the point is sufficiently the same (namely, that Wisdom did not learn his Wittgenstein well enough) to undermine Diamond's claim to freshness of approach in his discussion of Wisdom. Neither Phillips nor Diamond, however, seems to recognize that Wisdom did not fail to understand Wittgenstein; Wisdom, that is, both understood the radical character of the paradigm shift Wittgenstein called for and rejected it. I shall attempt to support this claim by providing an alternative reading of Wisdom's philosophy of religion. I shall show first, contrary to Diamond's claim that Wisdom was psychologically incapable of committing himself philosophically,[9] that Wisdom was in fact clearly committed to the belief in the cognitivity of religious discourse, even though he denied the claim that religious discourse is 'experimental/ scientific' in nature. I do not deny Diamond's claim that Wisdom's position is ambiguous. Indeed, his introduction to *Paradox and Discovery* is deliberately paradoxical in expression:

> In these essays it is submitted that questions which neither observation and experiment, nor yet further thought will settle may yet present real problems and even problems as to matter of fact. It is submitted that questions which 'have no answer' may yet present problems which have solutions.[10]

But the ambiguity, I suggest, hides a subtlety of argument that has misled his interpreters, and in particular Diamond. The ambiguity derives from the not altogether happy distinction that Wisdom draws between 'experimental' knowledge which is the substance of science (for Diamond, presumably 'bad positivist science') and 'factual' but non-scientific knowledge. Diamond fails to see the point in the distinction and consequently conflates the two 'kinds' of knowledge and concludes that with his rejection of a positivist interpretation of religion Wisdom really (although perhaps unconsciously), in the final analysis, rejected a 'cognitivist' interpretation of religious discourse. Certain modifications of Wisdom's position however – modifications derived, ironically, from the philosophy of science of Thomas Kuhn – will show the soundness of Wisdom's concern for the factual meaningfulness of religious discourse.

II

Diamond is quite right to claim that Wisdom was somewhat at odds with the positivists. Wisdom, it seems, understood positivists to have assumed the assertions found in religious discourse to be of an 'experimental' (normal-scientific) nature. Wisdom, however, quite emphatically maintains that it simply will not do to claim, as they do, that 'a statement hasn't really a meaning unless it can be settled either by observation or by the sort of definite procedures by which questions of mathematics or logic are settled....'[11] There are questions, and a whole number of them at that, he claims, which call for *reflection*, rather than *investigation*, and religious questions are included in the former group. Moreover, he claims, questions requiring reflection are on that account to be considered nonfactual. He explicitly rejects a suggestion to that effect by R. M. Hare in the 'University Discussion' articles.[12] He outrightly disagrees with Hare's claim that religious beliefs and convictions ought to be seen as *bliks*; as policies or attitudes towards the world which are neither verifiable nor falsifiable. *Bliks*, according to Hare, are assertions not factually meaningful, yet expressive of a deeper meaningfulness than factual assertions.[13] Wisdom's claim is that however much we emphasize that such belief assertions as 'there is a God' express an attitude or policy of action or some such thing, (and it is important to notice that Wisdom does not rule out the multiplicity of functions that theological utterances can perform),[14] they do more than this. Such beliefs also evince 'some recognition of patterns in time easily missed and that, therefore, differences as to there being any gods is in part a difference as to what is so and therefore as to the facts.'[15] In an article on religious belief he writes:

> Can we say that it is not of the essence of what we mean by a religious pronouncement that it should express some belief as to what the world is like? ... I believe the answer is no. It seems to me that some belief as to what the world is like is of the essence of religion.[16]

Of Jesus' words to the effect that in his Father's house there are many mansions, for example, he claims that there is a very important element, that these words and many others like them refer to something 'in the universe'. 'Words which do not do this', he writes, 'are *ipso facto* profoundly different. And they will lack ... what is of the essence of religion.'[17]

Such theological (religious) questions and utterances then are not beyond the scope of reason, even reason of a quasi-scientific sort. They are perfectly respectable as factual assertions, moreover, because as he puts it elsewhere, 'the reflection they call for may be carried out in a definite procedure which gives results Yes or No ... [which] takes us towards a better apprehension of reality....'[18] They may be subtle and slippery questions but are not such that nothing is more relevant to them than anything else. For example, to claim that God was incarnate in Christ, he asserts, is not to utter a meaningless string of words, but rather to make a claim to which every incident in the life of Christ is relevant. Thus in 'Gods' he points out that the disputants in a theological debate 'speak as if they were concerned with a matter of scientific fact or of trans-sensual, trans-scientific, and metaphysical fact, but still of fact and still a matter about which reasons for and against may be offered....'[19] However, he also claims here, a little ambiguously I think, that these utterances, even though factual in character, are *not* experimental in character as are scientific utterances.[20] That is, theological statements are not genuine hypotheses about something as are scientific statements. As he puts it, again in 'Gods',

> The existence of God is not an experimental issue.... In spite of this persistence of an experimental element in some theistic belief, it remains true that Elijah's method on Mount Carmel, of settling the matter of what god or gods exist would be far less appropriate today than it was then.[21]

In order to bring out this point clearly. Wisdom relates a parable, the well-known parable of the garden, which needs no repetition here. I shall however quote at some length the conclusions he himself has drawn from it:

> ... *we can easily recollect disputes which though they cannot be settled by experiments are yet disputes in which one party may be right and the other wrong* and in which both parties may offer reasons and the one better reasons than the other. *This may happen in pure and applied mathematics and logic.* Two accountants or two engineers provided with the same data may reach different results and this difference is resolved not by collecting further data but by going over the calculations again. Such differences indeed share with differences as to what will win a race, the honour of being among the most 'settleable' disputes in the language.

*But it won't do to describe the theistic issue as one settleable by such
calculation*, or as one about what can be deduced in this *vertical*
fashion from the facts we know. No doubt dispute about God has
sometimes, perhaps especially in medieval times, been carried on
in this fashion. But nowadays, it is not and we must look for some
other analogy, some other case in which a dispute is settled but
not by experiment.[22]

Wisdom finds that analogy in the procedure to be found in courts of
law where opposing counsel, who are often agreed as to the 'facts'
of the case at issue, yet find that they disagree as to the conclusion of
it. Argument in such a situation, he says, is not a chain of demon-
strative reasoning, but rather 'it is a presenting and representing of
those features of the case which severally co-operate in favour of the
conclusion.... The reasons are like the legs of a chair, not the links of
a chain.'[23] Although this might suggest that the argument lends
itself to description in terms of conflicting probabilities, this is a
muddle, for it is in fact wholly *a priori*. And it is *a priori* basically
because the dispute does not lead one to expect something further –
something beyond the facts already at hand. For example, the issue
at stake in this rather queer kind of question is not at all like that in
the question, 'Has Jack diphtheria?'[24] The latter question can easily
be settled by taking a swab from Jack's throat, for if he does have
diphtheria we expect to find a particular type of medical analysis of
the swab. Thus whether or not Jack has diphtheria is confirmable by
reference to such further empirical observations. There are, he
claims, no such conceivable future tests however with respect to
theological claims. (I will, below, voice some disagreement with this
claim but will also show that the disagreement need not amount to a
rejection of Wisdom's thought.)

Yet the decision taken here is not arbitrary. It involves making a
declaration and taking up an attitude as the result of argument or
reasoning. There are, that is, peculiar epistemological techniques
whereby reasoned conclusions can be reached on issues such as
these. These are the connecting and disconnecting techniques of
which Wisdom speaks in 'Gods'. The procedure is straightforward
and fairly simple. In using the connecting technique the disputant
concentrates his/her attention on the overall picture which is of significance to him/her, attempting to throw light on particular aspects
of it by showing how the various aspects of the whole are connected
in specific ways so as to produce a pattern or some semblance of

order that one's antagonist might see as well. The disconnecting technique is simply the reverse, namely, an attempt to persuade one's opponent that he/she has been making 'unwarranted' connections – connections that somehow did not add up to a significant overall picture of the situation. Each of the disputants, therefore, in the use both of connecting and disconnecting techniques attempts to bring about a gestalt-switch, so to speak, in the other; to provide the other, if possible, with a totally different perspective in which to view the 'facts' – indeed, which even, in some sense, changes the 'facts.'

III

In rejecting the 'Mount Carmel' model of religious discourse it is true that Wisdom rejects modern experimental science as in any sense paradigmatic of religious discourse. However, in insisting on the factual character of religious claims Wisdom also seems to be suggesting some analogy between scientific and religious discourse and therefore quite consciously rejecting the Wittgensteinian paradigm shift. The tension generated by this duality of vision in Wisdom is reduced by Diamond in reading him as a naive philosopher who had not learned his Wittgenstein well. Such a reading, however, does not do justice to the texts, nor, I think, to the intentions of the author of the texts. I shall look briefly at some of the evidence that might substantiate that judgement.

In his attempt to show that theological issues are not merely time-consuming blind alleys, Wisdom draws some very important parallels between science and theology which clearly suggest that the theological issue is indeed a scientific one, although a scientific issue of an *extraordinary* kind. This qualification will likely be claimed to be an evasion of the original problem faced by Wisdom in his rejection of positivism. But this is not in fact the case, for as Kuhn has shown in his *The Structure of Scientific Revolutions*, not all scientific issues are ordinary scientific issues soluble in the same logical or mathematical fashion. Even the natural sciences, that is, have both an ordinary and an extraordinary aspect. And the latter aspect of the sciences is as much 'scientific' as is the former. Some elucidation is appropriate here although I shall in no wise attempt a defence of Kuhn in the space available to me here.[25]

'Normal science' for Kuhn means research based firmly on some past scientific achievement seen as paradigmatic by the entire community of researchers. The transition of allegiance on the part of scientists from one paradigm to another (due to certain inevitable developments in normal science) constitutes extraordinary science, for it seems to 'occur' outside of any and all rational frameworks. Normal scientific research is guided by the framework provided by the paradigm; extraordinary scientific decisions, since they involve paradigm change, cannot be so guided. Kuhn summarizes the situation thus:

> These three classes of problems – determination of significant fact, matching of facts with theory, and articulation of theory – exhaust, I think, the literature of normal science, both empirical and theoretical. They do not of course, quite exhaust the entire literature of science. There are also extraordinary problems, and it may well be their resolution that makes the scientific enterprise as a whole so particularly worthwhile.[26]

In the light of this understanding of the nature of science furnished us by Kuhn, it is extremely interesting to note that Wisdom compares the type of apprehension of reality that the theologian provides with that given to us by Newton:

> Newton with his doctrine of gravitation gave us a so much greater apprehension of nature not so much because he told us what we would or would not see, like Pasteur or one who predicts what will be first past the post, but because he enabled us to see anew a thousand familiar incidents.[27]

To be sure, such a description (or evaluation) of Newton's contribution to the world of science is correct, but it is not the whole story. Newton did make it possible to predict events not predictable by his predecessors and he did so in fact precisely because he provided us with a new interpretation of 'a thousand familiar incidents'. Similarly Einstein has revolutionized our understanding of a myriad 'facts' and yet his conceptual revolution too has led to new discoveries. Wisdom overlooks this very important aspect of the conceptual revolutions that have taken place in science. And these extraordinary scientific 'discoveries' (?), it is important to note, are of the essence of science, even though the disputants in the debate during the revolution cannot settle their differences in a logical step-by-step procedure. Argument in extraordinary science that is, is less like the links of a chain and more like the legs of a chair – but it is still science. The extraordinary scientific 'discovery' then is not irrational. Argument is still important in attempting to get one's opponent to see one's own point of view in the matter – to get him/her to experience that all-important 'gestalt-switch'.[28] One could well apply Wisdom's terminology in a discussion of Kuhn's work at this point – that is, Kuhn's talk of the role of argument in such a situation resembles what Wisdom calls connecting and disconnecting techniques and both agree that whatever the role of argument is here, it is not a strictly deductive affair.

It is here then that I think Wisdom is misled into claiming that religious questions are not all experimental or scientific. Wisdom, on the explicit level of his argument, assumes that all scientific argument is a logical step-by-step affair – like the links of a chain. But this is in fact so only for a part of science, only for 'normal science'. Furthermore, there are undercurrents in his thought that seem to break away from the structures of his explicit argument. And the reasoning employed in 'extraordinary science' is precisely that described by Wisdom in those undercurrents. I do not say that the dispute over religious questions is, for Wisdom, like that over issues in 'normal science' but that they are, in a broader sense, scientific nevertheless. And an understanding of Wisdom that sees his experimental/factual distinction in this way, I maintain, does less violence both to the text and the intention of the author than does the Wittgensteinian, non-cognitivist interpretations offered once again to us by Diamond.[29]

IV

A brief comparison of Wisdom and John Hick on the question of the cognitivity of religious assertions will support the analysis just given and will highlight the 'undercurrent' argument in Wisdom to which I referred in the preceding section. Hick, it is fair to say, is much more sensitive to the positivist challenge to religious belief than is Wisdom and yet, as I shall attempt to show, there is not a vast difference between the two philosophers.

In *Faith and Knowledge* and 'Theology and Verification', John Hick maintains, and with some plausibility I think, that the theistic position is indeed an experimental (scientific) one because it does in fact *predict* a future state of affairs different from that predicted by an atheistic or humanistic view of 'the world'.[30] Initially it might seem that Hick's view of the matter is almost identical to Wisdom's when he writes: 'The monotheist's faith apprehension of God as the unseen Person dealing with him in and through experience of the world is from the point of view of epistemology an interpretation ... of the world as a whole mediating a divine presence and purpose'.[31] The atheist, in Kuhnian fashion, lives in a 'different world' while yet living in the 'same world' as the theist – that is, he/she places a different interpretation on the 'same facts.' Hick does not, moreover, see this activity of interpretation or significance-attribution as at all like the scientist's positing of micro-entities such as electrons, for example, to account for macro-phenomena. It is rather, he says, more like 'seeing-as' – a coming to appreciate familiar data in a fresh way.

Nevertheless, the issue between the theist and the atheist is yet, according to Hick, a decidable one in much the same fashion as are scientific disputes. It may not be a here-and-now, conclusively decidable question, but rather one that will be settled by certain events of the future. Hick, like Wisdom, makes this point in parabolic fashion. This parable too is familiar enough that it need not be repeated here. The thrust of the story is simply this – at the end of one's 'life's journey' the issue as to whether or not there is a God-created world will be settled by, first, whether one lives on after death and second, by the nature of the life that one then enjoys. In 'Theology and Verification' he summarizes as follows:

> ... a survival prediction such as is contained in the *corpus* of Christian belief is in principle subject to future verification. But this does not take the argument by any means as far as it must go if it is to succeed. For survival simply as such, would not serve to verify theism. It would not necessarily be a state of affairs which is manifestly incompatible with the non-existence of God.... The mere fact of survival, with a new body in a new environment, would not demonstrate to him that there is a God.... There are ... two possible developments of our experience however such that if they occurred in conjunction with one another (whether in this life or in the life to come) they would assure us beyond rational doubt of the reality of God, as conceived in the Christian faith. These are, *first*, an experience of the fulfilment of God's purpose for ourselves, as this has been disclosed in the Christian

revelation: in conjunction *second*, with an experience of communion with God as he has revealed himself in the person of Christ.[32]

It is possible that one might argue that this is still not an experimental issue as are issues in the natural sciences because in this case one does not actively set up an experimental situation whereby nature is forced to answer questions but rather sits and waits until death delivers the answer. Thus it might be claimed that the latter issue is an *experiential* one and not *experimental*. This difference exists, to be sure, and yet, in so far as the issue is that of positivism and the cognitivity of religious assertions the difference is negligible. The point quite simply is this, does the sentence, 'There is a God' predict any future state of affairs other than those expected by the atheist or humanist, and is the prediction in principle verifiable? Hick's answer to both these questions is 'Yes'.

Wisdom, it must be admitted, seems to ignore the force of such arguments and in this he seems to confirm some elements of Diamond's interpretation. In 'Gods' he simply pronounces:

> ... I do not want to consider here expectations as to what one will see and feel after death nor what sort of reasons these logically unique expectations could have.... I want to consider the difference between atheists and theists insofar as these differences are not a matter of belief in a future life.[33]

Nevertheless, his position is not as clear as this remark might suggest for he does not here categorically deny, as does Wittgenstein, that it is appropriate to consider the differences between the atheist and the theist as a matter of belief about a future state of affairs. Moreover, in 'The Logic of God', he himself suggests that theological utterances are indeed eschatologically verifiable and claims that if they were not, they would be meaningless. The positivist interlocutor who asks what difference the statement 'There is a God' would make – who asks whether any agreement as to the character of the order of events is necessary to affirm the statement – receives this reply: 'If there were *no* agreements that *would* make the question meaningless. But it is not true that there is no agreement. One could describe a future for the world which, were it to come, would prove the triumph of the Devil'.[34]

In light of these comments on Wisdom then, it seems to me that Antony Flew's interpretation and extension of Wisdom's parable in the 'University Discussion' in *New Essays in Philosophical Theology* is, in essentials, legitimate despite Wisdom's rejection of it in his 'Religious Belief'.[35] According to Flew, if the difference between one who accepts belief in the existence of God and one who does not is not a matter of the one rejecting something in the pattern of things somewhere which the other does not, it is informationally vacuous. In the adaptation of Wisdom's parable, the believer in the invisible gardener is hard pressed to show how this belief leads him/her to expect something not predictable by the atheist. 'Just how does what you call an invisible, intangible, eternally-elusive gardener differ from an imaginary gardener or even from no gardener at all', asks the interlocutor.[36] What therefore began as an assertion, claims Flew, is reduced 'step by step to an altogether different status, to an expression perhaps of a "picture-preference."'[37] And this is the danger endemic to all theological utterance which, I suggest, Wisdom wished to avoid. With Flew I too would wish to argue, therefore, that theological statements can die the death of a thousand qualifications.[38]

V

It is quite obvious that Diamond as theologian and philosopher of religion has no use for positivism or its influence in recent theology. It is that bias which I have intimated, allows him to see Wisdom as a second-rate Wittgensteinian still mired in a nasty positivism and its obsessive concerns with facts, although he does grant that Wisdom was groping for a position *beyond* positivism. I have argued that that view of Wisdom is not only unflattering but wrong. There is no doubt but that Wisdom was not a positivist *simpliciter* but neither did he reject their challenge to religious belief by simply accepting an easy non-cognitivist interpretation of such belief.

Contrary to Diamond, the conclusion I find implied in Wisdom's work is that the legacy of positivism for religion and theology is still very much alive.[39] A perusal of the relevant literature will reveal philosophers and theologians who, despite the long and tangled disputes over the proper formulation of the positivist 'principle of meaning'[40] insist on the legitimacy of the positivist challenge to religious belief. They do so because they, like Wisdom, understand religious assertions to be *bona fide* factual assertions which, consequently, require some verifying/falsifying procedure for determining the truth status of the claims espoused.[41] Therefore, as James A. Martin pointed out long ago, 'if one looks to a scientific inquiry as the most reliable means to knowledge of the world, then the definitions and proposals of the positivists are reasonable and fruitful.'[42] And to deny that science does provide us with reliable knowledge of the world in which we live, or to deny that religious devotees consider their theological claims to hold ontological/ metaphysical import, is I think, unreasonable.[43] As a result, theologians must recognize, as R. Jenson has put it in his *The Knowledge of Things Hoped For*, that they (we) cannot forever evade Flew.[44]

And with this note I shall conclude. Contrary to Diamond's Wittgensteinian intuitions, let me reiterate, I think it obvious that with respect to the question of the cognitivity of religious utterances the issues are clearly, precisely and correctly formulated by Flew. But I also believe that one can disagree with Hare who claimed that 'on the ground marked out by Flew, he ... is completely victorious'.[45] (It is the fear that Hare's assessment is right, of course, that sends a chill of fear down the backbones of the theologians.) Flew, that is, makes two errors: first, he shows a poor understanding of the nature of religious assertions, and second, he fails to see that scientific statements or assertions cannot be restricted simply to what has been referred to above as assertions of 'normal science'. Flew is misled in these respects, I suggest, by his modification of Wisdom's parable. In the revised form the parable is far too anaemic to convey the real nature of theistic utterances. The explorers in his parable are far too detached from the issues of the garden and gardening for their beliefs to be taken as analogous to religious beliefs. They have no real life and death concern with the garden as the believer/devotee does with God. In this respect B. Mitchell's parable, a part of the same 'University Discussion', comes far closer to revealing the nature of religious beliefs.[46] And it is for this reason, it seems to me, that Mitchell's analysis of the problem is more sound and provides, in the light of the above analysis of Wisdom, at least programmatically, an answer to Flew's challenge. According to Mitchell, the belief of the religious person, although open to possible falsification, is very difficult to falsify absolutely for it is not such as to be abandoned each time an awkward or ambiguous situation is encountered. In this sense religious beliefs resemble Kuhnian paradigms, the paradigm is not overthrown each time an anomaly crops up, but rather is reformulated and refined in an attempt to account for the now 'apparent' anomaly. Indeed, unless this were to occur, paradigms would be of little interpretive or heuristic value.[47] Religious beliefs, then, are more than 'provisional hypotheses to be discarded if experience tells against them', and yet other than 'vacuous formulae (expressing perhaps, a desire for reassurance) to which experience makes no difference and which make no difference in life'.[48] I conclude, therefore, that positivism's challenge to theology is by no means dead or insignificant but I am also ready to maintain that it is not successful in that challenge. To deny that the challenge exists, however, is crippling to theology. The evasion of the challenge is, no doubt, motivated by fear that to countenance the relevance of positivism must inevitably lead to the dissolution of the power of religion. I suggest, however, that theology is a cognitively committed enterprise and that it is dangerous to future theologizing to isolate it from the critical temper that characterizes other intellectual enterprises.

4

Explanation and Theological Method

Religion, Hans Reichenbach has claimed, 'is abundant in pictures that stimulate our imagination but devoid of the power of clarification that issues from scientific explanation'.[1] Philosophers of science have in general found themselves in agreement with this evaluation of religious discourse. Science, they have almost unanimously claimed, has achieved a generalized theoretical knowledge of the fundamental conditions determining the events and processes of the world whereas religion has simply spotted superficial analogies which it has confused with proper generalizations and consequently erroneously regarded as explanations. It would appear, therefore, that the long and often acrimonious debate as to the cognitive status of religious belief must, upon analysis of the concept of explanation alone, be concluded. Thus it appears also that the philosophers of religion who have argued that religion's concern lies exclusively in providing humanity with a 'way of life', rather than a speculative 'scheme of things', must carry the day.

Nevertheless, there is, to my mind at least, a certain uneasiness that attaches itself to such a conclusion, and that for two reasons. First, to advocate a 'way of life' involves, I think, an implicit view of reality – the perceiving of a 'scheme of things'. It hardly seems possible, that is, to preach an ideal way of life without concomitantly raising questions about the 'real' or 'ultimate' nature of the individual encouraged to undertake that ideal and of the world in which that ideal is to be put into practice. Second, seldom have the philosophers who have boldly claimed religious discourse to be pseudo-explanatory lavished the same attention upon the theologian's use of the concept 'explanation' as has been received by the scientist's use of it. Almost no attempt has been made by the philosophers to establish the precise nature and structure of 'theological explanation',[2] and, unless and until this is done, one can hardly justifiably conclude that 'explanation' is not a legitimate theological category and that religious discourse is not informative.

I shall in this chapter therefore attempt a defence of the concept of 'theological explanation' or 'religious explanation' – to play the devil's advocate, as it were – in order to redress this imbalance. Although I shall refrain from claiming that my analysis of the concept is wholly acceptable even to scientists, I shall nevertheless suggest that, upon completion of the analysis, the negative conclusion advocated by many to the question of the cognitive status of religious belief is wholly unacceptable. Before I proceed with this task, however, some critical remarks on the generally accepted analysis of 'scientific explanation' itself are required. If these remarks are in principle acceptable, and if the analysis of 'theological explanation' which follows is free from serious flaw, I suggest that the whole complexion of the science/religion controversy in its methodological form must change. Instead of conflict, one will find that science and religion are essentially similar enterprises.

SCIENTIFIC EXPLANATION

The aim of philosophical discussion of explanation and particularly of explanation in science is to establish what one might refer to as an operational understanding of the concept. By this I mean simply that the concept is so defined or delineated as to permit one to distinguish in a non-subjectivistic way between good and weak explanations – that is, by means of logical or at least quasi-logical criteria, rather than merely personal and psychological ones. If, for example, an explanation is explanatory only if it removes the obscurity of the matter under analysis for some particular person, then the notion of explanation becomes psychologically relativized. In so far, then, as the philosophical discussion of the concept has been an attempt to provide some explicit criteria, so that what counts as an explanation is not wholly dependent upon the person for whom the explanation is offered, I think it is a legitimate and necessary enterprise. However, to admit that such non-psychological criteria do exist is not to suggest that a proper understanding of 'explanation' will or can provide strictly logical criteria which alone will enable one to make the choice between or among alternative explanations in a somewhat mechanical fashion. And yet this seems to be the conclusion reached in many a recent analysis. Most such analyses find their inspiration in the covering-law theory of explanation (or deductive-nomological model) of Carl G. Hempel.[3] According to Hempel, explanations must display the form of a subsumptive argument. That is, the explanandum sentence must be entailed by the explanans sentences. Thus something has been explained only when it has been subsumed under, accounted for by, a law – when it can be shown to have occurred according to some general regularity.

For the formalist, then, the psychological sense of 'intellectual satisfaction', of having achieved some understanding of an otherwise puzzling situation, is entirely irrelevant. It is certainly not, according to them and as I have admitted, a sufficient condition for explanation[4] or even a necessary condition of explanation. Indeed, the whole point of the philosopher's task, it is maintained, is to abstract the notion of '*scientific* explanation' from the common-sense conception of explanation so as to free it from this kind of subjectivistic context. The scientific verb 'to explain' is not, that is, a triadic predicate like the common-sense form of the verb. The pragmatic element of the latter involving the notion of 'understanding' can consequently be dismissed as entirely irrelevant.

If such an understanding of 'explanation' is acceptable, I think it is obvious that religious explanations, so called, are not really explanations at all. But then neither are historical or teleological explanations – as still used in (organismic) biology, for example – for they do not conform to this pattern either. Indeed, the fact that such a model of explanation rules out historical and teleological explanations as non-scientific has often been raised as an argument both against the subsumptive model and for the possibility of legitimate types of religious explanation. Such claims, however, have raised rather complicated debates which I cannot enter into here.

Nevertheless, there is yet another kind of criticism raised against the subsumptive model. Michael Scriven, for example, argues that the subsumptive model is too formal and 'mechanistic' to do justice even to what is accepted as explanation by scientists.[5] In lieu of a full-scale, critical attack on the imperialism of this model, therefore, I shall limit myself to further elucidation of Scriven's thesis.

What is meant by 'explanation,' according to Scriven, is a gain in understanding. The weakness of the subsumptive model, therefore, is to be found in its rejection of the psychological criterion as unnecessary to real explanation, in its too easy rejection of the triadic character of the verb 'explain', involving reference to someone explaining something to someone. As Scriven puts it, the mistake 'lies in the supposition that by subsumption under a generalization one has automatically explained *something*, and that queries about this "explanation" represent a request for *further* and *different* explanation', adding that 'sometimes these queries merely echo the original puzzlement, and it is wholly illicit to argue that the original matter has been explained'.[6] Moreover, claims Scriven, 'an explanation that fails to measure up to its standards may be a great deal more complete than one that does, i.e., it may identify the relevant effective variables and ignore the ineffective ones.'[7]

The subsumptive model, then, claims Scriven, fails to distinguish between 'explanations' and 'the grounds of our explanations' and so errs in assuming that an explanation must include its grounds within the explanation – that is, laws or law-like statements. The grounds of an explanation, however, are no more part of an explanation than the grounds for thinking a statement is true are a part of that statement itself. Indeed, if the grounds of an explanation were part of it, no explanations could ever be complete, for, if one insists upon the inclusion of laws in the explanation, one would also have to insist upon the inclusion of the relevant data to justify our beliefs in the initial conditions.

Whereas the subsumptive theorists maintain that one must have in mind laws that exhibit the necessary connections among the phenomena, Scriven maintains that, even though such regular connection is involved, one need not necessarily be able to state it. He writes: 'The explanation requires that there be a connection but not any particular one – just one of a wide range of alternatives'.[8] Consequently, having reasons for causal claims does not imply the ability to quote laws. This does not deny a stable pattern to scientific explanations, although it does deny the appropriateness of the 'mechanical' model of the Hempelians.

A proper scientific explanation, then, according to Scriven, is constituted by a set of propositions which, if false, make the argument incorrect; by the assumption of connections between phenomena, which, if irrelevant, make the argument incomplete; and by a context within which an explanation is either appropriate or inappropriate. To give an explanation is therefore to commit oneself to the truth of the propositions involved, to the adequacy of the supposed causal connections, and to the appropriateness of the explanation as an answer to the question asked (considering the position of the questioner) without, however, having explicitly considered in advance grounds justifying the position or answer in the face of possible criticism. Although such justifications are not to be found within the explanation itself, nevertheless access must be had to them: to truth-justifying grounds, role-justifying grounds, and type-justifying grounds, as Scriven labels them.

RELIGIOUS EXPLANATION

In the preceding part of this chapter I have concerned myself with the question of what patterns of reasoning can provide one with 'scientific explanation', denying with Scriven that such patterns need be deductive. 'Explanations' which have available various sorts of defence in response to a variety of possible objections – even though all such defences may not be embodied in the explanations themselves – have full claim to the title 'scientific'. Thus one can, I suggest, weaken the deductive model without simply rejecting it outright since this could well lead to a complete psychological relativization of the concept of explanation.

Having outlined (there has been no space to argue the matter in detail) what can with good reason be considered a respectable understanding of 'scientific explanation', I shall now move on to the main part of my argument; that is, to a discussion of the possibility of 'religious explanation' – the possibility of religious beliefs supplying us with explanations of some puzzlement or other. The specific indictment that religious beliefs (if they make any claim to being cognitively significant whatsoever), provide us with but pseudo-explanations – with explanatory power only in the spurious sense of 'analogism', wherein 'our imagination is held in thrall by an awe-inspiring picture'[9] – must now be more closely examined.

Several questions have been raised legitimately by philosophers on the theological reaction to the displacement of religious explanation by scientific explanation: Has not the abandonment of the 'God-hypothesis' been a boon to the development of many of the natural sciences? Has not religious explanation been parasitic upon scientific explanation in that religious beliefs have provided explanations for events inexplicable only because of the primitive state of empirical knowledge? What precisely is lost in the abandonment of the concept of religious explanation? Of what precisely do the believers suppose their religious beliefs to be explanatory?

My answer to the first two questions is a simple yes. There is abundant evidence in the history of the relations of science and theology to indicate that the abandonment of the 'God-hypothesis', as Laplace referred to it, has been extremely beneficial to the development and progress of the natural sciences – not only in physics but even more so in biology, geology, paleontology, etc. Religious explanations, that is, have been used erroneously, it turns out, to fill in the gaps left by an immature science. From the religious perspective, this type of understanding of religious beliefs as explanatory was a special object of wrath for Dietrich Bonhoeffer. According to Bonhoeffer, it meant the death, if only gradual death, of theism.[10] Although such gaps in our scientific knowledge do exist, religious explanation of the phenomena is ruled out; for scientific explanations, though neither complete nor exhaustive, are in principle, so it is argued, sufficient in themselves to account for the data. It is claimed that there is no need or value connected with invoking religious hypotheticals and developing 'religious explanations' even with respect to the 'great questions' facing humanity.

But if this is indeed the case, then just precisely what religious beliefs explain is a somewhat puzzling affair, for, surely, the questions of life, death, and humanity can be and have been raised as specifically religious questions requiring a peculiarly religious answer. Such religious answers, it is generally agreed, are those which have had an 'integrative' function in the individual's life as well as in that of the community, giving meaning and perhaps viable behaviour patterns to one's individual and communal existence.

Consequently, on the understanding above of scientific explanation as a potentially adequate account of all states of affairs in the world, it would appear that religious explanations are of little cognitive value and hence not really explanations at all, despite their value in the past in providing a principle of personal and social integration. What is being argued here is that, although this is an important reason in favour of religious explanations, it is not sufficient; for the same function, it could be argued, could be filled by 'a likely story' or an 'awe-inspiring picture' as by an acceptable explanation – a sound and acceptable hypothesis or theory. Whether scientific explanations are better accounts of the states of affairs in question – that is, logically more connected and empirically better justified – is not the question at stake here. What I am trying to show is that the form and structure of religious explanation are essentially similar to those of scientific explanation properly understood and not in a league by themselves, as has so often been claimed. (And unless religious explanations are at least possible in the sense discussed here, it is unlikely that their value to society in the past will continue into the future.)

The first task for the theologian, it appears, is to establish the possibility and describe the nature of the object of religious explanation. Several possible alternatives are open and I shall look critically at three of them. The most obvious response to the criticism of religious explanation above is to find an object of religious explanation wholly different from the object of scientific explanation. There are two possible routes in this direction which the theologian might follow.

The first is 'the world,' that is, both the empirical world in its totality and the sum total of our personal experience (i.e. of human experience, in contrast to the events *in* the world explained by science). That either of these concepts of the world is not an object of scientific explanation, as defined by the deductivists above, seems plain. If explanation is subsumptive, then the whole is inexplicable, for subsumption in this case is impossible. R. B. Braithwaite makes the point clearly.[11] But this does not, I think, necessarily preclude the idea that ultimate questions are meaningless and without 'explanation', as redefined above. But more of this later.

Believers or theologians of this bent maintain, then, that our religious beliefs explain not some fact in the world but, rather, why there is a world at all. And this, it is claimed, is done by means of reference to that which lies 'outside of' or 'beyond' the world – reference, that is, to the trans-empirical. Thus, as Ian Ramsey puts it, the task of religious explanation is in effect to aid science in obtaining 'that one cosmic map which remains the scientific ideal'.[12] To fail to recognize this type of explanation, therefore, is to fail to fill in certain deficiencies of our scientific explanations, although these deficiencies are of an order different from those consisting of gaps in our present scientific knowledge. Scientific explanations on this account, then, are exhaustive only in a specific, not in a general, sense.

Such a position, however, is not without difficulties. As I have already intimated, to talk of 'the world' is not a straightforward procedure; nor is it a simple matter to speak of the principles of the world as somehow 'outside of' the world itself.[13] If, for example, it is denied that the world itself is ultimate, then it might just as easily be denied that the ground of the existence of the world itself requires explanation. To deny the claim is to be arbitrary and irrational, for, as Ernest Nagel puts it, it is 'theological gerrymandering... dogmatically cutting short a discussion when the intellectual current runs against them'.[14]

A second route open to the theologian bent on finding an object of religious explanation other than the object of scientific explanation is that of the 'religious experience argument'. This argument claims that there is a category of experiences which is other than mere sensation (sense experience). Religious explanation then explains – systematically explicates and accounts for the fact of – this other kind of experience. John Baillie, for example, claims that:

> our lives would indeed be poor and savourless if we had no awareness, in which we could repose the least degree of trust, of anything in reality save what we can see and hear and touch and taste and smell. My contention will be that we have even what can properly be called *sense* experiences for other things than these. The human spirit, I shall say, develops certain subtler senses or sensitivities which go beyond the bodily sense. They carry us far beyond such experiences, making us sensitive to aspects of reality of which these, taken by themselves, could not conceivably inform us.[15]

Or again in his criticism of Kant: 'the root of all my difficulty with it [i.e. his theory of religion] lies in the fact that, having accepted the irreproachable doctrine that all our knowledge derives from experience, he then confines our "experience" to that gained through the bodily senses'.[16] We have, then, by faith (according to Baillie) a direct and immediate 'sensory' awareness of God which it is the theologian's task to explicate. The certitude with which this experience is transfused, however, is never capable of being distilled into the particular affirmations made about it. Baillie writes: 'We are convinced we are in touch with reality, we do know something assuredly, but when we try to express in theoretical terms what we know and are sure of, we never have the same assurance that we have got our answer quite right.'[17]

This position, however, as Baillie admits, is not without weaknesses. As C. B. Martin points out, 'The addition of the existential claim "God exists" to the psychological claim of having religious experiences must be shown to be warrantable.'[18] The fact that these objects influence people's lives is not to provide such warrantability – for very often imaginal and ideal objects when believed to be actual have profound and fruitful effects. Indeed, this is precisely the point of Curt Ducasse's criticism of religious beliefs as having an explanatory function; that is: 'In order to be capable of performing the social or the personal functions distinctive of religious beliefs, beliefs having contents suitable for those functions need not be objectively true nor even clear; they need only be fervently held. If so held, they will work, no matter how vague, crude, or even absurd they may happen to be.'[19]

A third possible reaction to the charge that religious explanations are superfluous, because they really have no object of explanation, is that which claims that religious explanations also explain the phenomena within the world. That is, it is maintained that, if religious explanations are to explain anything at all, they ought to explain the daily round of experiences of which our life is made. This approach does not deny altogether the idea that our scientific explanations are adequate but claims, rather, that the adequacy is of a specific sort and restricted to a certain level of understanding. Alternative and complementary explanations of the same phenomena from other points of view are not therefore ruled out *a priori*. The point is simply this: when we have finished with our physical analysis of the phenomenon in question, there remains a fresh sense to be made out of the pattern of events – a fresh sense which is necessary for a proper (total) understanding of the phenomenon in question. A flashing light, for example, may be adequately explained on a physical level in terms of wavelength, emission rate, frequency and various other characteristics; and yet this may not be exhaustive in an absolute sense, for the same flashing light might also be explained in terms of Morse code as communicating a message. The two explanations of the flashing light, that is, are both acceptable and necessary for a fuller understanding: they are complementary. In a similar way, therefore, so claims the theologian, both a biological and a religious explanation are required for a complete understanding of issues such as birth, life, death, etc.

It might well be argued that for the religious believer to adopt such a view of 'complementarity' in explanatory schemes may be simply to use it as an escape hatch when the pressure of scientific progress on religious belief becomes very great. Yet the complementarity of two descriptions can be guarded against admitting nonsense. According to D. M. MacKay, who advocates such a view of complementarity, there are four conditions that must be fulfilled for two such descriptions to be logically complementary. I shall but list them here. First, they must have a common reference. Second, each must account for all the elements of the common reference exhaustively or at least in principle be able to do so. Third, they must make different assertions because, fourth, the preconditions of the use of the concepts in each are mutually exclusive, so that the significant aspects referred to in one are necessarily omitted from the other.[20]

This does not mean, however, that this approach to religious explanation altogether evades the difficulties encountered in the other two or that they give no account of our experience in this world, for this latter view is, in a sense, only a more comprehensive view that includes the other two. Its approach, however, is a little more 'down to earth', so to speak, than theirs. The first position, for example, in explaining 'the world' simultaneously 'explains' things in the world by giving them a broader location or placement. It provides a broader perspective, that is, for viewing events in the world. Similarly, it may include the 'religious experience' approach, for, although religious experience is not directly concerned with our sensory experience, it is nevertheless inseparably related to it. As even Baillie admits, even though God confronts us more than any other presence, God is never present to us apart from all other presences. Only '"in, with and under" other presences is the divine presence ever vouchsafed to us'.[21] However, the advantage of the third approach is its directness and inclusiveness, as I shall delineate somewhat more fully in what follows.

It might be argued that even such a direct approach to the problem of the object of religious explanation, however, cannot guarantee even the possibility of religious explanation. Although religious explanation might have a useful role or function at present, it has been argued that it will not do so as our scientific knowledge grows. The claim is that religious explanation, even in the sense described above, is but a neatly disguised variant of the old 'stops in the gaps in our knowledge' type. Thus, although religion may now provide a complementary argument for a certain phenomenon, there is no guarantee that that explanation will not eventually be reducible to a non-religious or non-supernatural explanation. There is nothing in the idea of complementarity to exclude the possibility of a higher (scientific?) mode of representation, synthesizing the two complementary ones. The present debate in biology as to whether organismic biological explanations are irreducibly fundamental or in fact reducible to molecular biological explanations may well illuminate the problem. Although at present the particular type of explanations used in organismic biology are essential, it is argued that new knowledge ultimately make them superfluous.[22]

The question, then, of just what it is that religious explanations are explanatory of is rather complex and difficult to answer straightforwardly. I have in effect suggested that they somehow concern all three 'objects' discussed above – that, although they concern such ordinary questions of happenings in the world as 'What is life?' or 'What is death?' they do so only in the sense of creating a broader context in which these questions might be asked. In creating that context, they legitimately raise questions about the world as such, as well as about a species of experience to which the label 'religious' peculiarly applies. In creating this broader context, the quest for religious explanation is an attempt to go beyond scientific explanation, seeing the latter as somehow inadequate. The question to which religious explanation is the answer, then, may not be a question that has a straightforwardly empirical and logical answer. Nevertheless, the answer provided by religious explanation may still be a 'scientific' one (i.e. in the broad sense of rational or reasonable) in that it is directed toward legitimate why-questions and bears in all essentials the same general structure as answers to scientific questions. Consequently, religious explanations function in the same way as do scientific explanations. Religious explanations, too, are concerned about what there is and are concerned about it in a critical fashion. I shall now focus attention on this latter aspect of the rational structure of the religious explanation.

The question of whether religious explanations are both rational and objective, as are their scientific counterparts, can perhaps best be answered by means of an analysis of some particular religious explanation. This analysis need not show whether the explanation proffered is true or false, but it must show that a decision as to truth or falsity is applicable to it. The structure necessary for this need not, as I have already suggested, be of the deductive type. A looser structure will do, as long as a justification of the explanation has recourse to sound defences against the three types of possible attacks listed by Scriven: charges of inaccuracy, inadequacy and inappropriateness.

An appropriate example might well be the explanation of the contingency of the empirical world, since, according to the theist, natural science that stops short of theistic culmination has the appearance of an arbitrarily arrested growth. James Richmond outlines the essentials of such an argument as follows:

> the more we contemplate the natural order in its entirety, the more we are impressed by the remarkable order, value and regularity we find there; the prolonged contemplation of this gener-

ates in us the conviction that the sheer quantity of intelligibility we find throughout the natural world (despite disorderly and dysteleological elements) requires some kind of explanation other than mere fortuitousness ... and the 'explanation' ... must somehow be in terms of a transcendent, personal (because intelligent) being involved in, yet unobservable within the spatio-temporal natural order.[23]

One's system of religious beliefs or theology, then, must in some sense be an explanation of a puzzling world – a world, moreover, that can be satisfactorily explained only by reference to that which is 'beyond' and 'other than' the world. If the world were in no sense a puzzle, there would be no need at all for explanation; and if, providing the world were puzzling, the questions raised by it were answerable from within the world process, the explanation would not be a religious or theological one. Thus, if theology is to be significant, claims Richmond, 'it must by necessity refer to the divine existence in order to explain what would otherwise be left puzzling and unclear; its intellectual attraction must reside in its power to make plain what is obscure.'[24]

We must now examine whether such an argument contains any blatantly inaccurate statements, fails to explain what it is supposed to explain because it does not bear on the matter at all (for example, in terms of causal connections between the apparently disparate elements), or is irrelevant to the context in which the question was asked, as to the existence and nature of the empirical world.

There is, I think, little question as to the access to type-justifying grounds in connection with this argument or explanation. A why-question about the existence of the empirical world, as long as by 'world' one does not mean 'all that there is', is certainly not in itself absurd. This may be seen in contrasting it with what Paul Edwards refers to as 'the super-ultimate why-question'. In the latter, claims Edwards, the word 'why' has simply lost all meaning, rather than exchanging its old meaning for a new one. He writes:

In any of its familiar senses, when we ask of anything x, why it happened or why it is what it is – whether x is the collapse of an army, a case of lung cancer, the theft of a jewel, or the stalling of a car – we assume that there is something or some set of conditions, other than x, in terms of which it can be explained. We do not know what this other thing is that is suitably related to x, but unless it is in principle possible to go beyond x, and find such another thing, the question does not make any sense.[25]

Therefore, if in asking why 'the world' exists, rather than nothing, meaning by 'the world' the totality of all things, the question is so all-inclusive as to make it *'logically* impossible to find "anything" which could be suitably related to that whose explanation we appear to be seeking'.[26] It is at least conceivable, therefore, that there may be contexts in which questions such as 'Why does the world exist?' or 'Why am I here?' can legitimately be raised. They are raised, in fact, in an effort to find out just what one is faced with in existence.

Truth-justifying and role-justifying grounds may be a little harder to come by, but they are by no means non-existent. On truth-justifying grounds, the argument against religious explanation is not so much that the statements used in the argument are false but, rather, that they are statements of a kind that can be neither true nor false – that they are, rather, meaningless. This, of course, was raised in its most vehement and perhaps crudest form in this century by the positivists of the Vienna Circle, although it has seen some refinement since then. On role-justifying ground, one would be required to show how reference to some trans-empirical reality, if possible, would bear on empirical reality. I shall not in either case develop detailed replies to such criticisms but, rather, shall indicate how they might be answered.

The first objection might well be labelled 'the cognitivist challenge'. It can be dismissed if it is possible to show that such trans-empirical statements, 'God-sentences', for example, can be made checkable or falsifiable in at least an indirect, if not in a direct, way. And this can be done by distinguishing between 'criteria' for a truth statement and 'evidence' for the same – a distinction not generally recognized by the positivists. It is another matter for something to be the case than for one to know or have reasons to believe that it is the case. 'Criteria', then, concern the conditions determining the meaning of a cognitive sentence, and 'evidence' concerns the conditions under which the truth or falsity of the statement is ascertained. It is possible, that is, to state what the truth conditions of a sentence are, independently of the availability of evidence. Such criteria, as R. S. Heimbeck points out, can be derived from entailment or incompatibility relationships that such trans-empirical sentences have with more directly empirical statements. He writes:

An entailment-rule, therefore, of the form 'p entails q' can function as a rule for the meaning of the sentence employed in making 'p' a rule in which 'q' exhibits at least part of the meaning of the sentence 'p.' And incompatibility-rules also can function to demarcate the meaning of 'p,' but they do so negatively by laying down what meanings are rejected by 'p'.[27]

Trans-empirical sentences, therefore, are capable of being cognitive because they are open to empirical falsification, even if only indirectly.

The second objection to the relevance of such odd statements to empirical reality is, then, also answered by the foregoing discussion. I shall elucidate this aspect of relevance even further by brief reference to Richmond's attempt to show that there are occasions in our experience which bring us to using equally 'odd' assertions and explanations – explanations that require a move to concepts such as 'beyond this world', 'outside of the world', etc. Richmond claims to have found in talk about 'selves' a justifiable analogy upon which to rest his case for a transcendent explanation of the world. A consistent empiricism, he points out, finds it extremely difficult to talk adequately of 'selves' or 'souls' as a result of 'illegitimately forcing upon a hugely significant area of our experience an epistemological straitjacket – namely, an epistemological account formulated specifically for the areas of the natural and human sciences'. If, however, one comes to the discussion of the self via *'one's own inner experience of what is involved in thinking and living'*, he claims, one can only conclude 'that there is a certain irreducible *duality* attaching to our understanding and explanation of ourselves', so that not only physical but also spiritual attributes must be used in our description.[28] He concludes, therefore, that we cannot say of human beings that they are either inside or outside the spatio-temporal world – that they are, in a sense, both inside it and outside it. Here, then, we have a case in point, he claims, in which the logic of inside and outside is understandably applied; and this 'makes intelligible the use of such words within the context of a metaphysical explanation of the world as whole in terms of an ultimate non-spatio-temporal being'.[29]

Enough has been said, I think, to show that religious beliefs or religious explanations are in some senses similar in structure and function to scientific beliefs and scientific explanations. They, too, have recourse to justificatory arguments when subjected to criticism from without. Although they emphasize the importance of the psychological criterion, they nevertheless do not make it the only necessary requirement of explanation. Whether they do in fact withstand the criticism is not a matter of concern at the moment. It might be argued, for example, that Richmond's talk of duality with regard to persons does not really escape Gilbert Ryle's criticism of 'the ghost in the machine' types of dualisms, although Richmond thinks it does. But this would be a matter of argument over whether Richmond's explanation was a good one or a weak one and not an argument over whether it could be accounted as an explanation at all.

5

Science and Religion: Is Compatibility Possible?

COMPATIBILITY SYSTEMS

To raise the question of the possible compatibility of science and religion must, in light of the historical relations of the scientific and religious communities, seem utterly naive. Since the days of Galileo and Urban VIII, it can be argued, the image of conflict has appropriately dominated all discussion of the relation of religion to science. The dominant picture, as Andrew White's famous *History of the Warfare Between Science and Theology* (1896) illustrates (although somewhat onesidedly), has been one of the religious faithful fighting the progress of the sciences, particularly when new discoveries threatened the security of cherished dogmas. And today the image of conflict is reinforced, despite the fact that contemporary scientific beliefs are more congenial to religious (and especially Christian) doctrines than those of a few generations ago,[1] for the conflict, it is maintained, is basically methodological. Both science and religion, that is, seem to be playing the 'cognition game' and yet religion, so it is claimed, seems to follow an entirely different set of rules in its achievement of 'knowledge' from those of science.[2] The point of the modern view of the conflict image, is that science provides us with a clear and straightforward paradigm for knowing – a 'morality of knowledge'[3] – which religious thinking obviously contravenes. Despite such claims, however, there is a reluctance on the part of many to accept the image of conflict as an appropriate category in discussion of the relations of science and religion, for both science and religion have made valued contributions to our lives and neither is likely to whither away in the very near future. That reluctance to deny the value of either community has inspired alternative interpretations of the meanings of science and religion that 'entail' compatibility. And it is the variety and significance of these various 'compatibility systems' that I wish to look at in this chapter.

A 'compatibility system' is essentially a justification of accepting two apparently conflicting systems of thought.[4] If no *prima facie* conflict existed, there would be no impetus to construct such a system. The growth of science in the West, however, with the gradual 'disenchantment' of the universe attendant upon that growth (i.e. the increasing superfluity of religious hypotheses in the attempts to account for or describe the world) suggests a radical discontinuity between science and religion – it suggests, in fact, that to do proper science one must give up religion. Such a 'conflict interpretation' of the relation of religion to science rests on two assumptions: first, that science alone provides us with the paradigm of *all* knowledge-gaining procedures; and, second, that religion is correctly or appropriately characterized, at least in part, as a system of beliefs. Compatibility proposals, consequently, rest on challenges to either one or both of these assumptions.

I shall look briefly at four kinds of compatibility proposals:[5] (1) science and religion are wholly incommensurable; (2) science and religion are complementary but provide us with radically different kinds of knowledge; (3) science and religion are complementary because science itself reveals elements of ultimacy and, consequently, exhibits a religious character; and (4) science and religion are complementary because archaic systems contain genuine cognitive insights although they need to be re-expressed in terms of contemporary scientific thought.

The classic 'compatibility system' – namely, that science and religion are complementary because they are logically similar 'enterprises' – however, challenges neither of the major assumptions of the conflict interpretation. Accepting both assumptions, it nevertheless differs drastically upon their interpretation: science, it agrees, provides us with a 'morality of knowing' but it hotly disputes the nature or significance of that morality. Extending that metaphor, one might say that the compatibility argument here does not involve the denial of an ethic of belief but rather suggests that the ethic is a contextual or situational one rather than an absolutist ethic. That is to say, just as ethical judgement is more than mere 'ethical calculation', so knowing is more than mere logical or 'epistemic calculation'. I will consider briefly the merits of this claim following the description of the four above-mentioned alternatives.

SCIENCE AND RELIGION AS WHOLLY INCOMMENSURABLE

Many philosophers reject the conflict interpretation in the discussion of science and religion because, according to them, science and religion are incommensurable; they are incapable of even being compared. Thus religion cannot be either compatible or incompatible with science; nor can it complement science in the sense of providing a different or higher kind of knowledge that science cannot achieve. The assumption that religion is appropriately characterized as knowledge or as a system of beliefs, it is argued, reveals a naive understanding of religion. Religion is a 'way of life' and not a source of knowledge. Religion functions in society in a different capacity altogether than science – it grounds the *meaning* of human existence. Religious language, therefore, is not the language of knowing but rather the language of commitment;[6] it is parabolic,[7] self-involving,[8] convictional,[9] symbolic,[10] etc., but not epistemic. T. R. Miles neatly summarizes the essential point of this position in his *Religion and the Scientific Outlook* as follows:

> On the general question of a conflict between science and religion there is a central part of the problem which we can safely claim to have settled once for all. This claim is not the presumptuous one that it sounds, for the matter is one of logical necessity and it would be muddled thinking to claim anything less. Religious language is of many different kinds; there is the language of parable, the language of moral exhortation, the language of worship and so on. Only if what is offered in the name of religion is factual assertion can there be any possibility of a head on conflict.... To insist that such (religious) language is parable and not literal truth is to ascribe a recognizable and legitimate function to a group of basic religious assertions and the result is to supply a permanent guarantee that these assertions cannot be refuted by the findings of science.[11]

SCIENCE AND RELIGION AS PROVIDING RADICALLY DIFFERENT KINDS OF KNOWLEDGE

Proponents of this kind of compatibility system do not deny that in some respects religion and science are incommensurable. They deny

that science is the *only* paradigm for all knowledge-gaining procedures and so admit that science and religion are methodologically
incommensurable. By suspending belief in the first assumption of the
incompatibility thesis, they insist, it can be shown that there are non-
scientific ways of knowing – ways of knowing that transcend and so
complement the knowledge of science. Karl Heim sets forth a persuasive argument in support of such a thesis.[12] According to Heim,
existentialism has discovered a whole new world of non-objective
experience. Consequently, it opens up the possibility of knowledge of
a non-objective space that is wholly other than the knowledge of the
objective space of the natural sciences. Heim calls this first non-
objective space 'ego-space', for it is first discovered in the discovery of
the inner Self – in the inward awareness of one's Self.

New spaces, according to Heim, are discovered when they make
possible something which is undeniable in our experience, although
within the space or spaces thus far discovered it appears self-
contradictory. The (inner) Self which must, in light of our experience, be part of our general picture of the universe is, for example,
invisible in the objective space of the natural sciences but becomes
'visible' in the non-objective ego-space.

Still other spaces, according to Heim, are revealed when questions
of ethics and origins are raised. We find in these issues that what is
necessary for a comprehensive picture of the universe is in the
objective space of the natural sciences (as well as in the ego-space,
for both these spaces are species of the genus 'polar-space') problematic. For example, in the area of ethical action, the ego is para-
lysed by the relativism and positivism that characterizes all our
decision-making. Within the 'polar-spaces' no goals are absolute
except those chosen by the human will. Consequently, action is
bound either by indecision as to which goal to direct one's action
toward, or it is plagued by the sense of arbitrariness in the goal
chosen. What is needed, therefore, is a new space wherein both the
indecision and arbitrariness can be avoided since both undermine
the ethical life. Such a possibility, Heim insists, can be seen only in
'supra-polar space':

> Unlike all human ethical doctrines, which are historically and cul-
> turally conditioned and possess only limited validity, Christ,
> according to the conviction of the primitive church, is the Kyrios,
> the only one entitled to the name which is above all names, the
> supreme authority, above which there is no higher power and by

which the final decision is taken with regard to every value that comes within our field of vision – the supreme yardstick by which all things are measured. This authority is like the lighthouse by which ships may steer their course when they have to pass by night through a dangerous channel which is full of rocks. If such a paramount authority is found to exist, then the aim of positivism too is achieved, for positivism seeks a supreme value, the antecedents of which do not require investigation.[13]

The Universe, then, consists of *spaces* rather than merely *objective* space as is assumed in the secular philosophies. *Knowledge* of the other spaces, particularly of the 'supra-polar space', however, cannot come via reasoning or thinking which finds its chief application in objective space – one simply becomes (or does not become) aware of such non-objective spaces:

> we are not ourselves able to force open the gate which leads to a space that has so far been closed to us. Whenever we experience the discovery of a space, the discovery always simply falls into our laps as a gift.[14]

From the standpoint of the polar spaces, this experience is totally incomprehensible.[15] That knowledge comes, then, by revelation – the scales must fall from one's eyes before one is able to 'see' it. Consequently, faith is the condition in which the person who lives completely immersed in this supra-polar space finds him or herself. Such a person has the same security and confidence as does the secularist who lives wholly within the polar spaces.

This is a kind of two-level theory of knowledge (truth) and, as M. Diamond points out, it 'is the major strategy of religious existentialists in coping with the challenges of a scientifically oriented culture'.[16] Other similar compatibility proposals, as Diamond points out, can be found in Buber, Bultmann, Barth and Tillich. The classic statement of this school of thought, perhaps, is to be found in Kierkegaard's *Concluding Unscientific Postscript*,[17] in his talk of 'truth as subjectivity'. Of kindred mind is Pascal's reference to the reasons of the heart of which reason knows nothing.

In all such two-level theories, Diamond points out, a compatibility and complementarity between the lower and higher levels of truth is claimed but, at the same time, a greater importance is claimed for the higher (or religious) level of knowledge and truth.

SCIENCE AND RELIGION AS COMPLEMENTARY BECAUSE SCIENCE IS VERY MUCH LIKE RELIGION

Stated somewhat crudely, compatibility systems of this order claim to show that science functions not only in a cognitive capacity but also, although in an inferior way, in a religious one; that is, science is a kind of surrogate religion. L. Gilkey's *Religion and the Scientific Future* is an apologetic of this kind.[18] Although 'secular man' (*sic*) believes one thing – namely, that he is irreligious – his existence, claims Gilkey, reveals a dependence on elements of ultimacy. Gilkey makes this point in a broad and general way in his *Naming the Whirlwind*[19] but there points up three specific characteristics of ultimacy in science.[20] The first, he insists, is found in the unremitting *eros* to know. Further, the assumptions of some ontological generality about the character of reality as such and of the possibility of a relationship between it and the knowing mind is a leap beyond the evidence – it is a step beyond the bounds of science to that which ultimately makes sense of the scientific enterprise in the first place. The third hint of ultimacy in science, Gilkey claims, is to be found in the structure of scientific judgement, a structure that reveals, in the final analysis, the ultimate awareness of oneself as a knower. In this regard he writes:

> [The] personal affirmation of oneself as a knower is ... the foundation of the possibility of all rational judgement and in the end it grounds all science. In turn this awareness of oneself as a knower cannot be doubted. The sceptic, in affirming his scepticism also is aware of himself and affirms himself as *understanding* the view that he now asserts; he is also aware of himself as judging that this view is in fact true.... No movement could take place without this element of indubitable certainty, without this unconditioned assertion of the actuality of knowing ourselves.[21]

According to Gilkey, then, modern science and human trust in science results in the adoption of a new myth – a quasi-religious myth – which he calls the 'myth of total awareness'. The myth asserts that:

> man becomes *man* and can control his life and destiny if he is educated, liberal, analyzed, scientific, an 'expert,' etc ... that knowledge and awareness can turn whatever has been a blindly determining force on and in man and so a *fate* over man, into a new instrument of man.[22]

The emergence of the myth, Gilkey claims, shows humanity's need for 'ultimacy' and an attempt on the part of science itself to fulfil that need after having contributed to the loss of ultimacy in contributing to the decline or 'demise' of religion.[23] Gilkey sees the new myth, however, as dangerous, for, according to him science and technology, which are to be the source of human salvation (according to the new myth), are in actuality the source of the threat to humanity's ultimate well-being.[24] Science, therefore, 'reaches out for' ultimacy yet is unable within itself to provide it. Consequently science requires religion – religion however that goes beyond the 'broken images' of past tradition. Thus Gilkey concludes:

> The dilemmas of even the most secular of cultures are ultimately intelligible only in the light of faith; the *destiny* of even a scientific world can be adequately thematized only in terms of religious symbols; and the confidence of the future even of technological man can be creatively grounded only if the coming work of the Lord in the affairs of men is known and affirmed.[25]

SCIENCE AND RELIGION AS COMPATIBLE BECAUSE THERE ARE GENUINE COGNITIVE INSIGHTS IN ARCHAIC RELIGIOUS SYSTEMS

Compatibility systems of this sort attempt to salvage folk-wisdom of archaic cultures. Philosophers admit that there is a radical methodological incompatibility between the two – that religion has gained its insights in 'unacceptable' ways – but they attempt also to point out that, somehow or other, the insights of religion are of importance to humanity. Thus religion can complement science in a cognitive way (although only heuristically so), but its insights will require the services of a 'translator' – the insights, that is, require support in terms of a scientific justification. R. Burhoe's aim in his 'Concepts of God and Soul in a Scientific View of Human Purpose', contains the germ of this kind of compatibility system. He writes:

> I seek ... in this paper to show how belief in a reality sovereign over man (a god) and a belief in the essential immortality or eternal duration of man's basic nature (a soul) not only are necessary for human motivation but are indeed credible on the very grounds

of science, which confirms insights common to the higher religious traditions of the world.... I think in the modern sciences we have far surpassed earlier methods by which man finds knowledge. However, I have already pointed out that the scientific method does not shun looking into and taking advantage of more ancient accumulations of wisdom such as the genetic 'wisdom of the body', or the traditional wisdom of human cultures.[26]

SCIENCE AND RELIGION AS LOGICALLY SIMILAR ENTERPRISES

This, the boldest of the compatibility systems, lays claim to a complementarity relationship between science and religion on the basis of a logical similarity between the two communities – on the basis of the claim, that is, that religion, like science, has cognitive significance and that its claims to knowledge have the same 'foundation' as the claims to knowledge by science. Like the proponents of the conflict thesis, the exponents of this understanding of science and religion assume both that religion is appropriately characterized, at least in part, as a system of beliefs and that science provides us with the paradigm for our knowledge-gaining procedures or activities. However, although agreeing that the 'morality of knowledge' that governs activity in the sciences has full sway in theology or 'reflective religion', it differs radically with the conflict theorists on the interpretation or description of that morality.

The indictment by the rationalist is that the recourse to faith by religious believers in their 'religious knowing' permits them to evade the force of the standards and canons of rational assessment which the rationalist recognizes to be binding in other areas of cognitive concern, such as, for example, history[27] or the natural sciences.[28] This, the rationalist insists, corrodes the 'machinery' of coming to a sound judgement whereby truth might be separated from falsehood and so calls 'into question the very conception of scientific thought as a responsible enterprise of reasonable men'.[29] It is assumed, therefore, that science can *prove* its knowledge claims (i.e. *justify* them),[30] while religion cannot. Scientific method, therefore, can provide impersonal, objective, and hence reliable *knowledge* while the non-scientific 'disciplines', and religion in particular, can provide us with mere opinion, or, at best, illuminating visions.[31] In science there is *convergence of belief* which one fails to obtain in religious matters, for 'belief' (knowledge) in science is a matter of evidential appraisal and logical assessment, whereas 'belief' in religion depends upon persuasion and rhetoric aimed at conversion – that is, it is based upon extra-logical and non-evidential bases. The adoption of religious beliefs or a change of religious beliefs, consequently, is a matter of intuition and is, in some sense, a mystical and subjective affair, a matter for psychological description only. But the adoption of new scientific theories, or a change of scientific belief, is a matter of proceeding according to strict logical and methodological rules.

Such a view of science and scientific rationality, it is argued, is naive. The dominant attitude which distinguishes scientific thinking as presenting us with objective knowledge from non-scientific thinking which is emotive or conative is fundamentally wrong-headed. It is so, however, not because religious thinking resembles scientific thinking in its logical rigour but rather because scientific thinking is a good deal less rigorous than it is generally supposed and hence that it is in some respects like religious thinking.[32] The rules of logic and/or evidence that have been suggested as charac-terizing scientific thought as wholly rational, it is claimed, cannot account adequately either for the existence of our knowledge or its growth. Such an account can be provided only if science itself is seen as a 'fiduciary' enterprise – that is, involving personal judge-ment (*fiducia*, trust/faith) that of necessity exceeds the grounds of evidence from which it first arose. Since purely logical procedures or evidential appraisals cannot 'guarantee' one's conclusions, it is 'wrong' to place the responsibility for their acceptance upon a set of eternal rules.[33] The acceptance of not only specific scientific conclu-sions, therefore, but even the so-called rules of scientific procedure involve an element of 'faith' in their adoption.

This kind of attempt at establishing that science and religion are compatible is extremely common. Historically, however, the claim was that religion was structurally similar to science and now the claim is that science is structurally similar to religion. The position is adequately represented today, I think, by H. K. Schilling.[34] Accord-ing to Schilling, each of the communities constitutes a kind of enter-prise concerned with: (1) a (empirical or factual) description of the universe; (2) an explanation or theoretical account of the universe; and (3) a transformation of human existence in the universe (i.e. with an application of the insights achieved). After analysis of each of these concerns within each of the communities he concludes:

out of this analysis there emerges the idea of a continuous spectrum of cognition and knowledge, extending from the physical sciences, through biological and social sciences, through the arts to religion. It is proposed that some characteristics of knowledge and of the cognitive process vary continuously within the spectrum from one end to the other, but that others remain constant. Thus we can speak of 'knowledge' in all these fields and assert that in an important sense the way it is attained is the same for all of them. There is therefore no discontinuous separation of science and religion as far as cognition is concerned.[35]

THE SCIENCE OF RELIGION

The majority of the compatibility proposals of the past have been concerned largely with reducing the tension (doctrinal and methodological) between religion and the natural sciences. With the increasing attention that the social sciences have received in recent years the question of compatibility has been further complicated – particularly in respect to the science and/or sciences of religion. The social sciences, in providing us with a knowledge about ourselves and the world around us, provide us also with a scientific knowledge of religion. Religion itself is an object of study and consideration by science. Consequently one has two views of religion to consider when talking of the relations of science to religion – that of the insider, the committed believer, and that of the outsider, in this case the objective scientist revealing to us the truth *about* religion. Compatibility as it has been discussed above hardly seems a possibility now, it would seem, for the scientific view of religion requires the adoption of assumptions inimical to religion. Sociologists, for example, maintain that the study of religion can be undertaken only in so far as it is a cultural system and not treated as a divine or supernatural institution.[36] As one sociologist puts it, a scientific understanding of religion presupposes a 'methodological atheism'.[37] And another writes:

Science inevitably takes a naturalistic view of religion. This is a necessary *assumption* not a demonstrated truth from which all science proceeds. Religion is in man; it is to be understood by the analysis of his needs, tendencies and potentialities.... For those who identify religion with supernatural views of the world it must appear that scientific analysis must weaken religion.[38]

Yinger assumes here, as did Durkheim, that

> That which science refuses to grant to religion is not its right to exist, but its right to dogmatize upon the nature of things and the special competence which it claims for itself for knowing man and the world. As a matter of fact [Durkheim goes on to say] it does not know what it is made of, nor to what need it answers.[39]

Religion *properly* (i.e. scientifically) understood, therefore, is real and is compatible with science. Religion and science, that is, are compatible since they are coexistent realities, but there is no compatibility between religion's understanding of itself and the social-scientific understanding of religion (and, consequently, none between the religious view of the world and the scientific – physical and chemical – view of the world). To quote Yinger again:

> Science disproves religious beliefs, but it does not disprove religion. There may be conflict between science and a given religion, if part of its [the given religion's] total system is a series of propositions about the nature of the world, but there is no general conflict between science and religion defined in functional terms.[40]

The compatibility systems discussed above seem to be undermined by the claims of the social scientists. At first it might seem that the incommensurability thesis remains 'undamaged', but the judgement is mistaken; for although the two communities are indeed incommensurable there is no doubt in the mind of the social scientist that science is the superior community. The value of religion, that is, is revealed by science – a conclusion far removed from the claims of the incommensurability supporters of the religious camp (such as T. R. Miles). It would seem, therefore, that even though the conflict thesis is only weakly supported in the contrast between religion and the natural sciences it is thoroughly established in the contrast between religion and the social sciences.

Two important questions need to be raised with respect to the social sciences and the science of religion in particular. The first concerns the descriptive sciences and especially the phenomenology of religion. It is important to know precisely the nature and structure of the historical religious traditions. The study of the various religious traditions shows them to be very much concerned with a knowledge of the world, both mundane and supermundane. In the religious traditions of Judaism, Christianity and Islam, for example, the belief element is of considerable importance and has, in good measure, accounted for the force and power those traditions hold in the world today.[41] It is a fact then (revealed by a phenomenological study of religion) that religion consciously provides, or attempts to provide, explanations of the world.[42] Moreover, persons proposing religious explanations are cognizant of the possible conflict between their explanations and those provided by the sciences and have developed compatibility systems to overcome or mitigate the conflict. To ignore this primary cognitive interest is simply not acceptable – it is to overlook one of the key elements of several major religious traditions.

The second major question that needs to be raised concerns the methodological assumptions of the social sciences – particularly the assumption of atheism as it is enunciated, for example, by Berger.[43] It is possible, it seems, to distinguish Berger's 'methodological atheism' and atheism *tout court*. Such an atheistic (naturalistic) assumption is really a theological assumption, although in a negative mode, that is no more acceptable than the theological bias of the religiously committed person; either assumption introduces 'distortion' in the study of the data.[44] Smart brings the point out clearly when he writes:

it happens that the dominant theories in sociology have allowed at most a partial autonomy to religion itself; and this may be a justifiable conclusion. However, it is not at all clear that the whole question of autonomy has been dealt with in a proper manner.... It has not been easy for the human sciences outside religion to rid themselves of an explicitly theological Discipline.[45]

The conclusions about religion reached by the social scientist, therefore, have no more inherent validity than do the conclusions reached by the critical study of the religiously committed. Consequently, the supposed conflict between religion's self-understanding and the social scientific understanding of religion is not automatically resolved in favour of the social sciences.

A RENEWED UNDERSTANDING

The proliferation of compatibility systems suggests the emergence of a renewed understanding of both the scientific and religious communities. None of the systems, I think, is without flaw. All of them are helpful in one way or another, although some only negatively so in that they force us to examine old assumptions and presuppositions about religion and/or science. It is obvious, for example, that the early 'skirmishes' over cognitive matters between the scientific and religious communities led to a hardening of the lines of opposition in which those in the religious community seemed to forget that religion is a matter of life and not only a matter of cognition – that religion is a matter of existential decision and commitment and not *merely* a matter of knowing the nature and structure of the universe. Furthermore, science, encouraged by its early victories in such 'skirmishes,' came to see itself as a wholly rational enterprise which could easily be broadened to include *all* of life – to apply to every aspect of human existence. The non cognitivist systems of compatibility, with their emphasis upon the moral/emotional aspects of religion, function, then, to place limitations on this scientific (scientistic?) rationalization of human existence.

In so far as religion is not logical or epistemic calculation it has something to contribute to life that science does not possess. By denying cognitive import to religion, therefore, the non cognitivist avoids debate with the sciences and reveals the enriching effect that religion can have for individuals and for society. The claim on the part of the scientific community to have no need of such enrichment – that is, that science would eventually rationalize or make meaningful the whole of our existence – has really not undermined the non cognitivist compatibility system, as one might suspect, but rather has further weakened the conflict theory. Gilkey, it will be remembered, points out that such a claim on behalf of science is really a 'mythification' of science – a substitution of the scientific 'myth of total awareness' in place of older religious myths. And in this science reveals elements of ultimacy such as characterize religion. Gilkey's attempt at reconciling the two communities is extremely important for it suggests that compatibility systems may need as much scrutiny and analysis of science as of religion, for the real nature of science has yet to be revealed. Too much has been assumed about the nature of science too soon. Gilkey's own kind of compatibility system is not wholly adequate, however, for his suggestion that science needs necessarily to reach out to religious myths of ultimacy hardly follows from the fact that some have made of science a quasi-religious myth.[46] Furthermore, Gilkey fails to reveal whether this completion of science in the (revitalized) religious myths is a cognitive completion. It seems to me that it is not and therefore suffers the weakness of all non cognitivist proposals.

The claim that religion provides us with a radically different kind of knowledge than that provided by science parallels the claim of the non cognitivist in one respect. The non cognitivist completion of religion is not subject to scientific critique because it is 'beyond' cognition. Similarly the claim to 'super-knowledge' is beyond scientific critique, for the criteria of knowledge do not apply to the knowledge obtained in the 'realization ' or experience of the Ultimate. As one scholar puts it in criticism of those who assume *all* knowledge subject to the same criteria:

> What can one say of all those treatises that attempt to make the religious doctrines a subject of profane study, as if there were no knowledge that was not accessible to anyone and everybody as if it were sufficient to have been to school to be able to understand the most venerable wisdom better than the sages understood it themselves? For it is assumed by 'specialists' and 'critics' that there is nothing beyond their powers; such an attitude resembles that of children who, having found books, intended for adults, judge them according to their ignorance, caprice, and laziness.[47]

This kind of compatibility proposal, however, fails to recognize that religions make ordinary as well as extraordinary knowledge claims. Furthermore, many of the extraordinary knowledge claims seem to have implications that bear upon the states of affairs in the world and so involve implicit knowledge claims about the empirical world. Such beliefs can conflict with other non-religious claims about the world and these are not accounted for within this compatibility system. However, even though it is inadequate as a compatibility system, it is nevertheless a salutary warning against scientific arrogance. Whether or not such super-knowledge exists cannot be proven by science but neither can science disprove its existence.

The claim that there are genuine cognitive insights to be found in archaic religions that are capable of being re-expressed in modern scientific terminology hardly constitutes a compatibility system. It suggests the substantial or doctrinal compatibility of science and religion – or at least the possibility of a doctrinal or cognitive supplement to science by religion. How this is possible – except by happenstance – unless there is also a methodological compatibility is left unexplained.

COGNITIVE SIGNIFICANCE OF RELIGION

A compatibility system, it seems to me, is required only if religion actually claims cognitive significance and in particular claims knowledge of the nature, structure and meaning of this world and our existence in it. If religion makes no cognitive claims or only purely trans-empirical (i.e. supraworldly) cognitive claims, then it is in a different league altogether from scientific discourse and can never conflict with it. But religions do make empirically significant claims and so *can* conflict with science. In the history of Christian thought, for example, there has often been a conflict of theories or views of the world or some particular aspect of the world. That such cognitive disagreement is less noticeable today than in the past (that is, less so after the overthrow of Newtonian physics[48]) shows some possibility of a compatibility between the two. That there is not complete agreement, and never has been, does not preclude that there cannot be. Scientific theories cannot be espoused as final truths for science is progressive. Similarly, religious doctrines have often been inadequately interpreted. Since there is less than omniscience in either of the two communities, a complete agreement of thought between them is hardly to be expected.

Mere doctrinal agreement between science and religion is not enough, as I have already intimated above. The knowledge claimed by religion must be testable or checkable in the same (general) way as is scientific knowledge. An adequate compatibility system, therefore, must show that religion in its cognitive aspect has a similar logical structure to science. In the past such proposals have been unacceptable for they assumed the complete rationality of science and then attempted to show religion to be as rational as science. However, the recourse to faith – the lack of absolute objectivity in religion – repeatedly dashed all hopes of success in this endeavour. As I have already pointed out, however, the procedure is now reversed due to new revelations about the nature of scientific thought. Crudely put, the methodological similarity is now seen to exist in the fact that scientific thought is really as 'irrational' as theological thought. Much philosophical analysis of science and recent history of science seems to reveal that science is not a strictly logical and wholly empirical affair as it was once conceived to be. The work of philosophers and historians such as M. Polanyi, T. Kuhn, P. Feyerabend et al., reveals a fiduciary character to science.[49] As Kuhn puts it, scientific thought is characterized both by 'ordinary scientific thought' and 'extraordinary scientific thought', but only the former can be characterized as wholly rational: a 'deductive affair'. Extraordinary scientific thought does not move in a logical step-by-step fashion but rather has the character of a 'cumulative argument' and is, consequently very like theological argumentation.

NO NECESSARY CONFLICT

Whether science and religion are compatible, it should now be obvious, is a question that transcends the framework of thought of both these communities. That religion can enshrine superstitions or unfounded beliefs that can come into conflict with scientific doctrine cannot be disputed. But that there is a necessary and general conflict between science and religion has nowhere been shown. Doctrinally there have often been arguments between the two communities. And shifts of doctrine that bring about such agreement have not always been made by the religious community. Further, the claim that science and religion are radically different in method has until now been *assumed* on the strength of the modern reputation of science and has never been established. The various compatibility systems outlined above reveal a variety of challenges to the claim itself, or to the significance or meaning of the claim. The claim of an inherent and all-pervasive conflict between science and religion, I suggest therefore, is an *assumption*, not wholly groundless but not a *conclusion*. The uncritical tenacity with which it is held at times suggests, moreover, that it is a modern myth. That none of the compatibility proposals outlined all to briefly above has achieved universal agreement among philosophers or even among theologians does not make the assumption more than an assumption. The dissolution of long-standing myths is never likely to be the result of direct attack, but rather the product of a steady erosion, over a long period of time, of the uncritical foundations upon which they rest. The insights *vis à vis* science and religion gained from the various compatibility proposals discussed hint at the groundlessness of the conflict assumption and, as a result, suggests the possibility of compatibility. Indeed, a thorough analysis of the classical compatibility system to which I have referred above will show, I think, not only the possibility of compatibility but also its plausibility.

Part II
Beyond Legitimation: Compatibility Systems Reconsidered

6

Religion Transcending Science Transcending Religion ...

The nature of the relationship between science and religion has long been a central concern to both philosophers and theologians. For the most part, the relationship has been described in warfare imagery. Until this century, moreover, it was generally assumed that science and religion were locked in mortal combat with victory assured to science. However, some modifications of this simple picture emerged with the birth of post-Newtonian physics, and particularly so with the ascendancy of the Copenhagen interpretation of indeterminacy in quantum physics. This did not, as some thought, bring about a reversal of the fortunes of religion in the discussion, but the ambiguity of modern physics did spawn a *détente* between the two communities.[1] Indeed, the stage was set for the construction of 'compatibility systems' designed to show how science and religion constitute an essential unity – each incomplete in itself and a complement to the other.[2] Some who are involved in the ongoing discussion, in fact, have gone so far as to claim that earlier analyses of the relationship between the two communities in terms of warfare imagery were simply wrong. In support of their claims they point to the espousal by some in the religious community of the very scientific discoveries that the philosophers have seen as destructive of religious belief.[3]

In this paper I *suggest* that the *détente* between the two communities, even though real, is a matter of convenience, and merely temporary; that the 'compatibility systems' built are, ultimately, incoherent; and that the 'revisionist history' that would banish warfare imagery in recounting the history of the relationship between science and religion, or in predicting its future, is deceptive. There is, I shall attempt *to show* an unbridgeable gulf between religious knowledge, so-called, and science. Religion and science, that is, constitute two radically different modes of thought – mutually exclusive modes of thought with each transcending the other. Such transcendence makes it impossible to hold to both at the same time (although the impossibility is purely a logical one and must not be taken to mean that persons cannot, in fact, perform this 'feat' in their personal and social lives).

To *argue* the claim I have just put forward constitutes a task that cannot be undertaken within the bounds of a single chapter. I propose, therefore, to 'illustrate' the claim in a comparative analysis of the thought of the little-known Russian existentialist Lev Shestov and philosopher/social scientist Ernest Gellner. On one level their respective philosophical projects appear to have nothing in common. Closer analysis, however, will reveal an identity of structure in their thought that can provide the foundation of an argument for the claims made here. I begin with Shestov.[4]

Shestov boldly proclaims the incompatibility of religious and scientific modes of thought. In his *Potestas Clavium*[5] he describes the move from religious (mythopoeic) to rational thought as a 'bewitchment' of the human mind for it involves a loss of Freedom through an acknowledgement and acceptance of (scientific) Necessity. He maintains, therefore, that 'the "logic" of the religious man ... is quite different from the logic of the scientist.'[6] To know, according to Shestov, is to be subject to the 'laws of the universe' which, in the final analysis, predict the death, and therefore the insignificance, of persons, and so, ultimately, of ourselves. To cry to the gods (God) for help against that Fate is, of course, simply absurd in a world of science – it is against reason – and yet that is precisely what religion, and in particular the religion of the Bible, is all about. Such 'help' could only be possible in a world not fully accountable in terms of necessary and binding physical 'laws.' And, as Shestov puts it, 'The Ancient Greeks were already obviously afraid to leave the universe to the sole will of the gods for this would have been equivalent to admitting arbitrariness as the fundamental principle of life.'[7] To accept the 'necessity' of scientific laws, therefore, is the destruction of a peculiar religious mode of thought and existence; this is, as he states it in *Potestas Clavium*, a millennial struggle between Jewish and Greek genius.[8]

In *Kierkegaard and the Existential Philosophy*,[9] Shestov presents the same argument but uses the story of 'the fall of man' as symbol of this change in the style of thinking. God had warned Adam and Eve not to eat of the tree of knowledge of good and evil lest they die. and Shestov sees that death symbolically in the 'Necessity' which is the essence of our knowledge: 'Knowledge enslaves human will, making it subordinate to eternal truths which by their very nature are hostile to everything that lives and is at all capable of demonstrating its independence and which cannot bear to have even God as their equal.'[10] As in the former volume so also here Shestov maintains that the knowledge sought by us in a bid for power to control our own lives independently of the gods (God) is an intellectual vision of inevitable destruction of all that has ever come to be. The principles of causality are, if they are to be of any 'value', inflexible but as such can only account for the universe as a relentless round of birthing and dying. Consequently he once again concludes that 'science' – the philosophic vision – makes nonsense of the human cry for help that is the centre of religion for, he writes, 'when love comes face to face with truth, it is love that must retreat.'[11]

In both these volumes Shestov maintains that the belief in the eternal validity of the principles of knowledge means that even the gods (God) are (is) subject to such principles and that because of this humanity is 'enchanted' into believing that 'salvation' is to be found in the loss of the self in the impersonality of law.[12] What I have referred to above as the disenchantment of the universe by philosophy, Shestov refers to as a 'bewitchment' and an 'enchantment' of the human mind by God.[13] And theology, the Hellenized thinking of the fathers of the Church, is an element of that enchantment/bewitchment by God:

> theology itself which, as I have already indicated, was even in the Middle Ages, at the time of its highest flowering and triumph, the servant of philosophy (*ancilla philosophiae*), wanted absolutely to be above and beyond God. The entire *potestas audendi* of the philosophers and theologians expressed itself chiefly in the endeavour to subordinate God to man.[14]

'Religious thought' – that is, faith – is, however, quite opposed to this way of thinking; it is a 'religious philosophy', he argues in *Athens and Jerusalem*, that surmounts such knowledge, for faith is the *deus ex machina* that smashes Necessity.[15] 'God's thunder,' he writes, 'is the answer to human wisdom, to our logic, to our truths. It breaks to bits not man, but the "impossibilities" placed by human reason – which is at the same time human cowardice – between itself and the Creator.'[16] Either one follows reason by which reality is revealed according to scientific laws or one follows the biblical revelation of God. The dichotomy of the two ways of thought is unmistakable in Shestov:

if reality is rational, if we can derive truth only from reality, then elementary consistency demands of us that we pass Biblical revelation through the filter of the truths obtained from reality. And conversely, if revelation receives the sanction of truth, it must bear the halter of reality.... [R]evealed Truth engulfs and destroys all the coercive truths obtained by man from the tree of knowledge of good and evil.[17]

The task of thinking – religious thinking – is not to attempt to justify the revelation of God for that is but to submit to reason; rather, one is to dispel the power of reason through faith which is a renunciation of the tree of knowledge and a return to the tree of life.[18]

According to Shestov, then, Religion (Christianity) transcends (and therefore abrogates) reason because a proper understanding of 'biblical (religious) thinking' precludes the philosophy of the Greeks and the modern philosophy and science to which it has given birth. An analysis of the notion of Christian philosophy, especially as it arose in the Middle Ages, will clarify and confirm that interpretation. In his analysis of E. Gilson's Gifford lectures, *The Spirit of Medieval Philosophy*, Shestov maintains that the philosophers of the period, in attempting to bridge the gulf between the Bible and Greek philosophy were unwittingly recapitulating the sin of Adam and Eve: '... the medieval philosophers who aspired to transform faith into knowledge were far from suspecting that they were committing once again the act of the first man.'[19] They were, that is, being seduced by the promise of knowledge; hoping to transform the truths received from God without attendance of proofs into proven and self-evident truths. Medieval thinkers were incapable of removing the influence of their classical training, of giving up their Greek heritage, and consequently took their task to be the grounding, through rational argument, of the revealed truths of God, or what Gilson referred to as 'created truths'. This, however, subverted the 'created truths' for, as Shestov puts it, 'the principles of the Hellenic philosophy and the technique of Hellenic thought held them in their power and bewitched their minds.'[20] But this, Shestov maintains, is not possible, for the God of the Bible is a God who creates and destroys everything, even the eternal laws of the Greeks, and therefore God has nothing in common with either the rational or the moral principles of ancient Greek wisdom. Espousal of Greek metaphysics, therefore, means a rejection (i.e., an ignoring) of the Bible: 'The principles for seeking truth that it had received from the Greeks demanded imperiously that it not accept any judgement without having first verified it according to the rules by which all truths are verified: the truths of revelation do not enjoy any special privilege in this respect.'[21]

For medieval philosophy, then, the goal was clearly set out: it must, at all costs, defend the truths of faith by the same means by which all other truths are defended or else find themselves in an unbearable intellectual situation. But this is not really a 'bridge' between the Bible and Greek philosophy but rather a transformation or transmutation of the Bible in that it makes the Christian faith – the 'created truth' of God – another kind of human knowledge:

> The philosopher seeks and finds 'proofs', convinced in advance that the proven truth has much more value than the truth that is not proven, indeed, that only the proven Truth has any value at all. Faith is then only a 'substitute' for knowledge, an imperfect knowledge, a knowledge – in a way – on credit and which must sooner or later present the promised proofs if it wishes to justify the credit that has been accorded to it![22]

But faith, and especially the faith of the Bible, he insists, has nothing to do with knowledge. Not only is faith not knowledge, and here Shestov invokes the authority of the life of faith of Abraham and St Paul, but rather stands opposed to knowledge.[23] The knowledge of the Greeks is 'impersonal knowledge' – a recognition that all of life is subject to Necessity (of law) and that it is, therefore, 'indifferent to everything, truth that we raise above the will of all living beings.'[24] Biblical faith quite to the contrary extends the life of possibility and thereby transcends the death of Necessity. This is the theme tirelessly repeated by Shestov in all his writing, the force of which can hardly be captured in so brief an account as this. To *trust* the possibilities that faith opens up, lacking all proofs as did Abraham, for example, is foolishness to philosophy and knowledge; it is contrary to reason. Indeed, in his book on Kierkegaard, Shestov interprets Abraham's transgression of the law of ethics as the essence of the movement of faith, pointing out that the Bible glorifies him rather than seeing him as a disgrace.[25] Faith therefore is not 'credit knowledge' but rather a mysterious and creative power, 'an incomparable gift'.[26]

For the Greeks (that is, for rational thought in general) such obedience to God is 'war' – it is to find oneself in that unfortunate condition described by Socrates in the *Phaedo* of being a *misologos*.[27] But to follow Reason is to deny Possibility and to destroy the power of God. Consequently, it is impossible to 'defend' the God of the Bible through rational argument, for that would amount to a destruction of rational argumentation itself.[28] 'We must', Shestov therefore urges, 'before everything else, tear out from our being all the postulates of our "natural knowledge" and our "natural morality."'[29] Salvation must (as Plotinus had already recognized centuries back) seek salvation outside of knowledge and outside of reason.[30]

As has already been intimated above, E. Gellner, a philosopher and social scientist of a radically different frame of mind to that of Shestov, has a surprisingly similar understanding of the nature and history of human thought. For Gellner too there are 'modes of thought' and modern-Western-scientific thought is incommensurable with earlier forms of thinking; the 'modern mind,' as he puts it in the title of an essay ('The Savage and the Modern Mind'[31]), is clearly distinguishable from the 'savage mind'. The move from the latter to the former constitutes, he says, a 'Copernican revolution' because it shifts the *ultimate* seat of legitimacy of belief(s) from 'visions' to 'epistemology'. The difference between the two, therefore, as with Shestov, hinges essentially on the quest for knowledge – scientific knowledge – to which Gellner refers elsewhere as the 'leap of science'.[32] What the leap amounts to, he suggests, 'is that the world is seen *within* knowledge, and not the other way around?'[33] It is a search for the 'validity' of knowledge-claims that will provide an 'entry permit' to our world.[34] In summary: 'The great transition between the old, as it were nonepistemic worlds, in which the principles of cognition are subject to the pervasive constitutive principles of a given vision, and thus have little to fear, and a world in which this is no longer possible, is a fundamental transition indeed.'[35] In an essay on 'An Ethic of Cognition', Gellner describes the difference in the 'modes of thought' as even more glaringly obvious: 'The biggest, most conspicuous simple fact about the human world is the Big Divide between what may rightly be called the industrial-scientific society and the Rest,'[36] and the difference is one of morality and cognition.

In his book *Legitimation of Belief*, from which I have already quoted here, Gellner sets out this difference of mind and cognition in terms of two epistemological models – there are, that is, two theories concerned with cognitive legitimacy, namely 're-endorsement' theories and 'selector' theories. The former are 'mentalistic' in that their distinguishing feature is the acceptance of mental powers as self-explanatory. The latter are 'empiricistic' and they deny that consciousness is an explanatory principle rather than something itself in need of explanation. In the essay on an ethic of cognition also referred to above, he writes: 'The essence of empiricism is that all, but *all*, theoretical structures are accountable; that none can claim such an awful majesty as to be exempt from the indignity of inquiry and judgement; and that substantive theoretical systems as to elude and evade this indignity are out. *Out*,'[37] Selector theories and, consequently, knowledge, for Gellner, as for Shestov, thoroughly 'disenchants' the universe and seems to stand opposed to 'life' in the sense of a 'meaningful existence'. This, perhaps, requires a little further elaboration.

Selector theories, based as they are upon empiricist principles of legitimating knowledge claims, are, according to Gellner, essentially mechanistic: 'The growth of knowledge presupposes its communicability, storage, public, and independent testing, independence of anyone's status, moral or ritual condition and so forth. This is what makes such knowledge powerful, and it is also what makes it "cold", disenchanting, "mechanical".'[38] Such a view I would be willing to argue is already perceptible in the philosophy/science of the Milesians in their attempt to account for the existence and nature of the universe not through divine agency as in mythic forms of thought but rather in terms of substance and causal transformations of that substance.[39] And it is that same scientific view, it seems to me, that animates the radical disenchantment of the universe in the 'philosophy/science' of Watson, Skinner, et al. This subsumption of persons under impersonal explanatory principles is dehumanizing because it seems to remove any element of purposive activity, and hence meaning, from human existence. A meaningful universe, that is, is one amenable to human concerns and purposes; one that is sympathetically in tune with our human fears and anxieties. The pre-scientific world, therefore, is meaningful because it is still 'enchanted'. 'Mechanism' as in that of the selector theories of knowledge destroys all this, for 'enchantment works through idiosyncrasy, uniqueness, spontaneity, a magic which is tied to the identity and individuality of the participants, and all these are excluded by orderly regularity.'[40]

The agreement here between Shestov's existentialist perspective and Gellner's empiricist stance is remarkable. The language of 'life' becomes problematic in light of the language of knowledge. Since general 'visions' of life in archaic cultures and 'religious systems', or 'views' of life in modern ones provide meaning in a picture of the universe as enchanted, where agency, whether transcendent or purely immanent, is in no need of explanation. They stand opposed, however, to science and its causal understanding of that same universe. And the conflict is not merely contingent but necessary: 'There is no escape: it is not the content, the *kind* of explanation which de-humanizes us; it is *any* genuine explanation, as such, that does it.'[41] As Gellner puts it elsewhere and in more detail:

> the disenchantment is not a contingent consequence of this or that specific discovery, but inheres in the very method and procedure of rational inquiry, of impartial subsumption under symmetrical generalizations, of treating all data as equal. Reductionism is not an aberration. it is inherent in the very method of science. If we 'scientifically' establish the reality of some 'human' and seemingly reduction-resisting element in the world, we would *ipso facto* thereby also 'reduce' it, in some new way.[42]

Although Gellner's description of our present state of affairs is almost identical to that of Shestov, his evaluation of that 'condition' in which we find ourselves is radically different. There is a sense in which, like Shestov, he sees the quest for knowledge as a 'fall': 'All in all, mankind has already made its choice, or been propelled into it in truly Faustian manner, by a greed for wealth, power, and by mutual rivalry.'[43] The style of knowing that is chosen commits one to a particular kind of society, he suggests here, and all we can do is try, in looking back at the 'Copernican revolution', to understand what happened.[44] But such pessimism is not, I think, characteristic of Gellner's view. On epistemological grounds it seems we are forced into opting out of the world – our moral world included – in order to evaluate it because neither our 'selves' nor our cultures are unproblematic, or solutions to problems, but rather are problems themselves that require elucidation and explanation.[45] And the only way to achieve that understanding is to break free from our ethnocentrism and anthropomorphism and to adopt a 'non-circular' framework of reasoning in which 'human requirements are not allowed to limit or even create presuppositions, in the sphere of scientific theory?'[46]

Gellner does admit that the empiricism he advises is, in the final analysis, a choice; an arbitrary decision. In this he seems to echo Shestov's *charge* of the arbitrariness of reason/rationality. However. Gellner's stance is much more positive. There may indeed be no 'proof ' of the rightness of this empiricist 'knowledge' but it is still, nevertheless, the best ideology available to us, for its prejudge-ments, as he puts it, are indirect and negative. And this ideology, he further maintains, is supported by the argument from illusion and the important difference between its success and that of other abort-ive styles of thinking.[47] In this, the scientific 'attitude' *transcends* that of religion.[48]

Unlike other positions regarding the nature of modern science, Gellner's stance cannot, I think, be charged with naivety. He is quite aware, for example, that the viewpoint of the 'surrogate angel' – the opting out of the world in order to evaluate it – is not actually poss-ible. He admits convergence, that is, between re-endorsement and selector theories. It is obvious that no particular explanation at any given moment is absolutely acceptable and yet the principle of mechanism itself is not questionable. Consequently, when particular explanations are in question it is *persons* who make judgements about them. He concludes, therefore, that:

> we shall never find ourselves without either ghosts or machines, or without the tension arising from their joint presence. Knowl-edge means explanations and explanation means the specification of a structure that will apply generally and impersonally to all like cases. The mechanistic vision of the world is the shadow of this ideal, our ideal, of explanation. Yet at the same time, no par-ticular explanation is ever permanent or sacred; it is judged by us ghosts.[49]

But, as he points out elsewhere, this does not mean that one must, because of this, rule out altogether the possibility of a non-anthropomorphic account of persons. The fact that the 'study of humanity' is 'human beings' does not, that is, entail that the explan-atory concepts must also be 'human'; the account may quite reason-ably be causal in form.[50]

It is obvious from this discussion of Gellner, then, that even though he provides an account of modes of thought that parallels that of Lev Shestov, his evaluation of the situation that ensues is rad-ically different. He affirms scientific as opposed to religious thought and its vestiges in humanism and humanistic thinking. 'The requirements of life and thought?' he writes 'are incompatible,'[51] and on this he is in agreement with Shestov. But Gellner refuses either to give up thought and the quest for knowledge or to allow it, for non-epistemological reasons or ends, to be adulterated by the 'mentalism' of theological/religious thought (and for Gellner all theology is voluntarist theology), or of contemporary idealistic social sciences which are but contemporary attempts to 're-enchant' the universe.[52] For Gellner, therefore, science *transcends* religion.

The conclusion that presses itself upon us on completion of this analysis is that plain coherent thinking cannot operate in terms of the principles inherent in both faith (religion) and reason (science). To proceed upon such an assumption is to admit that religion *transcends* science and that science *transcends* religion where transcendence of principles implies their abrogation. But we must also conclude that mutual transcendence is not logically possible.

7

Is Science Really an Implicit Religion?[1]

Our modern Western (that is, European/Anglo-American) civilization has come to be what it is, a religious and, scientific structure, both at once. It cannot be denied that it is both a religious and a scientific culture, but neither can it be denied that there has existed a constant tension between its scientific and religious communities at least since the emergence of modern Western science at the close of the Middle Ages. Indeed so often has that tension deteriorated into outright hostility that it is not at all inappropriate to describe the relationship between them in warfare imagery.[2] And that has made us rather uneasy, for we suspect that the conflict between the two communities is indicative of a more profound and significant conflict of concepts and ideas – indicative of the fact that science and religion provide not just different sets of concepts for coming to terms with the world but rather mutually exclusive conceptual structures or frameworks for doing so. Thus, even though there can be no doubt that a *modus vivendi* between the two communities and, in a sense, between the two sets of concepts, was achieved and gave birth to our simultaneously scientific and religious civilization, there is no longer the confidence that once existed in its validity. The perpetual conflict between the two has come to constitute a kind of *prima facie* case against it. And there is some apprehension – given that in our society we tend to think more like scientists and less like the religious devotees of bygone days – that religion will somehow succumb to science; that our culture will 'degenerate' into a purely scientific culture. We are loath to give up the benefits that either the one or the other of the structures of thought has conferred upon us – religion having provided us with meaning (meaningfulness) and science with knowledge (power) – although even putting the issue that way may be to draw the distinction too precisely between the two for us to feel comfortable with it. And so we seem to be committed to finding some new interpretation of science, or religion, or both, so as to entail their compatibility and complementarity, both substantively and methodologically. Anything less would force us to acknowledge a fundamental contradiction at the core of our cultural inheritance and existence.

If science, however, were itself to be shown to have a religious quality – to be, at least implicitly, religious – the apparent conflict between science and religion, especially at the methodological level, in the history of the relations of the two communities of thinkers could then be chalked up to simple misunderstanding. Though science and religion might be in conflict over substantive matters of belief – in just the way that religious traditions appear to differ on matters of belief – there would be no *necessary* conflict in the way those beliefs are derived and adjudicated. And in clearing up misunderstanding over such methodological matters one would also make available the fruits of both science and religion, free of any intellectual misgivings.

Such an approach to resolving the science/religion question has been proposed in recent years by the Chicago theologian Langdon Gilkey. Gilkey, although not referring overtly to science as an implicit religion, argues that science functions not only in a purely cognitive capacity but also in a religious one, even though it functions in the latter capacity in a distinctly inferior way. Given the history of the relation of religion and science, Gilkey's claims about the nature of science as implicitly religious is of considerable apologetic value. Whether the argument he provides to support the claim is adequate, however, is very much open to question.

According to Gilkey, secular, scientifically oriented persons genuinely believe themselves to be irreligious (or areligious) but analysis of their scientific existence reveals a dependence upon elements of ultimacy usually characteristic only of the religious devotee. Gilkey sketches out his argument in support of this claim in a broad and general way in his *Naming the Whirlwind*.[3] There are, he maintains in that essay, three elements of ultimacy that characterize science. The first is the unremitting *eros* in the scientist to know the world. Secondly, the assumption by scientists of the ontological reality of what they study and of the possibility of a relationship between that reality and the knowing mind, he argues, involves a necessary leap beyond the evidence available to science and is, therefore, a kind of faith which ultimately (i.e. which alone) makes sense of the scientific enterprise itself. The third hint of ultimacy in science, he maintains, is to be found in the structure of scientific judgement – a structure that in the final analysis reveals the ultimate awareness of oneself as knower. In his later *Religion and the Scientific Future* he summarizes his position in the following way:

> [The] personal affirmation of oneself as a knower is ... the foundation of the possibility of all rational judgment and in the end it grounds all science. In turn this awareness of oneself as a knower cannot be doubted. The sceptic, in affirming his scepticism also is aware of himself and affirms himself as *understanding* the view that he now asserts; he is also aware of himself as judging that this view is in fact sure.... No movement could take place without this element of indubitable certainty, without this unconditioned assertion of the actuality of knowing ourselves.[4]

For Gilkey, then, the modern person's trust in science really constitutes the adoption of a new myth – a quasi-religious myth – which he calls the 'myth of total awareness'. As he puts it, the myth asserts that 'man becomes man and can control his life and destiny if he is educated, liberal, analyzed, scientific and "expert", etc ... that knowledge and awareness can turn whatever has been a blindly determining force on and in man and so a *fate* over man, into a new instrument of man'.[5] The emergence of the myth Gilkey claims, however, shows one's need for ultimacy and the attempt by science to satisfy a need which, ironically, it contributed to creating by undermining traditional religious belief. But Gilkey also sees the new myth as dangerous, for the technology that science presumes will 'save' humankind in fact constitutes its greatest threat. For Gilkey, therefore, science 'reaches out for' ultimacy and is, consequently, implicitly religious; yet science, he also insists, is unable to provide the ultimacy which it (implicitly) seeks. Thus, he insists, science needs religion although, to be sure, religion that goes beyond the 'broken images' of past religious traditions. In *Religion and the Scientific Future* he concludes:

> The dilemmas of even the most secular of cultures are ultimately intelligible only in the light of faith; the *destiny* of even a scientific world can be adequately thematized only in terms of religious symbols; and the confidence of the future even of technological man can be creatively grounded only if the coming work of the Lord in the affairs of men is known and affirmed.[6]

The tension in Gilkey's understanding of science as implicit religion is obvious for it involves seeing science as both a quest for and a denial of ultimacy; as both a proto-salvific possession of ultimacy and a damning deprivation of it. And such contradiction within his analysis radically undermines his claim to have shown science and religion to be compatible. Gilkey's analysis of the character of science, moreover, is also suspect and fails to persuade. That some persons may have fastened on to science in a religious fashion hardly grounds the claim that science seeks a saving ultimacy; that some have made of science a quasi-religious myth does not imply that science is a myth. According to Gilkey, the scientific 'myth of total awareness' asserts that humankind can control its destiny if only it becomes properly educated and so claims that knowledge can change what has been a blind determining force over humankind into an instrument for its ultimate benefit. But such a portrait of modern, secular, scientifically oriented persons is more a distortion than a representation of the truth of the matter. Secular persons committed to science, properly understood, are not persons who believe that they can totally control their destiny by means of it. Rather, such persons simply recognize that there is no one else around to look after them, and that to resolve problems concerning their continued existence they must do the best possible with the knowledge available. It is assumed that the best way of proceeding with any task in life is to know as much as possible about the nature of the physical, psychological, and social worlds we encounter. As Karl Popper puts it, to suggest that we cannot and must not attempt to 'remake' the world in which we live in order to provide ourselves a more significant existence is to offer a very poor solution, or none at all, to the problems faced not only by the human race but by 'the world' in general.[7] Gilkey fears that those who 'control' the institutions of science directed towards this end will themselves be without control and therefore dangerous to us – as if those in control are always 'sinister others' different from ourselves. He seems somehow to think that religion, in placing such institutions under the control of the representatives of religious institutions, puts science under non-human or divine control. On that score Gilkey seems to me to be politically naive. To be sure, control must be wielded over the *direct* controllers of science and technology as Gilkey suggests but that control, it must be recognized, will also be a human control (or what the theologian might wish to refer to as divine control humanly mediated). A human control of these institutions that pretends to be divine is, it seems to me, far more dangerous than the one that does not so pretend.[8]

Gilkey's talk of ultimacy in science is also misleading. Ultimacy is in no sense a goal of the epistemology that characterizes science; nor is it a goal of the political institutions committed to making use of science in tackling problems in human affairs. Popper, for example, does not search for an ultimate salvation of humankind. Rather, in stark contrast to Gilkey's assertions about such philosophers, Popper claims on behalf of the scientific rationalist the lofty, but not ultimate, aim of bringing about a more reasonable world – that is, of creating a society that aims at humaneness and reasonableness; at a reduction of strife and war; at equality and freedom; a world in which one day, as he puts it 'men [and women] may ever become the conscious creators of an open society, and thereby of a greater part of their fate'.[9] To seek to create an 'open society' in which individual persons come increasingly to direct their fate rather than to have that fate determined by others in their community is hardly to seek eternal salvation or some other equivalent religious goal. And to suggest, as Gilkey does, that such a quest, which calls for critical reflection at every step rather than submission to the authority of the revelations of others, necessarily leads to tyranny strikes me as ludicrous.

Given this analysis of Gilkey's claims, we can only conclude that his attempt to show an essential harmony between science and religion on the basis of an essential 'religiousness' of the project of science itself is unpersuasive. That some have made of science a religion, or that science can be treated in that fashion, I would not deny. But that does not justify the further claims Gilkey makes. Indeed it can be shown, I think, that science is not only *not* an implicit religion, or implicitly religious, but that it is in important respects both *incommensurable* (at the level of intention) and *incompatible* (at least potentially so on the substantive level and necessarily so at the methodological level) with religion. Furthermore this is so notwithstanding the fact that the scientific and religious communities have, until the recent past at least, created the conditions for their cultural coexistence. An uncritical acquiescence in that cultural achievement gives rise to the assumption that if, to put it crudely, we need both science and religion in order to exist, the scientific and religious modes of thought must be commensurable and logically compatible or, if incommensurable, in some important sense complementary. That is to say, since we desire the fruits of both science and religion we therefore feel it impossible to exist without either one or the other, and so the assumption of their complementarity or compatibility – contrary appearances notwith-standing – is taken for granted (i.e. as justified). Yet it is quite obvi-ous to most of us that the achievement of a *modus vivendi* between scientific and religious modes of thought could well be rationally explained even if the two structures of thought presented by those communities should be logically incompatible. A matter of logic is not necessarily reflected either in psychological or social realities however: logically incompatible modes of thought and outright contradictions often coexist in one and the same individual; and communities of persons can similarly harness together what on the logical level are mutually exclusive structures of thought.

I am aware, of course, that there have been many accounts of the natures of science and religion and their mutual relations that claim to prove or to show that scientific and religious modes of thought are not logically incompatible but complementary. It is not possible here even briefly to deal with all of them, although some general comments may be helpful.

'Compatibility systems', as such accounts have come to be called, can be divided into two major groups according to the nature of the complementarity between science and religion that is being argued – that is, as to whether religion complements science in a cognitive or non-cognitive fashion. There are those who insist that religion is not concerned with obtaining knowledge – that it is not a matter of logical or epistemic calculation but rather entirely a matter of com-mitments, decisions and, in general, life. Science, on the other hand, aims simply at obtaining a knowledge of the structure and nature of 'the world'. The two are therefore, incommensurable and logically could never find themselves in conflict with each other. Being incommensurable they can never be incompatible. Though it does not make sense to talk of them as being compatible either (that is in the logical sense), it is obvious that they are complementary, for each provides something the other does not and both individuals and society, it is assumed, would be the poorer without either of them.[10]

Not all who argue that science and religion are incommensurable, however, hold religion to complement science in an extra-cognitive sense only. Some religious existentialists, for example, have argued that religion does make a cognitive contribution to life but point out that the knowledge it provides is radically different from and supe-rior to the propositional knowledge of the sciences. So different a knowledge exempts it, so it is claimed, from the standard criteria by which scientific claims are adjudicated, thus making it logically impossible for the two sets of claims ever to be in conflict.[11]

Whether this latter strategy is really different from the non-cognitivist complementarity one, however, is very much in doubt. It parallels the non-cognitivist move in that both the non-cognitive complement and the 'super-cognitive' complement in some sense lie beyond ordinary scientific knowledge and so beyond adjudication by the criteria applied to scientific knowledge-claims.

Compatibility systems based on subjectivist interpretations of science *à la* M. Polanyi and T. Kuhn – of which there have been not a few – argue that science and religion are commensurables and that religion complements science both cognitively and non-cognitively. Such systems differ little from traditional apologetics which attempted to prove that religious beliefs constituted knowledge of the same order, and every bit as creditable (or justified) as the knowledge provided by the sciences.[12] There is general agreement, however, that such traditional argument was vulnerable to criticism – that in that framework religious belief claims were not justified and so pointed to the commensurability *and* incompatibility of science and religion. But the 'new apologists' claim to be able to show such incompatibility to be the consequence of a false understanding of science that makes of it a more rational enterprise than it really is. Based on the 'new philosophy of science' referred to above, they argue a kind of inverse commensurability in which science is shown to be – putting it bluntly – as irrational as religion. Religious and scientific beliefs, therefore, are still structurally identical but the significance of that identity is now radically altered. Scientific belief-claims are now no longer seen as purely cognitive and wholly non-ideological; they are seen, that is, to function in *more than* a cognitive fashion, and in doing so reveal elements of ultimacy that – as with Gilkey – bespeak a quasi-religious quality. And religious beliefs, though primarily concerned with commitment, decision and life, also provide an understanding in which that life is lived. Science, therefore, is quasi-religious and religion quasi-scientific. Consequently they are commensurables and so can be found to be either compatible or incompatible with each other. But given the nature of this commensurability it is much more difficult to show incompatibility either on the substantive or on the methodological level.[13]

None of these so-called compatibility systems is finally persuasive. The non-cognitivists fail, for example, to persuade us that religion really is a wholly non-cognitive enterprise; of that the phenomenological study of religion leaves us in little doubt. That would seem a denial of religion's reality, for in disengaging it from the world it makes it wholly the product of the human imagination, and therefore a fictive reality.[14] That is not a denial of value to religion but it does seem radically different from the value that religious devotees see in it. (The value of religion for them lies in the extra-mental reality to which the religion refers, whereas the social reality of religion requires only that it is believed by them to be extra-mentally true.) The 'super-cognitivists' (i.e. the existentialists referred to above), on the other hand, offend science and logic in their special pleading for a 'religious knowledge' alongside that of common sense and scientific knowledge. And the new apologists, it seems to me, are handicapped by a deficient philosophy of science that precludes any serious distinction between referential and non-referential uses of language which suggests that we live in a wholly textual or intertextual world.

The attempt to construct the ideal compatibility system either by showing science to be implicitly religious or by showing science and religion to be necessary and logically consistent aspects of some more general and fundamentally religious reality leaves us with rather inconclusive results. Given the types of systems that have been proposed, one is forced to deny that religions and religious persons make knowledge-claims; that the knowledge-claims made by religion in some systems have anything in common with those made by science; that religious knowledge-claims stand justified precisely as scientifically valid knowledge-claims even though they have no obligation to measure up to what has been called the requirements of the morality of scientific knowledge. The failure to achieve an adequate compatibility system does not, of course, prove that it can never be achieved – that could be chalked up to present ignorance or to the immense complexity of the problems its construction encounters. Nevertheless it does seem to me that the persistent lack of success in compatibility system construction constitutes sufficient grounds for seeking a different kind of understanding of the relations of science and religion. And that is what I propose to do now in a preliminary way.

On the basis of the negative results of the foregoing analysis I shall begin by abandoning the assumption embedded in our culture and operative in those constructing compatibility systems, namely, that because science and religion are both fundamental elements of our civilization they must also be compatible with each other in all respects. However, before being able genuinely to raise the question as to whether or not science and religion present us with conflicting and possibly mutually exclusive modes of thought, a further widely held anthropological assumption – namely, the assumption of the rational unity of humankind, which insists that all human thought, whether magical, mythical, religious or scientific, is essentially alike in structure – will have to be shown to be equally suspect. Without that assumption, that is, the apparently *a priori* knowledge regarding the ultimate reconcilability of science and religion, of reason and faith, is transmuted to the level of an empirical question, and only then open to serious criticism. Once free of those two assumptions, I shall argue, there is a possibility of achieving a truer understanding of the logical relation of science and religion that will do justice to the peculiarities of each, as well as to what is genuinely common between them. And with that understanding established, the perpetual tension and conflict between science and religion will no longer need to be explained away in tortuous and over-elaborate fashion; for conflict, it will be seen, is precisely what one ought to expect, theoretically speaking, in any institution attempting to combine the two within a single framework.

There are good grounds – though at best I can only suggest their nature here – for rejecting the 'uniformitarian assumption', often referred to as the assumption of the rational unity of the human race. They can be found in a careful re-examination of Lévy-Bruhl's thesis that a kind of logical gulf separates primitive ('archaic', 'savage') thought from modern, Western, scientific thought. I have argued for the soundness of the Lévy-Bruhlian dichotomy thesis in a recent essay entitled 'The Prelogical Mentality Revisited',[15] and shall not recapitulate that argument here. In an unpublished essay – 'In Two Minds: Religion and Philosophy in Ancient Greece' – I have argued that we can see in the Presocratic philosophers the 'birthing' of the modern mind.[16] The thinking of the Presocratics, that is, constitutes a revolution in thought that even though what follows is not wholly discontinuous with what precedes it, it still makes sense to claim that from this point on the Greeks are 'in two minds'. Their philosophy, in progressively abandoning the medium of myth, created a mode of thought that transcends the essentially mythopoeic thinking of the traditionally religious mind. It is not that philosophy simply replaces mythopoeic/religious thought but rather that it gradually emerges as another alternative form of knowing the world. Changes in the economic, political, and social complex of ancient Greek society provided opportunity for a truly cognitive interest, distinct from other concerns, to flourish.

The easiest way to summarize this discussion is to say that the emergence of philosophy signals the emergence of a more purely cognitive intentionality in human thought. 'Beliefs' come to function in an *essentially* cognitive capacity rather than in what has been called a 'catechismic' one.[17] Primitive thought certainly produces and operates with beliefs, but their beliefs function primarily socially rather than epistemically; they function as a social bond amongst the members of the group rather than merely supplying them with knowledge. Scientific knowledge-claims do not function in such a catechismic fashion. In drawing this distinction I do not mean to suggest that catechismic beliefs have no cognitive function as well, but only that their cognitive function is blurred and of subordinate interest – the cognitive element of such beliefs is not a conscious concern.[18]

Given this description of Lévy-Bruhl's 'dichotomy thesis' with respect to the nature of human thought, it is obvious that the two modes of thought are incommensurable. Though not absolutely different enterprises, of course, they nevertheless fulfil significantly different functions that require radically different structures. Though primitive thought provides the community with knowledge, its central, though perhaps unconscious, intention is to provide the community with a meaningful world picture that facilitates the structuring of individual and social existence. The cognitive baselines of such thought, as Ernest Gellner refers to the beliefs it contains, simultaneously constitute the framework of a social and moral order.[19] And concepts behave very differently when governed by such normative concerns – when indeed they are tools for the engineering of meaning and for structuring a meaningful existence – than when they operate merely as tools of explanation. In the latter sense they possess what Gellner refers to as 'diplomatic immunity' from the 'entrenched clauses' that determine the social, moral and political obligations of society and that give us the meaning of a world picture.[20] But it is because the 'knowledge' provided by the primitive mode of thought lacks such 'diplomatic immunity' that it is likely to be incoherent and unsupported, and so in all likelihood *incompatible* with that provided by the modern scientific mind.

I shall try to clarify what I mean here by responding briefly to a recent attack by I. C. Jarvie on those 'who try to make a case for some qualitative difference between systems of superstitious [mythopoeic] thought and science', for, as he puts it, magic and religion, as examples of superstitious thought, are, like science, 'attempts at cognition'.[21] However I suggest that his understanding of the notion of 'attempts at cognition' is seriously and misleadingly ambiguous. Jarvie adopts his position on the basis of the assumption that magic and religion are cognitive or scientific even if there is no conscious intent to be so. Though I have already made clear that I do not deny that in a very important sense primitive persons know the world that they inhabit – and by that I do not mean only the world of their world picture but the objectively, independently existing world in which they subjectively exist – and therefore find myself in agreement with Jarvie on the truth of this claim, nevertheless I disagree as to the significance of what precisely that claim implies. As I have intimated above the 'cognitive intention' that first emerges with the Greek (Presocratic) philosophers involves the creation or construction of a new and radically different set of intellectual techniques and procedures that distinguishes it from the intellectual activities engaged in that undifferentiated thinking that embodies an apprehension of the world indissolubly with a projection of meaning upon it, from the thinking that is an amalgam of cognition and fabrication resulting in the production of meaning. Non-human animals, as Jarvie knows, also learn from their experience in the world. Animal behaviours, that is, also constitute 'attempts at cognition'. That, however, does not prevent us from distinguishing the peculiar character of consciousness in human knowing, making human knowledge significantly different from, even though not wholly discontinuous with, those attempts at cognition. Similarly the explicit, conscious intent to know the world rather than to interpret it – to discern its meaning for us (which is what mythopoeic thinking is all about) – introduces a radical distinctiveness.

In so far as I agree with Jarvie that primitives 'know' the world in which they live, I also find myself in agreement with his claim that science 'deserves credit for being nearer the truth than the world-view systems that preceded it'.[22] That would appear to put me into some difficulty: in agreeing that science and magic (or myth, or religion) are *incompatible* they cannot be incommensurable because questions of compatibility or incompatibility, it is generally argued, presuppose commensurability. The difficulty is more apparent than real, however, since we can, etically – that is, as outsiders to the archaic/primitive world-view – compare its unintentional cognitive component, isolated by us from its richer matrix of fabrication and meaning-construction, with the achievements of science, all the while recognizing that this constitutes a kind of distortion of the primitive/archaic world view as a whole. The distortion is, however, only the product of an analytical exercise and is not taken to represent the actual mind of the primitive cognitively speaking. But through that exercise we can arrive at their cognitive understanding of the nature of the world, at what would constitute the only knowledge of the world of which they were capable. And that knowledge we now know stands in conflict with the explicit, scientific knowledge succeeding it. As distilled from a much richer context of thought, that knowledge, of course, is not their knowledge – it is their knowledge only in so far as it is seen from our perspective of what constitutes knowledge. Proceeding with such an interpretation of primitive thought, however, it becomes clear that the two modes of thought, mythopoeic and scientific, are incommensurable with respect to intention but commensurable with respect to function.[23]

In talking of scientific thought succeeding mythopoeic modes of thinking, I do not mean to imply that it also supersedes mythopoeic thought, save with respect to cognition. Since the two modes of thought differ radically in intention they are incommensurable values. Neither requires justification outside itself – they simply are what they are, neither better nor worse than the other. On that score it might well be argued that they transcend each other.[24] In so far as they are incompatible – in the sense I have just now described – they cannot be espoused simultaneously with logical consistency.

If the arguments I have sketched above are successful, and if it is possible to show that religious thought is more mythopoeic than scientific, then it will also have been shown that science *and* religion are both incommensurable and incompatible and, consequently, that one cannot with consistency espouse both at the same time. (My concern here, it should be remembered, has not been whether one should believe in either religion or in science but whether it is possible with logical consistency to believe in both at the same time.) There are good *prima facie* grounds to indicate that religious thinking generally is mythopoeic in structure and not simply from existentialist quarters but also from the phenomenology of religion. But the existence of theology might appear to confirm quite the opposite conclusion, though I think it can be shown that theology is not really a religious mode of thought – theology, in fact, is a mode of thought ultimately detrimental to religion and religious thinking. This claim, however, is not something I can prove here.[25]

If the suggestions I have put forward and developed briefly can be persuasively argued – and I think they can – the only conclusion we can come to is that the search for the perfect compatibility system is misdirected and the attempt to show science to be a species of religion futile. Moreover, a reasonable account of the relation of science to religion will have been provided – or at least the possibility will have been created of such an account that will be able to do justice to what is peculiar in each of these institutions as well as to what little is common to both. Such an account will also be able to provide a persuasive explanation for the perpetual tension between the scientific and religious communities. Pursuit of the ideal compatibility system, even though logically unobtainable, nevertheless seems to fulfil a social function for many in our society and that is bound to keep it alive; the quest itself, that is, keeps alive the assumptions essential for the perpetuation of our scientific-cum-religious culture that so many of us are reluctant to give up. And those committed to science will not, therefore, be seen as a threat for they will have somehow or other, to be religious – at the very least implicitly or anonymously religious.

8

Religion, Science, and the Transformation of 'Knowledge'

Despite the work of recent revisionist historians concerned with the relations between science and religion in modern Western society, I believe most students of Western culture would agree that there has been a persistent tension – even warfare – between the scientific and religious communities in the West, at least since the emergence of modern Western science in Europe at the close of the Middle Ages.[1] I would argue, moreover, that that tension is already to be found in the very roots of European thought in ancient Greece.[2] Indeed, had no such tension existed it would be difficult, if not impossible, to make sense of the rather pervasive enterprise amongst Western intellectuals – especially philosophers and theologians, including ourselves – of constructing compatibility systems that will somehow harmonize science and religion. Nor could we make much sense, I think, of the pervasive experience of 'the eclipse of meaning' so widely addressed in modern and contemporary European philosophy. This is not to say that the existence of such tension is itself indisputably indicative of the incompatibility of science and religion and therefore a clear indication of a fundamental contradiction at the heart of our simultaneously religious and scientific culture. However, neither does the fact that our modern Western civilization is at once a religious and scientific culture imply that science and religion are compatible structures of thought. That a *modus vivendi* between the two communities was achieved in the Christian West is obvious, but what needs also to be recognized is that what is socially compatible, so to speak, is not necessarily logically or epistemologically compatible.

I do not intend here either to present a proposal for the construction of a compatibility system or to analyse the compatibility systems proposed by others.³ My concern in this chapter is, rather, with the question of the status – with the possibility of – all attempts to construct a unified system of thought intended to harmonize the religious and scientific elements of our culture without subordinating one to the other. At first blush it would appear that compatibility systems will but reflect the very ambiguity and tension they are invoked to resolve, for they must necessarily be both an aspect of religion and of the edifice of scientific knowledge. To put it bluntly, compatibility systems must constitute a contribution to scientific knowledge in that religious knowledge claims are given cognitive legitimation, and an extension of the realm of religion in that science is made meaningful and is therefore recognized as at least implicitly religious. Further analysis of this ambiguity, however, will reveal that the building of compatibility systems is always religiously rather than scientifically motivated, which involves a subordination of the scientific impulse, so to speak, to the religious vision, thereby making of science an implicit religion.⁴ However, I do not think it possible to set out the evidence for that claim in a direct and straightforward manner that is likely to be wholly persuasive here. I do think it possible, however, to provide sound reason to question the very project of searching for a compatibility system. Though not an *argumentum ad absurdum*, absurdity constitutes a significant part of the case I wish to make here. I begin with referring to Max Weber's judgement about the relation of scientific argument to religious belief that suggests that the quest for the perfect compatibility system is simply absurd. In his 'Science as a Vocation', Weber, in attempting to distinguish his own analysis of the meaning of science from what he refers to as 'earlier illusions', writes:

Who – apart from certain overgrown children, who are indeed to be found in the natural sciences – still believes today that a knowledge of astronomy or biology or physics or chemistry could teach us anything at all about the *meaning* of the world? How could one find clues about such a 'meaning', if there is such a thing? If anything, the natural sciences tend to make the belief that there is something like a 'meaning' of the world die out at its very roots. And finally, science as the way 'to God'? Science, that specifically irreligious power? Nowadays nobody can doubt in his heart of hearts that science is irreligious, whether he wishes to admit it or not. Deliverance from the rationalism and intellectualism of science is a fundamental precondition of a life in communion with the divine.[5]

For Weber, as this passage makes clear, the *knowledge* provided by the sciences and *the meaning of the world* presented by religious systems of thought are incommensurable. (They are also, obviously, quite incompatible although I shall not pay attention to that aspect of his claim here.) Though Weber does not argue the matter here, I think his claim can be persuasively argued. And it is to that end to which I wish to direct my attention in this chapter. I shall attempt to show that the emergence of scientific thought entails so drastic a transformation of the notion of knowledge that it virtually creates a new cultural value which, to say the least, stands in tension with the 'knowledge' – that is, the religious meaning and values – already possessed by society.[6]

II

'Knowledge', obviously, predates what I am referring to here as 'scientific knowledge'. Persons in pre-scientific cultures know (knew) the world in which they live(d), otherwise they would surely have perished. This kind of knowledge might best be referred to as 'traditional knowledge' or, following Clifford Geertz, as 'local knowledge' because its shape, as Geertz puts it, is 'always ineluctably local, [and] indivisible from their instruments and their encasements'[7] whereas scientific knowledge presumes the existence of a kind of neutral epistemological framework that transcends all such cultural particularity. Scientific knowledge, as I shall point out below, although it emerges within a particular cultural context, is a new form of knowledge dependent upon a new mode of thought that, I think it can be persuasively argued, transcended such localization and became tradition-independent and in an important sense, therefore, objective. Until a clearer understanding of these forms of knowledge and the modes of thought underlying them is achieved there is no great likelihood that we will come to an understanding of what we mean when we talk of 'religious knowledge' nor are we likely to understand the nature of and account for the science/religion controversy in Western society. I shall begin with a discussion of the nature of pre-scientific traditions of knowledge, drawing primarily on a recent contribution to the comparative anthropology of knowledge by Fredrik Barth entitled *Cosmologies in the Making: A Generative Approach to Cultural Variation in Inner New Guinea.*

In his attempt 'to identify the developments, departure, and dogmatisms of each of the small centres *within* [the Ok] tradition of knowledge', as Barth puts it, he discovered that their rituals constitute 'major occasions', so to speak, in the genesis of that knowledge.[8] The task of the ritual expert in this culture, he points out, is to make present the immanent mystery of life and that in order to do that the ritual master must spellbind both himself and the novices with the experience he creates in the ritual action. This, he claims, introduces a fundamentally subjective element into the knowledge the ritual action transmits. 'Without any awareness of innovatively changing a received tradition', writes Barth,

> but merely by trying to communicate it more truly and deeply, such elaboration is profoundly stimulated by an organization where the ritual leader is required to 'show' the secrets of the cult to regularly recurring sets of new novices every ten years or so.[9]

Given that there are only a small number of ritual experts with whom these 'cultural materials' are stored for safekeeping in the long interval between ritual occasions and performances, the cultural materials undergo a kind of subjectification. Without wholly rejecting Durkheim's insights regarding the influence of social organization on individual creativity and performance, then, Barth maintains that, amongst the Ok people of New Guinea at least, the vision and commitment of the ritual expert is of central importance in the structuration of the knowledge that sustains the group's collective identity. There is, to be sure, an interaction between the knowledge presented by the ritual expert and the novices for whom the ritual is performed which presents certain constraints upon the ritual expert. Nevertheless, there is a peculiar individuality that characterizes this knowledge, given the nature of the oscillation it undergoes between the periods of collective ritual performance and secretive private thoughts.

In analysing the substance of Ok knowledge, Barth shows how centrally important it is that Ok knowledge is not simply a knowledge about a world 'out there' and wholly distinct from the self. It certainly includes a kind of knowledge about nature – an ethno-zoology and ethno-botany, for example – but not in the modern scientific sense of knowledge that lays claim to being a universal science of those aspects of the world. Their knowledge here is, rather, metaphorical – the world is seen as 'a multi-layered structure of mystical relationships, associations and equivalences between the numerous taxa'[10] in which nature is seen as a kind of alchemy of life forces. Ok knowledge is not, therefore, causal and scientific but rather symbolic in that it is a set of *meanings* that is established in the statements of associations, connections and disjunctions in nature, especially given that the latter must be understood in the light of the meta-premise of the secret cult of the ritual expert that, as Barth puts it, things are never what they appear to be. Ok knowledge then, according to Barth, 'provides a web of concepts, connections and identities whereby one's own attitude and orientation to the various parts of the world are directed and moulded.'[11]

Although Ok knowledge includes a kind of natural knowledge in its ethno-zoology and ethno-botany, etc., it is much richer than merely being a knowledge of nature. It is a knowledge that involves other forms of understanding that provide 'direction' to the lives of those who find themselves living within it. Ok 'knowledge', therefore, is more like 'culture' in the sense given it by Max Weber – that is, it is the *meaning* conferred on a segment of the meaningless infinity of the world. Ok 'knowledge', that is, is a cosmology – and even though it is not necessarily a wholly coherent and unified structure of thought agreed to by all, it nevertheless allows the members of the community which it characterizes to be moved by the same symbols and thoughts; it permits a bridging of the gap between self-integration and orientation to the world around one. Barth therefore recognizes that Ok knowledge is a knowledge that is, methodologically speaking, 'almost the obverse of our own'.[12] What knowledge of nature it contains that 'overlaps' our 'scientific knowledge' of nature is learned from experience but is not, so to speak, purely an intentionally cognitive product even though it may be, when 'abstracted' from its richer matrix, compared with such knowledge. But to abstract it from that matrix would be to destroy it as Ok knowledge. Barth insists, therefore, that to understand Ok knowledge (and by extension, all pre-scientific and non-scientific knowledges), it must be seen as the particular living tradition that it is and 'not as a set of abstract ideas enshrined in collective representations'.[13]

III

It is in ancient Greece – as I have intimated above, and argued at length elsewhere – that the transformation of 'knowledge' began. With the Milesian philosophers, I have suggested, a new cultural value was born, namely, the desire for a kind of general, abstract, and non-local knowledge of the world; a desire, to put it crudely for the moment, for knowledge for the sake of knowledge alone.[14] The intellectual revolution of the Milesians, it could be said then, introduced a division of labour in the work of the mind by distinguishing the descriptive and explanatory functions of traditional knowledge from its evaluative and identificatory functions. And with that division of intellectual labour the Greeks clearly distinguished science from myth – scientific knowledge from traditional knowledge. Whereas the local/traditional knowledge of society operated on at least two levels – the descriptive/explanatory and the evaluative/identificatory – the new knowledge they sought would operate only on the descriptive/explanatory level. With scientific knowledge clearly distinguished from the knowledge that is intimately concerned with meaning there emerged a new mode of thought from the mode of thought that antedates it, directed specifically to this end. It is, to use a Popperian phrase, a conjectural/refutational mode of thought in contrast to the narrative mode of thought of local knowledges that not only contain what we might consider 'scientific knowledge' but also provide a framework for structuring a meaningful existence. Not only is it discontinuous with such narrative thinking, it puts to question all such speculative narratives of meaning, in so far as they are considered, in whatever sense, representations of the world rather than merely as orientations to the world (reality). The contrast in methods between these two modes of thought, and the tensions between them, is clearly articulated by Plato in the *Phaedo* in which Socrates, in providing for his interlocutors an account of his intellectual development, sets out his reasons for rejecting the scientific path to knowledge which he had espoused in his youth. Though at first 'keen on that wisdom they call natural science',[15] he eventually came to see that science could not contribute to the understanding he sought because it could not give the 'reasons for' things in the world. The promise of a meaningful account of life that seemed to be offered in Anaxagoras's theory 'that it is Mind that directs and is the cause of everything'[16] came to nothing. 'I never thought,' Plato has Socrates complain, 'that Anaxagoras, who said that those things were directed by Mind, would bring in any other cause for them than that it was best for them to be as they are.'[17] 'Once he had given the best for each as the cause for each and the general cause of all,' Socrates continues, 'I thought he would go on to explain the common good for all, and I would not have exchanged my hopes for a fortune.'[18] But his hopes were dashed, for Anaxagoras proceeded, scientifically, to provide not a teleological account of 'the world' but only a causal one. And, like Weber, although long before Weber, Socrates saw the absurdity of trying to establish, scientifically, anything at all about the *meaning* of the world.

In his recent Lewis Henry Morgan lectures entitled *Magic, Science, Religion and the Scope of Rationality*, Stanley Tambiah seems to conclude that the anthropology of knowledge confirms such a dichotomy of mind and duality of knowledge. Scientific knowledge as distinct from the earlier and more pervasive traditional knowledge is indeed simply about objective features of a reality 'out there' and 'beyond' the human mind. Tambiah quickly adds, however, that such causal scientific thought has not displaced the traditional thought and knowledge that antedates it. Tambiah sees the two kinds of knowledge as being complementary, although not, it appears, cognitively complementary, in the sense that traditional knowledge adds something to the store of information, so to speak, about the world gained by science. Using Lévy-Bruhlian categories he writes:

> It is possible to suggest that a meaningful way to contrast participation [local knowledge] and causality [scientific knowledge] is through a comparison of religion and science as contrasting and *complementary orientations* to the world. What our discussion so far has led to is the plausibility of at least two modes of ordering the world that are simultaneously available to human beings *as complementary cognitive and affective interests* and which in the self-conscious language of reflexivity and analysis might be labelled as 'participation' and 'causality'.[19]

Tambiah recognizes of course, as must we all, that scientific knowledge amplifies and extends traditional 'informational knowledge', but maintains that it 'does not *necessarily* drive out or displace ritual and magical acts which combine the purposive aims of better mechanical performance, or larger yields of rice, with the aims of a moral and prosperous social and religious life'.[20] Consequently he also realizes that there is room for conflict between the two orientations; he is aware, that is, that science can undermine traditional knowledge because the affective interests of such local knowledges appear to require a particular cognitive/informational foundation. It may be true that, as Barth puts it, 'a narrowly "cerebral" and abstract interpretation' of traditional knowledge fails to capture the dignity and force that 'lies in how it directs and moulds the persons's subjective experience, and this creates emotions and sensibilities that are harmonious with a vast structure of precepts and events in nature',[21] but if that dignity and force involves the acceptance of untestable beliefs in extra-natural ontological realities then not only is there the possibility of a substantive conflict between scientific and traditional knowledge, there is also a serious 'conflict' of methodologies in regard to how the 'knowledge' is obtained.

IV

If the brief analysis I have provided here of the transformation of 'knowledge' has any merit whatsoever, a sufficient foundation has been provided for answering the question as to the possibility of constructing an adequate compatibility system raised above. It is clear, that is, that in this light the quest for a compatibility system that can harmonize science and religion without subordinating one to the other is futile. The two enterprises are simply incommensurable even though there are respects in which they overlap.

Religious knowledge, as I have argued elsewhere, is a 'local knowledge'. Though it may contain, so to speak, pieces of (scientific) information, (which may or may not be true), it is essentially a 'grand narrative' that creates a framework within which the world, and one's life in it, makes sense. Its concern is primarily meaning, though, as with all local knowledges, there is no reflective awareness of a distinction between meaning and knowledge – meaningful religious narratives, that is, constitute knowledge for those who espouse them. That the construction of such a matrix of meaning is essential to our existence, individually and socially, may or may not be true. But even if it were true, it appears that knowledge of that fact would be a kind of scientific information that could not help but undermine the very 'truth' of Religion by showing it to be other (i.e.

psychological or sociological) than what it presents itself as being –
namely knowledge (metaempirical or metaphysical).

It is no doubt true that society has other aims/goals/values than
simply that of scientific knowledge. And it is, perhaps, legitimate to
complain that a scientific society like ours is in danger of ignoring
those values and underestimating their significance.[22] However, if
my analysis of the transformation of 'knowledge' here is on the
mark, it seems to me that societies that have espoused scientific
knowledge have espoused a value destructive of the matrix of
meaning that has sustained those other values simply because they
have always constituted the knowledge (i.e. the cosmology) of those
committed to them. Scientific knowledge, that is, undermines the
cognitive legitimacy of the meaning structures of local knowledges
in somewhat the same fashion that a computer virus destroys the
meaning structure of the software program. Time does not permit
extensive elaboration of this point here but a brief reference to
Feyerabend's critique of science in his essay 'Notes on Relativism'
may be helpful in clarifying the nature of the dilemma scientific
societies face in this regard.

Feyerabend claims that he does not want to indict science but that
he rather wishes only to show 'that the choice of science over the
other forms of life is not a scientific choice'.[23] He admits that a new
form of knowledge did arise in ancient Greece – a knowledge, as he
puts it, that differed greatly from the knowledge 'in tradition and in
Greek commonsense [which] was a collection of opinions, each of
them obtained by procedures appropriate to the domain from which
the opinions arose'.[24] The new knowledge, he continues, not only
attempted to detach itself from, and so transcend, traditional knowledge but also sought to 'devalue, and push aside [the other] complex
forms of thought and experience'.[25] Espousal of this new knowledge,
he therefore argues, was tantamount to moving away from life itself.

Though I am in considerable agreement with Feyerabend's
description and evaluation of the structure and effects of the new
Greek mode of thought, my analysis of 'what it all means' nevertheless diverges considerably from his assessment. Feyerabend maintains not only that this new mode of thought attempts to establish a
tradition-independent view of the world but that it is *intent* on
destroying all local knowledges. As he puts it, such scientific knowledge cannot 'overrule' the traditions even though it can 'overrun'
them.[26] It cannot overrule them, he claims, because the choice of scientific knowledge over traditional knowledge is not, and cannot be,

itself a scientific choice. However, 'intent' is not relevant here (unless one feels no discomfort with such a grand conspiracy theory regarding the historical origins of the scientific temper). Though Feyerabend is right in claiming that the decision to espouse scientific knowledge as a value in itself is not a scientific decision, it is nevertheless still the case that that choice constitutes a massive intellectual challenge to traditional or local knowledge because it creates a new model for the very notion of knowledge. And the new mode of thought in which this new model is rooted involves a kind of revaluation of all other cultural values because the very notion of scientific knowledge implies its autonomy from that web of other values. Without what Ernest Gellner calls the 'diplomatic immunity of cognition' – i.e. the liberation/emancipation of the search for knowledge from 'the social, moral and political obligations and decencies of society'[27] – there would be no new mode of thought and no new knowledge. This does not, of course, scientifically justify espousing that new value but it does mean that having espoused it all other values are subordinated in the sense that they have lost all power to control the knowing process or of determining the results of the exercise of this new mode of thought. Cognitive legitimacy from this point on, that is, is no longer determined in terms of the web of values that otherwise characterize a society. It is obvious then, to put it bluntly, that traditional knowledge and scientific knowledge cannot, logically, be held together within a single coherent framework. A rationally persuasive compatibility system, therefore, is simply not possible no matter how much modern Western societies desire it, though this is not to say that the quest for that elusive structure will come to a halt. Society, if it is not to disintegrate, it appears, requires it – and it will, therefore, 'find' it. The 'discovery' of science and the transformation of the notion of 'knowledge' it entailed, it is now obvious, cannot be seen simply as an unalloyed good. Indeed, as I have already suggested, it may be quite detrimental in the long run no matter how beneficial it may have been in the short run. And whether a society once having espoused this new value can survive the logic with which it operates is a moot question. I conclude with Gellner's view on that matter in his *Plough, Sword and Book: The Structure of Human History*:

> Clearly there is a price to be paid here. Ordinary life, life as lived, has its crises and tragedies. When men [and women] face these, they need to be succoured by ideas they take seriously and hold

to be cognitively valid. Men [and women] can attend carnivals without necessarily endorsing the theological or magical beliefs which had inspired them. 'Ironic cultures', which are not granted serious cognitive respect, are perfectly practicable over a large part of life. Many of us live within them, often comfortable enough. But it is hard to be content with them when something very dear and important is at stake, or when tragedy strikes. One must distinguish between specific problems and generic salvation. Concerning specific ailments, men [and women] will no doubt turn to putative or genuine bits of science which offer help, or promise to do so. When it comes to generic salvation, the need to endow life as a whole with an acceptable meaning, they will continue to face the current options; they may hope to extract an overall vision from serious cognition (some men [and women] will continue to seek this); or they may turn to (usually bowdlerized and selectively reinterpreted) faiths surviving from the agrarian age, or from the transition period; or they may, perhaps, be satisfied with a candid and brave recognition that the age of cognitive validation is gone for ever.[28]

9

Has Philosophy of Religion a Place in the Agenda of Theology?

Accepting the invitation to comment on the value of philosophy and the philosophy of religion to theology was, it seems to me now, rather foolhardy. Assurances that a fully developed statement on the issue was not expected made the exercise appear far easier than I found it to be. The simple question presented for comment – Has Philosophy of Religion a Place in the Agenda of Theology? – is not so simple, for even what philosophy, religion and theology are in themselves is not at all clear – all three being hotly contested notions on which agreement is seldom achieved and never widespread. I shall, nevertheless, attempt an answer to the question, despite the difficulties, proceeding on the basis of provisional characterizations of its three central concepts.[1]

Popularly understood, philosophy is concerned with the meaning or significance of life and in that regard is usually associated with questions of ontology and metaphysics – with questions about the ultimate elements or building blocks of the universe and the processes of transformation they undergo. Its concern, so to speak, is with the world as a whole and with our place in it. Understood in this way it has very much a religious quality to it, for religion also is concerned with ultimacy and meaning – with the world and the meaning of our lives in it. On the other hand, there is good reason not to see philosophy essentially as a first-order activity concerned with determining the structure of a world that produces a body of doctrine to be affirmed, but rather as a second-order activity, essentially analytical, that reflects critically on the sciences (and metasciences?) that concern themselves directly with the world and the elements of which it is composed.

The division of philosophical labour by the use of the genitive structure – a modern development – only further complicates matters. Reflection on religion, to be sure, antedates the emergence of

111

the philosophy of religion as a sub-discipline in the university curriculum in the eighteenth century, but there is a sense in which religion did, for the first time, quite consciously and explicitly become a distinct focus of philosophical reflection. Philosophers like Hume, Kant and Hegel began to focus attention on religion as a distinctive social reality. Sense can be made of the paradox of philosophical reflection on religion antedating the emergence of the philosophy of religion, I think, by distinguishing the variety of meanings implicit in the genitive structure of the phrase 'the philosophy of religion.'

As a descriptive genitive, 'philosophy of religion' points to that systematic reflection on the world and the meaning of our existence in it that in some sense or other rests on the belief in a world *beyond* this world; it is a mode of thought that rejects a purely naturalistic view of the world. As a subjective genitive, 'philosophy of religion' is the application of rational reflection to and metaphysical elaboration on the notions, ideas and beliefs explicitly or implicitly contained in religious revelation vouchsafed to particular communities; it is, so to speak, philosophy done *by* religion. In this sense, I think, philosophy of religion is indistinguishable from what has come, relatively recently, to be known as 'philosophical theology'. (That phrase appears to be a pleonasm, however, for it is important to recognize that 'theology' already refers to the concern to rationalize – to provide a rational account of – theos, in the same sense that biology is the concern to provide a rational account of living matter.) Finally, as an objective genitive, 'philosophy of religion' clearly distinguishes the realms of religion and philosophy – as different from each other as language is from a meta-language in which that language can be discussed.

Consequently it becomes obvious that in the philosophy of religion in this instance, the results of philosophical reflection are not themselves religious products but rather, simply, objective statements *about* religion and religious concepts, ideas, beliefs, etc. In the etymological sense of 'theology', it needs pointing out, the philosophy of religion as just described is theology, for in so far as it attempts to explain the nature of belief in god(s) it is, even if only indirectly, rational discourse about god(s). It bears repeating, however, that such discourse about the gods is *not* a form of religious discourse and I suggest that we distinguish the religious from the non-religious form of god-talk by means of scare quotes. 'Theology' therefore is a religious undertaking, whereas theology/philosophy of religion is simply one of several approaches to be taken in the objective, academic study of religion.

Not only are 'philosophy' and 'theology' philosophical problems, the term 'religion' is as well. I shall not pay much attention to that here, however, for fear that I will not get down to answering the question of philosophy's role in the agenda of the theology. Suffice it to say that I do not see religion and theology as in any way identical; theology, that is, is not a religious mode of thought even though it is thought about religious events, persons, processes, etc. That much follows from the preceding discussion and will, I think, be borne out in the argument to follow. My concern in this chapter, then, is with the role of philosophy and the philosophy of religion within a Christian context and I shall, at least to begin with, assume we have a roughly similar notion as to what Christianity is. I shall in due course, however, suggest that what Christianity is is not what it was, nor, more controversially, what it should be. Moreover, I will suggest that, once having established what it was and still ought to be, the role of philosophy will be seen to be meagre indeed. All of this, however, can only be sketched out briefly and without developing the kind of argument required if it is to be fully persuasive.

The Christianity to which we are presently tied, and especially so in the seminary/divinity school setting, is, using Harry Wolfson's phrase, a thoroughly philosophized Christianity.[2] And if we are to *understand* it, philosophy, quite obviously, will be a necessary tool. Philosophy was introduced into Christianity in the second century and has had a continuous history, as Wolfson points out, among both the Greek and Latin fathers and beyond. Consequently, as Diogenes Allen has recently insisted, 'everyone needs to know some philosophy in order to understand the major doctrines of Christianity or to read a great theologian intelligently'.[3] Philosophical theology, he rightly claims, 'enables one to appreciate more deeply the meaning of virtually every major doctrinal formulation and every major theologian'.[4] This kind of engagement with philosophy, however, is not that in which the Christian fathers, or their successors, early or late, were involved. What Allen refers to is not the *doing* of philosophy but rather becoming aware of the philosophical views and methods of thought employed by philosophers and taken over by the theologians. The latter is a first-order philosophical activity concerned with the interpretation and elaboration of revealed truth, whereas the former is primarily a historical activity.

Whether the kind of constructive philosophical exercise adopted by the fathers ought to have been used, or ought now to have a role in the interpretation and elaboration of the Christian faith seems to me to be a much more difficult issue to decide. There is certainly no necessity laid upon us to accept the assumption of the fathers that philosophy is necessary, or even helpful, to understanding more deeply the Christian revelation. If that deeper understanding of the Christian revelation may be referred to as 'theology,' then, rephrasing the claim, it is not obvious that philosophy is necessary to the *'doing* of theology' even though it is necessary to understanding 'theology' since the time of the Greek and Latin fathers. Indeed, I think it can be shown that philosophical thought is both discontinuous and incompatible with religious thought in general and Christian thought in particular. Christian thinking – and religious thinking more generally – is mythopoeic and is not bound, nor can it be bound, by the logical structures of philosophical thought. I have, I think, shown the radically different natures of these two modes of thought in my book *The Irony of Theology and the Nature of Religious Thought*.[5] I will not attempt to spell out this argument in any detail here, but will try instead to illustrate its point, as found in Edwin Hatch's analysis and assessment of 'the influence of Greek ideas on Christianity'.[6]

That Hatch is at least vaguely aware of the different modes of thought is obvious from the fact that he also sees a stark contrast between 'Greek thinking' and what he calls the 'Palestinian thinking' which characterizes the early Christian community. For Hatch, the former is analytical, logical and metaphysical whereas the latter is pragmatic and practical in the sense of being concerned with ethics and behaviour. Furthermore, he notes that the latter recognizes an authority *outside itself* that the former, as autonomous, could not. It is true that despite the obvious tensions between Greek and Palestinian thinking, Hatch assumes that the rapid change of the centre of gravity of the Christian faith from ethics to belief and from practice to theory can only be explained by 'the fact' of 'a special and real kinship' between the leading ideas of current philosophy at the time and the leading ideas of Christianity. But it is also true that he is not sure that the Hellenization of faith does not really constitute a loss of faith. 'Christianity', he writes,

> has won no great victories since its basis was changed. The victories that it has won, it has won by preaching not Greek metaphysics, but the love of God and the love of man. Its darkest pages are those which record the story of its endeavouring to force its transformed Greek metaphysics upon men or upon races to whom they

were alien. The only ground of despair in those who accept Christianity now, is the fear – which I for one cannot entertain – that the dominance of the metaphysical element in it will be perpetual.[7]

Harry Wolfson's *sociological* accounting for the rapid rise of a philosophized Christianity is far more persuasive, I think, than Hatch's metaphysical/religious account of an essential identity of the two modes of thought and sets of doctrines. The change in Christianity occurred, Wolfson tells us, because: (1) pagans who had been trained in philosophy were converted to the faith; (2) because philosophy was useful in helping Christians construct a defence against a variety of accusations hurled at them; and, (3) because philosophy provided, or so it appeared, a kind of immunization against the heresy of Gnosticism.[8] More recently, however, Eric Osborn has argued an essentialist position that sees philosophy as integral to the Christian faith.[9] He maintains that in the religiously pluralistic context in which Christianity emerged it became increasingly difficult for Christians to be, as he puts it, 'ignorant of their faith'.[10] And in taking up philosophy as a means to deepen their knowledge of the faith, he sees its legitimate development because, according to him, it preserved the faith. He seems unaware of the distortion this may have involved, however: the irony of his claim that in combating heresy, Christianity more and more became 'a doctrine or a philosophy'.[11] In admitting that development he does not, like Hatch, have doubts about the value of the transformation. Rather, like A. H. Armstrong and R. A. Markus in their assessment of the value of Greek philosophy to the Christian faith, he sees the dialogue between the two as a model for contemporary Christian thinkers who face a similarly pluralistic world.[12] For Osborn then, philosophy and metaphysics are not unacceptable, or even only temporarily helpful transformations of the faith, but rather extensions of it. 'A lot of argument was necessary before a clear pattern of Christian truth could be found throughout the Church universal', he writes. 'The way was through argument, whether the threat came from Gnosticism or Marcion, just as the way to answer the Roman state, philosophers and Jews could *only* be through reasoning and evidence.'[13]

Although I find Wolfson's sociological thesis more persuasive as an account of that ancient development, I cannot entirely dismiss Osborn's view. I think, however, Hatch's hesitancy on the similar view he held far more appropriate. I believe there is some truth to the assumption that underlies Osborn's position: namely, that there is an affinity between Greek philosophy and the Christian faith. But the true nature of that affinity is not what it has been taken to be, due to the failure of most analysts to distinguish the varieties of Greek philosophy that existed. The affinity is not between the philosophic mode of thought that first emerged with the Milesians and their break with a mythopoeic tradition preceding it, but rather between post-Milesian thinkers like Plato and Christianity. That is not so surprising because Plato's philosophy is essentially a religious philosophy which emerged in reaction to the naturalism of Milesian thought. Unlike the philosophic thought of the Milesian tradition, Platonic thought rejects autonomy and deliberately subordinates itself to revealed truth of a pre-philosophical kind. As Michel Despland has put it, 'Plato's philosophy of religion strives to interpret the fears and hopes expressed in the Greek religious practice of his day and tries to set in motion a healing process'.[14] There is something of the paradoxical in this claim for, so it seems, Plato wishes to change religion while yet remaining schooled by it – seeming to require of philosophy both autonomy and subordination.

Seeing this diversity in Greek philosophy and the stark contrast between its embodiment in a naturalistic and religious form, it seems to me that we ought more carefully to talk not about the Hellenization of the Christian faith but rather of its Platonization. Then the affinity between Christianity and philosophy will be immediately apparent because of the religious nature of Platonic thought. Furthermore, it ought to be noted that Plato's form of philosophizing amounts to a distortion of philosophy as it first emerged as a distinctive mode of thought over against the mythopoeic.[15]

Plato's philosophy, I argue, is not really philosophy so much as religion. It is a hybrid mode of thought, combining elements of both religious and philosophical thinking. Since the two modes are logically/structurally incompatible, one is ultimately wholly subordinated to the other. The Platonic influence on Christianity, therefore, is twofold. On the one hand, the religious intent and other-worldliness served as a source for a systematic reformulation and elaboration of Christian belief. On the other hand, it introduced into Christianity a new mode of thinking incompatible with its own and which will ultimately be, it seems to me, destructive of it. The seeds of destruction are found in the autonomy of philosophy that is still implicitly present in Plato's thought. All trace of that Milesian character of philosophy has not, and cannot, I believe, be eradicated from such hybrid modes of thought. The philosophy now present in Christianity is bound eventually to reveal what Plato had so skilfully concealed. Indeed, that problematic autonomy begins to reemerge in the eleventh and twelfth centuries in the debates over the nature of theology, and with the emergence of theology as an academic discipline. There seems no sounder way to read the nature of the collision between Peter Abelard and Bernard of Clairvaux over the question of the nature of theology. Durkheim, in recounting the history of education in France, acknowledges that the scholastics no more than the monastics deliberately cast doubt or aspersion on the truth of the Christian faith but did so nevertheless because, he insists, the very need to examine and elaborate the faith implied doubt.[16] The need to understand the faith more deeply, that is, even without the question as to whether it might be false, constitutes a remarkable innovation that opened the door to a great deal more. As Durkheim puts it,

> the moment one introduces reason into a set of ideas which up to that time has appeared unchallengeable it is the beginning of the end; the enemy has gained a foothold. If reason is not given its fair share, then from the moment that it has established a foothold somewhere, it always ends up by casting down the artificial barriers within which attempts have been made to contain it.[17]

As in the past, theology today is frequently shaped by philosophical thought, and often takes philosophy of religion to heart. But the philosophy of religion of value to contemporary theology is, as I have suggested, characterized either as a descriptive or a subjective genitive. In either case it is a hybrid mode of thought taken over and used by the theologian – it involves argument constrained by commitments to pre-philosophical wisdom of some kind. Consequently, philosophy is still both a source for further reflection on the Christian faith and a potential disaster to it. Only if the distortion of its truly philosophical character is maintained by the commitment to some pre-philosophical truth will it be of value to Christianity – the value deriving not from philosophy but from its peculiar distortion. This becomes quite obvious, I think, in Etienne Gilson's discussion of the value of philosophy to theology in his *The Philosopher and Theology*.[18] Gilson there insists that it is really quite impossible for a Christian ever to philosophize as if she or he were not Christian. Can philosophy, he asks, 'be thus used by theology toward ends that are not its own without losing its essence in the process?' His answer: 'In a way it does lose its essence, and it profits by the change.'[19] Such distortion amounts to its virtual destruction, although Gilson maintains it is its reclamation. He elaborates on the nature of how philosophy profits as follows:

> theology is not a compound, it is not composed of heterogeneous elements of which some would be philosophy and the rest Scripture; all in it is homogeneous despite the diversity of origin. 'Those who resort to philosophical arguments in Holy Scripture and put them in the service of faith, do not mix water with wine, they change it to wine.' Translate: they change philosophy into theology, just as Jesus changed water to wine at the marriage feast in Cana. Thus can theological wisdom, imprinted in the mind of the theologian as the seal of God's knowing, include the totality of human knowledge in its transcendent unity.[20]

That nothing of original philosophy and its autonomy remains is doubtful however, for Gilson also maintains that philosophy needs to retain its rationality if it is really to be of service to theology, and the echoes of autonomy sound clearly in the claim. Philosophy of religion, then, taken as an objective genitive, is of little relevance to religion and theology for it rigidly maintains its autonomy from religion. Taken as a subjective genitive, however, it may be of benefit, but only because it has already been transformed from philosophy to something more nearly like religion. As a hybrid mode of thought it still retains traces of philosophic autonomy and its use, therefore, lays Christianity open to the threat of a re-emergent autonomous reason able to explain religion rather than simply providing a deeper understanding of it.

10

Postulations for Safeguarding Preconceptions

The study of religion in an academic/scientific setting is in need of close philosophical scrutiny. It is unfortunate, therefore, that philosophy of religion has for the most part been seen as an activity continuous with the religious life itself. It has usually been understood, that is, as a rational explication of the import of religious experience; or, perhaps, in a more critical vein, as an examination of the doctrinal/dogmatic contents (whether explicit or implicit) of religious traditions. Although I do not wish to argue that such activity is either unwarranted or of no value at all, it does seem to me that there are more pressing matters regarding religion for philosophy to attend to – namely, 'the study of religion' as a possible discipline, and the claims made on its behalf.[1] That kind of epistemological concern, with its 'turn to the subject', so to speak, will, at least in some senses, bring the philosophy of religion into the modern period and give it a relevance it seems to have lost in our own times.[2] Given the claims that students of religion have made regarding the scientific character of that undertaking, one might have expected the philosophers of science – and in particular the philosophers of the social sciences – to turn their attention in that direction. But they have not. It is quite appropriate, if not imperative, therefore, that the philosopher of religion take up precisely that task. Indeed, that kind of philosophy of religion, I venture to suggest, may have more to tell us about religion and the religions than can philosophy of religion as traditionally understood. This chapter, then, is intended as a first step in changing the focus of attention for the philosopher of religion, and in that process, to rejuvenate the philosophy of religion so as to make it, once again, an interesting and significant *philosophic* activity. In taking up the issue of the nature of the study of religion here, however, I shall pay particular attention to that study as it is undertaken in the North American academic setting.

The title of this chapter comes from Willard Van Orman Quine.[3] In his recent autobiography Quine recalls what he refers to as an 'eccentric assignment' in religion in his agreement to comment on a paper by Charles Hartshorne presented to a colloquium at Boston University in 1979. It was, according to Quine, an odd paper, filled with apparently meaningless or contradictory statements which forced him to question what he was doing there. Nevertheless, he says that he did learn something in the process, namely, why Hartshorne, and others, insist that sentences about the future are largely neither true nor false. Their claim, he found out, is made in order to reconcile God's omniscience with indeterminism. This, and the recognition of how heavily theology rests on the distinction between contingency and metaphysical necessity elicits from him the remark: 'such are the postulations for safeguarding preconceptions.'

Unlike Quine, I have worked all my academic life in the field of 'Religious Studies' but have only recently, and for reasons similar to Quine's, come to ask myself what I am doing there. There are, that is, contradictions to be found in the way the study of religious phenomena is undertaken, and which I have not until recently clearly recognized, that seem to suggest that certain religious preconceptions are being provided with safeguards. It would seem, therefore, that the academic study of religion is really scientific only in name and not in substance. If the scholar is to retain her/his integrity as a scholar in the field, therefore, s/he must provide a persuasive critique of the postulates that function to safeguard religion from the effects of the scientific study of religion.

Many, if not most, academic students of religion, it is becoming evident, wish to pursue their study of religion in an academic/ scientific context but wish to do so without placing in jeopardy the truth-claims of Religion. Talk of a 'science of religion' as a special discipline is affirmed by many in the field, therefore, in order to reconcile the 'perceived' sacredness of religion(s) with the secularity of the ordinary, non-partisan social-scientific study of human/cultural phenomena. This claim is not, however, made directly, but rather flows from a particular reading of what such students of religion refer to as the principle of the *epoché* which underlies all 'religious studies'. The *epoché*, it is argued, founds the non-partisan study of religion in that it is a conventionalist stratagem which calls for the 'bracketing' of the truth-question in the study of religion. The *epoché*, therefore, allows the student to replace the contentious philosophical/metaphysical study of religion of the past with a historical/empirical study of religious phenomena that can far more easily achieve 'a convergence of opinion' in the quest for an understanding of religion amongst the practitioners in the field. The new 'study' of religion that emerges from the adoption of the principle of the *epoché* has generally come to be known as the phenomenology of religion.

The claim that the phenomenological study of religion evades the metaphysical debates characteristic of the theological and philosophical approaches to the study of religions is, however, suspect. To restrict the study of religion to pure description precludes what seems to be of the essence of science, namely, explanation and theory. And to curtail so severely the activities of the 'scientists' in this field not only requires justification, but itself begs for an explanation. The justifications usually provided are not persuasive – in fact, the claims made on behalf of the phenomenology of religion appear to involve one in viciously circular thinking – which suggests that the champions of the phenomenological study of religion have adopted a set of postulations for safeguarding the presumptions of the value and truth of religion. To assume that the academic study of religion is exhausted in an empirical/historical analysis of a particular religious tradition or traditions only makes sense if one assumes 'the autonomy of religion'. If one postulates that religion is a *sui generis* phenomenon, that is, one can legitimately assume that it can only be properly treated 'on its own terms'. To understand the religions as psychological or sociological phenomena, therefore, is simply not 'taking religion seriously' because it allows an understanding of religious phenomena in terms of that which is not religion. Thus, unless the study of religion is anti-reductionist and therefore precludes all social-scientific analysis of religion, religion will simply disappear and the study of religion with it. To explain religion in such a social-scientific fashion, to put it another way, is really 'to explain away' religion as something other than what it really is, and is, therefore, a pronouncement about the 'truth of religion' which will simply return the study of religion to further fruitless metaphysical wrangling. Explanation and theory, therefore, are seen as contraventions of the postulate of the *epoché* which alone has permitted the emergence of a non-metaphysical study of religious phenomena. However, to preclude all possibility of explaining religion *a priori* is to assume that it can never be 'explained away' which implies, it appears, the assumption of an ontological reality for religion which it may not really have. And to do so without independent argument would be tantamount to accepting such a metaphysical conclusion on the basis of some intuition or other. Postulating the *sui generis* character of religion, therefore, it appears, is not free of metaphysical entanglements.

The explicit intention of the early students of religion to have the study of religion ensconced in the university setting, as I have shown elsewhere,[4] required convincing the legitimating authorities that the 'new discipline' did not simply duplicate the work of theology. The apology for a place for the study of religion in the university curriculum, that is, required what we might reasonably call the detheologization of the study of religion and religions. The postulates upon which the phenomenology of religion rest, however, amount to an implicit, although perhaps unconscious, theological agenda in the academic study of religion. And the recent discovery of that implicit agenda in the phenomenology of religion, I shall show in this chapter, has given impetus to a movement to retheologize the study of religion in the academy despite the fact that its inclusion in the university curriculum was based on the assumption of the non-theological character of the enterprise.

In a recent article reporting the results of a conference concerned with the question of the relationship of theology to 'Religious Studies', Professor Laurence J. O'Connell asks: 'Is it true that any attempt to reestablish an explicit role for theology within the boundaries of religious studies is fundamentally misguided and a repudiation of the scientific/academic aim of religious studies?'[5] Although claiming that the conference did not reach many theoretical conclusions, O'Connell leaves no doubt in the mind of the reader as to how the question ought to be answered. The practical solutions reached for the department of religion at St. Louis – the venue of the conference – involve the adoption of a first-level course with a predominantly 'religious studies' identity which, however, allows for it to be complemented in the future by second-level courses 'which would be *more frankly* theological'.[6] Several essays based on the conference papers and published in the *Journal of the American Academy of Religion* under the title 'Religious Studies/Theological Studies: The St. Louis Project'[7] for the most part adopt O'Connell's assessment that theology and religious studies can be successfully blended. For the majority of the participants at the conference there is a firm belief in an underlying congeniality between religious studies and theology, and they look forward to developing 'a closer working relationship' between the two enterprises at a future conference for which funding has already been obtained.

A very different answer to the question raised by O'Connell, is I think, in order. Indeed, I shall attempt to show here that the development of a 'closer working partnership' between religious studies and theology as sought by O'Connell and others will set the academic/scientific study of religion back a hundred years or more.

The formulation of O'Connell's question is subtle and intriguing. There is no presumption, it appears, that 'Religious Studies' has ever functioned without the assistance of theology, or that it ever intended to do so. It appears, rather, that theology's role in the study of religion has simply been somewhat submerged and out of view. Consequently O'Connell's response seems to concern only the question of bringing into explicit consciousness what is already implicit, and intentionally so, in the new (in the nineteenth century) discipline of 'the science of religion'. On such a reading of the question a negative reply would be most reasonable. However, if religious studies is a 'discipline' wholly different from theology, only an affirmative reply will do. To show the latter to be the case would require showing that the crypto-theological character of religious studies in its early days is not at all essential to that enterprise. To assume that the theological elements in the work of the early (nineteenth and twentieth century) 'scientific' students of religion are necessary components of their methodological framework derives rather from a misreading of the implications of the *epoché* and a serious misconstrual of the intentions of the 'founders' of that enterprise by contemporary students of religion.

In an essay on 'The Failure of Nerve in the Academic Study of Religion' I have argued, successfully I think, that the theological component which O'Connell finds to characterize the work of scholars in this field from its inception down to the present day is but the 'vestigial remains' of the evolutionary development of the so-called discipline of 'Religious Studies'.[8] This is quite obvious in even the most cursory reading of the writings of the generation of scholars intent on establishing the scientific study of religious phenomena within the university setting. Their primary argument in seeking such legitimation involved a radical demarcation between theology (which was already ensconced in the university context in Europe and Great Britain), and the new approach to understanding religion which they were proposing. To suggest that the crypto-theological agendas so often to be found in their work – as well as in the work of the subsequent generation of scholars in the field – is something they were not aware of is both reasonable and true. But to argue further that had those scholars been aware of this aspect of their work they would have made it an explicitly constitutive element of their methodology for the new 'discipline' is, I think, wholly unpersuasive. Consequently, any attempt to re-establish a methodological link of that kind between theology and religious studies today on the basis of theological statements in their published work would be unfair, for it would amount to a rejection of their expressed intention to establish a 'science of religion'; it would, moreover, constitute a 'failure of nerve' in the new undertaking in that it exhibits a fear of the effects such a new study might have upon religion when examined in this 'detached' fashion. I will not here recapitulate the arguments in support of this claim which were formulated in the above mentioned article but will rather illustrate that 'failure of nerve' in the study of religion, as I see it, in the academic setting in North America, and particularly in the United States. If one takes Claude Welch's assessment of the 'new discipline' presented in his presidential address to the American Academy of Religion more than two decades ago as a bench-mark of the academic/scientific development of religious studies in the United States, the 'failure of nerve' to which I have referred will be clearly evident in the increasingly significant and explicit role that theology is being given in the affairs of the Academy.[9]

Welch's address to the Academy directed the attention of its members to the question of a possible identity crisis in the study of religion emerging from an incapacity of the 'new discipline' to distinguish itself from theology. In this Welch seems, and correctly so I would maintain, to have accepted the assumptions about the scientific study made by the European founders of the discipline referred to above. According to Welch, no such crisis exists for the student of religion in the North American academic setting because religious studies in this context has moved away from a religious/denominational orientation by rejecting the 'confessional principle' operative within the religious community; the academy, as Welch alternatively puts it, has rejected 'the insider theory of religion' as an appropriate methodological structure for its work. The battle for recognition of religion as an appropriate field of objective, scientific study within the university, therefore, had been won. Welch clearly identifies the 'confessional principle' with theology and therefore insists that the new discipline is not only independent of theology but is wholly distinct from it. Indeed, he further insists that the temptation to look upon the academic study of religion as a means of redemption – whether of the world or simply of the university – had also, for the most part, been resisted.

In this light it is obvious that Professor O'Connell's article shows a decided drift towards, if not outright acceptance of, the 'confessional principle', although suitably 'de-denominationalized'. His essay, moreover, is but the tip of a very large iceberg, for there are, literally, scores of similar proposals in the journals that serve scholars in this field.[10] More importantly, however, the American Academy of Religion itself seems increasingly to take on the religious hue to be found in so many of its members. The Academy, that is, seems to take up a 'confessional stance', even though one might insist that such a stance constitutes only a 'small c confessional' theology which can be clearly distinguished from a historically specific, denominationally oriented theology. What the Academy 'permits', therefore, is the adoption of an assumption about the truth of religion in general even though it excludes the presumption of the truth of any particular, historical religious tradition. Transcultural theology, or 'perennial theology', however, is still theology and is not, therefore, an appropriate aspect of the academic study of religion.

There was, it is true, a hint of movement in the direction of Welch's ideal, by the 'reflective religious activity' that characterized many departments of religious studies on American university campuses. That much is recognizable from at least the time of Clyde Holbrook's presidential address to the Academy in 1964, entitled 'Why an Academy of Religion?', in which he dealt with the rationale for the 'emergence' of the Academy out of the substance of the National Association of Bible Instructors (NABI). The formation of the Academy was certainly intended to move the study of religion away from, as he puts it, 'the partialities which at present afflict the field'.[11] The report of the 'NABI Self-Study Committee', however, seems to present an understanding of the role of the Academy which stands in opposition to any such development taking place.[12] That report, it is correct to say, took as one of its concerns the question of the independence of scholarship, but it also foresaw an Academy concerned with 'public professional obligations' and with 'the commitment of faith'.

As I see the developments in religious studies on American university campuses, and in the various societies and associations for the study of religion – and particularly so the American Academy of Religion (AAR) – the more pervasive and significant concern on the part of the student of religion has been with the commitment of faith and the professional obligations and not with the study of religion as an academic/scientific undertaking. This is quite evident, I think, in recent 'moves' not only to retheologize religious studies within the academy but also to politicize it. I shall, for the sake of illustration of this general claim, draw brief attention to three recent presidential addresses to the Academy which clearly suggest that something of that nature is happening. In 'The AAR and the Anxiety of Nonbeing: An Analysis of Our Present Cultural Situation', Langdon Gilkey deplores the positivist inspired split between reflection and belief which, he insists, can only lead to the nonbeing – the death – of the AAR and of academic concern with religious phenomena. An analysis of our present cultural situation can only involve us, as he puts it, in 'seemingly inescapable, deeper questions than we expected, not only questions of fact and the scholarly interpretation of facts but reflective questions calling for new self-understanding and so for philosophical and theological creativity'.[13] Professor Gordon Kaufman in his 'Nuclear Eschatology and the Study of Religion' similarly complains of 'the artificial separation of theology from religious studies, which has come to define all too much of our work', and he looks forward to our overcoming it.[14] He concludes: 'Theology and the study of religion must together move forward into one discipline which draws on the deepest religious resources and reflection in human life as it tries, in face of a thoroughly threatening future, to provide orientation, and guidance for our contemporary human existence.'[15] For Kaufman, then, religious studies must necessarily be a means of redemption or a hindrance to it (*contra* Welch) and so cannot be an objective or neutral examination of religious phenomena. Finally, Professor Wilfred Cantwell Smith, in his address on 'The Modern West in the History of Religions', urges us to recognize that the very goals Welch thought we had already attained – and that Smith very much fears we might yet attain – are eccentric, bizarre, abnormal, aberrant, etc., and that they cannot possibly constitute a framework for understanding religion or religions.[16] Such a study, Smith maintains, is a wilful refusal to see the truth of the transcendent, and a dogmatic imposition of a naturalistic ceiling on the interpretation of religion and, indeed, of all human history. He concludes, and I think somewhat ominously so, that modern secularism is 'so important an error as to be socially and historically disruptive; not to say, disastrous'. And as an intellectual error, he continues, 'it is the task of the intellectuals to correct it'.[17]

This sample of opinion of the 'leadership' in the American Academy of Religion is slim, but very suggestive. The distance between these three and Welch is vast. The sample, in my view therefore, is indicative of a decline in the concern for the academic/scientific study of religion; a decline the root of which is to be found in the rejection of the assumption that we can come to understand religion by scientific means. The academic study of religion, it is being argued, is exempted from the ordinary obligations of neutrality and objectivity that attend our other academic/scientific activities but is still nevertheless to be accounted as if such exemptions had not been invoked given the expectation that it will be accorded a place in the university curriculum.[18] Special pleading, it seems, is deemed an acceptable form of argumentation in Religious Studies. It appears, therefore, that having achieved the desired political goal of the establishment of the study of religion as a *bona fide* element of the university curriculum, Religious Studies will now refuse to live up to the academic commitments it freely gave, or at least implicitly acceded to, in taking its place in the university community.[19]

It is in sorting out this rather complex apology for a theological study of religions that the philosopher of religion can, I think, play an important role. The philosopher's task here is, I would argue, twofold: the critical function of exposing the crypto-theological agendas that seem perpetually to infiltrate the academic/scientific study of religion and religions, and the constructive function of providing a methodological framework (or of fine-tuning existing methodological frameworks) so as to carry forward the intention of the 'founding (fathers) scholars' of the 'new discipline'. The task of the philosopher, therefore, is one of 'naturalizing' this field of research. The late Professor William Clebsch has quite rightly insisted that as a part of the curriculum of the modern university Religious Studies has become a 'naturalized citizen', and that like any other citizen of that community, it must live up to the obligations to which it has, so to speak, given allegiance.[20] For students in the field not to live up to that allegiance is simply to undermine the credibility of their work as a scientific activity worthy of academic consideration or legitimation. Special pleading of their case can, that is, only lead to the infection of Religious Studies by religion itself and so place in question the objectivity of the results of the research undertaken. Consequently, I would argue that the tack taken by O'Connell and company can only make of the study of religion an enterprise indistinguishable in structure and intent from the scientific-creationism that emerges from the religiously oriented study of biology. The development of evolutionary biology, as everyone knows, is the result of the detheologization, so to speak, of the study of biology. The 'retheologization' of biology, however, has given us scientific-creationism which, according to its practitioners, is a 'new discipline' which deserves acceptance/legitimation by the academic/scientific community. It has, I think most would agree, rightly failed to receive such legitimation. Those who wish to synthesize theology and the study of religion, however, maintain that the 'retheologization' of the academic study of religion ought not to be treated in the same fashion, even though no persuasive reasons have been provided for such differential treatment of scientific creationism and the religiously oriented study of religion. In any event, unlike 'scientific-creationism', a kind of 'scientific religionism', if we may so call it, seems to have achieved a place for itself in the university curriculum despite the fact that, methodologically speaking, its credibility does not exceed that of the scientific-creationists. And that, I suggest, is an important matter for investigation by philosophers as well as other concerned academics.

Part III
On the Incommensurability of Scientific and Religious Belief

11

Philosophical Reflections on Twentieth-Century Mennonite Thought

There is a sense in which one might reasonably query the possibility of the task suggested by the title of this chapter. One might justifiably argue, that is, that there is really no substantial body of thought both characteristically Mennonite and characteristically of the twentieth century upon which reflective attention might be focused. This is not to say that the intellectual is non-existent in the Mennonite community, for Mennonite artists, writers, musicians and various kinds of 'academics' abound. Nevertheless, it is extremely difficult to find 'the thinker' in contemporary Anabaptist/Mennonite circles. There are few Mennonite theologians with originality and flair and even fewer, if any, Mennonite philosophers. The *Mennonite Encyclopedia*, interestingly, boasts not a single entry under 'philosophy'; and theology, according to the *Encyclopedia*, seems to emerge only under the stimulus of an unacceptable 'liberal influence'.[1] My concern in this essay, however, is not with an examination of any particular expressions of the twentieth-century Mennonite mind but rather with the impoverished state of that mind.

In a recent article on the 'Cultural and Intellectual Aspects of the Mennonite Experience in Russia',[2] J. B. Toews describes the utter impoverishment of the nineteenth-century Mennonite mind. 'The village teacher', he writes 'was there to teach reading and writing, not art, literature, or liberating ideas.'[3] Heinrich Balzer's attitude in *Verstand und Vernunft* he claims, is typical:

> His appeal is to the past and his intellect, though of high quality, was of an ultraconservative turn. He possibly symbolized the Mennonite mind of the mid-nineteenth century – certainly not illiterate, but incapable of adapting a historic faith to new circumstances.[4]

131

Closed communities dictated rather extreme limits of intellectual inquiry. Learning and teaching were for the most part, Toews argues, but a reaffirmation of existing knowledge and experience; there was no 'quest for new frontiers'; indeed:

> self-doubt and personal soul searching, criticism of community values such as blatant materialism, the questioning of traditional teachings and practices as well as verbal or literary exploration in such areas – activities of this kind were out of the question.[5]

Such activities, I suggest, are still 'out of the question' and because they are so, I shall argue, the twentieth-century Mennonite mind represents no substantial improvement upon the nineteenth-century state of affairs described by Toews.

The first task of this chapter is to substantiate the claim just made. This will not be a difficult task, especially since I shall restrict myself in this respect to a discussion of the Mennonite Brethren community. A further and much more important task – and infinitely more difficult as well – is to inquire as to the reasons and/or causes for our present 'state of mind'. Is our impoverished condition merely the product of contingent historical events or social, political, and economic factors; or does it emerge out of the very essence of 'the Anabaptist vision'[6] itself?

The impoverished state of the twentieth-century Mennonite mind is twofold. Not only is there a dearth of theological and philosophical productivity but, more importantly, there is an almost total lack of freedom for critical thought. The former problem only, it appears, characterizes the Anabaptism of the first few generations whereas both aspects of impoverishment characterize both the nineteenth and twentieth centuries.[7]

C. Krahn in a 'Prolegomena to an Anabaptist Theology'[8] suggests that lack of theological productivity in the first few generations of the movement is not indicative of an antagonism to theological thought nor of a lack of interest, but rather simply the result of the lack of adequate time and resources of a people under constant harassment and persecution. Furthermore, he suggests, the community was early on deprived of its intellectual leadership through persecution and martyrdom. Given the laws and regulations under which most Mennonites were forced to live they became, he argues, largely a rural people whose interests were, quite understandably, rather different. However, even if Krahn's thesis were entirely verified, its explanatory capacity is almost entirely applicable only to the first few generations of Anabaptists. It cannot satisfactorily be invoked to account for the lack of interest and even hostility toward the theological enterprise in a community under strong urban leadership four centuries later.

Some, like Harold S. Bender for example, have implied in their treatment of Anabaptism that the emphasis placed upon Christian discipleship is largely responsible for the lack of theological output. 'It is evident,' claims Bender, '... that the Anabaptists were concerned most of all about "a true Christian life", that is, a life patterned after the teaching and example of Christ.'[9] He continues: 'The Anabaptists could not understand a Christianity which made regeneration, holiness, and love primarily a matter of intellect, of doctrinal belief, or of subjective "experience", rather than one of transformation of life.'[10]

Bender's suggestions here are certainly more persuasive than Krahn's, but still not wholly so. It is immediately apparent that an ethic itself implies a world-view; that discipleship draws its inspiration from a peculiar conception of the nature of the universe and people's place in it, even if that conception is not explicitly formulated. The centrality of the notion of discipleship in early Anabaptist life, therefore, *could* just as easily be used to explain the growth and development of a prodigious theological output.

The suggestions of Krahn and Bender are helpful in coming to some understanding of our present theological state, and I shall come back to them later in this chapter. The primary cause for the dearth of our theological and philosophical output in this century, however, must be found elsewhere. Its cause, I suggest here, is to be found in the radical rejection of free and critical thought, that is, in a rejection of 'modernity'. Although I shall attempt to account for this rejection in a later section, further comment is required here for clarification. It must be admitted that, as Jarold Knox Zeman argues,[11] the elements of personalism, pluralism, and egalitarianism in early Anabaptism give the movement a characteristically modern tinge. However, even though they are significant motifs of modernity they do not make Anabaptism a modern phenomenon. Indeed, Zeman himself recognizes other 'criteria of modernity' that characterize the nineteenth and twentieth centuries[12] but are not characteristic of Anabaptism. One of those 'other criteria' is autonomous and unhindered critical inquiry. And this does not characterize contemporary Mennonite thought. In this sense it seems to me that the *promise* of

Anabaptism as a 'prelude to the modern age', as Zeman puts it, has gone unfulfilled in the present century. It now remains to document this claim.

The lack of freedom for free and critical thought within the Mennonite, and particularly Mennonite Brethren,[13] community in Canada is seen most forcefully expressed in the establishment in 1968 of the Radical Mennonite Union on the campus of Simon Fraser University (British Columbia). John Braun in the *Manifesto* of the Union[14] sees the lack of freedom for critical thought of one's own community as the central problem for the Mennonite concerned with the problems of the twentieth century. In a short paragraph on the establishment of the Union he writes:

> Surely our greatest allies in building the movement are the Mennonite churches whose authoritarian structures continually drive free-minded people to despair and defeat. It is an ultra-conservative church, fighting determined rear-guard actions to defend not only its rigid theology and outdated social mores but also the status quo in the political sphere. The suppression of all human spontaneity is clearly evident to anyone [who] sees the passive docile idiots the church creates – human near-vegetables incapable of facing life with any kind of honesty.[15]

This demand, argues Braun, calls for reform of our educational institutions from 'indoctrination centres' to

> true educational centres where children (as well as young people and adults) learn to intellectually [*sic*] (i.e. critically) and not dogmatically deal with theological and religious matters. The same goes for the other 'educational' institutions – the private high schools, the Bible schools, and the various colleges. They must cease being dens of dogmatic stagnation and become centers of questioning, criticism, reflection, and action in meaningful social areas and become relevant in the context of the whole of society.[16]

The language is obviously inflammatory. There is less here of the quest for freedom of thought than of zealous reform. The movement appears more a concern for praxis than for critical thought. This comes out rather clearly in Braun's 'A Radical Confession of Faith',[17] written less than a year after the publishing of the *Manifesto*, although Braun recognizes that his argument here in fact constitutes, in embryo form, a new and modern attempt at theology, there is in much of this document, however, a repudiation of mere intellectualization.[18]

Ferment in this regard was not to be found only amongst Mennonite students on university campuses. There was a deliberate attempt on the part of the Winkler Bible Institute in the latter half of the 1960s to break traditional educational patterns. In an attempt to convey the meaning of the new patterns I described the intent of the new curriculum in a short article in the *Mennonite Brethren Herald*: 'It is obvious ... that a two year curriculum of studies cannot contain all the answers to life – no curriculum can. The curriculum, therefore, seeks to develop in the student a spirit of critical and wholesome inquiry and to develop techniques of research and communication, so that a student might learn to think independently.'[19] The faculty and Winkler Bible Institute Committee[20] agreed upon 'a spirit of critical, yet wholesome inquiry' as an acceptable objective, to be implemented by 'a search for the truth' through open confrontation among students and teachers and through 'a critical examination of contemporary thinking'.[21] The effect of the new developments and of the new approach to Bible Institute teaching was predominantly one of fear and mistrust of the faculty on the part of the Board of Christian Education of the Mennonite Brethren Churches of Manitoba. The minutes of the meetings of the Winkler Bible Institute Executive for 22 November 1968, list as items for discussion the following: '(5) re-assessing the aims and objectives for WBI (Winkler Bible Institute); (7) allowing for student criticism and questioning; and (8) allowing for different views and approaches without labelling them as conservative or liberal.'[22] The beginning of a rift between the Board and the Executive Committee is already apparent here. By 16 December 1968 conditions had noticeably deteriorated. The minutes for that meeting indicate that the new curriculum and style of teaching were critical problems. One key issue raised was 'the question whether our library should contain books which are not necessarily our point of view or our faith but which our students read in order to prepare them for the world which they will face, [which] was discussed at some length'.[23] By 7 February 1969 several faculty members described the situation in a letter to the Committee of Reference and Counsel as follows:

At present, the whole program of the school is deadlocked in an intense ideological struggle which resulted in the resignation of four (of five) members of the Executive of the Winkler Bible Institute as well as of several (four of five) faculty members.[24]

The official history of the Bible Institute published on the occasion of the Institute's fiftieth anniversary recalls the character of the conflict as follows:

> The latter part of the sixties posed a threat to man's traditional way of life and values of the past which man held dear. Changes came about ruthlessly and ferociously, without regard for anyone, sparing nothing. The effects of protest, revolt, rebellion and social upheavals managed to filter down irrevocably into the enshrined life structures of the past. The world seemed to shrink, the human race appeared like a leviathan which was difficult to govern and next to impossible to control. Undesirable influences, tangible and intangible, penetrated all realms of life. Cultures and establishments of former times began to crumble and went down in ruins. Unleashed and untethered heretofore, latent psychic powers from the mysterious depth of man's life clamoured for domination and control.
> Although the Bible Institutes by and large, were not the direct target of the onslaught of the spirit of the times, it would be less than truthful to say that they were not assailed indirectly.[25]

The melodramatic character of the description is hardly credible, and yet it reveals the utter revulsion with which the spirit of free and critical inquiry was repudiated. This repudiation found its final stamp of approval by the Manitoba Conference of Mennonite Brethren in the election of a new principal to head the school. In an interview with Principal elect, Rev. H. R. Baerg, in the *Alumni Newsletter*, Baerg is asked: 'We keep hearing that since most young people nowadays pursue higher education, the Bible Institute must upgrade its supposedly rurally-oriented, juvenile, curriculum. Does this rank high among your priorities?' His response runs as follows: 'To operate on an intellectual par with the university is not our aim. Nor are we out to equip students intellectually for the higher criticism of the university. Few issues are resolved by argument. Rather, we must zero in on the Bible and in this way foster an attitude of love for Christ and the Gospel, thus fortified a student will best face the attacks of the world.'[26]

The impoverishment of the Mennonite mind begins to emerge in incidents such as these. There is here no sensitivity to self-doubt and soul-searching, no room for the quest for new frontiers in Christian faith, no room for liberating ideas that may put in jeopardy past experience and knowledge. The limits to intellectual inquiry are as tight in the twentieth century, it seems, as ever they were in the nineteenth – despite the development of 'higher' educational institutions amongst the Mennonite Brethren.

A more recent incident must suffice in illustrating this lamentable state of the twentieth-century Mennonite mind. I refer here to a recent 'Study Conference on the Bible'[27] held by the Mennonite Brethren in Fresno, California, in December 1976. The announcement of the Conference in the *Mennonite Brethren Herald* itself indicates that the Conference was somewhat out of the ordinary, for it was restricted to teaching members of the Bible Institutes and Colleges and the Seminary of the Mennonite Brethren Conference. Indeed, it was the first time a conference of this kind had ever been convened. The announcement reads as follows: 'Growing differences in the way Mennonite Brethren are interpreting the Bible has prompted the General Conference Board of Reference and Counsel to call a study conference on the issue ... to develop better understanding between the schools ... [and to] strengthen the relationships.'[28] More disturbing than the restrictions on the number and 'make-up' of the participants, commented upon in an editorial in the *Mennonite Brethren Herald*, is the fact that observers were not permitted.[29] Even 'the editors of the Conference periodicals', writes Jantz in a later article, 'were allowed into the meeting with reluctance and only after submitting to some restrictions on their reporting.'[30] Jantz, nevertheless, reports fairly candidly the nature of the proceedings. It certainly seems that there is growing suspicion even of the Bible teachers of the Conference, let alone of theologians and philosophers. Jantz, however, does not use the word suspicion; he writes rather of 'a growing impression that Mennonite Brethren teachers of the Bible in Canada and the United States might be moving apart on their interpretations of the Bible....'[31]

J. A. Toews in the opening paper of the Conference sets, I think, a tone of anti-intellectualism which seems to reflect the stance taken by the Conference organizers. He emphasizes the need for a 'practical biblicism', without defining exactly what he means by that phrase, 'reminding' the participants that it is not the Bible that 'divides' the church but rather the hermeneutical frameworks adopted for its interpretation. Any philosophical or theological considerations of such a hermeneutical framework seem to be excluded when he 'points out' reasons for Mennonite Brethren unity to date. The last of four reasons, listed by Toews, is

> a wholesome aversion to dogmatism [which] has played an important role in our brotherhood unity. Our forefathers preferred to express their understanding of truth in biblical rather than in theological or philosophical terms. This is true also of our confession of faith. As a result, we have not capitulated to 'isms', such as an extreme Calvinism, a narrow Fundamentalism, or a Hyper-Dispensationalism.[32]

Many of the papers presented, Jantz points out, received sharp and challenging criticism from members of the Board of Reference and Counsel. The criticisms, however, do not appear to have been of a scholarly or intellectual character. The 'critical study' of the Scriptures came in for special mention: 'all seemed aware that the very term "criticism" was loaded and difficult to use, especially within the Church constituency.'[33] Nevertheless, a subsequent discussion of the tensions faced by professors of Bible in having to present one face to the constituency and another in the classroom drew the rather ironic response that 'it was dishonest to "hide what we are doing in the classrooms"'.[34] This response, it appears, drew a rather stern warning about 'possessing too many tools of scholarship', and Clarence Hiebert, in what is referred to by Jantz as a 'moving statement of counsel', 'urged that we recognize that some teachers just out of graduate schools are still in spiritual pilgrimage themselves [which] becomes the agenda for their classes'.[35] The note of fearful reaction is hard to miss. The call for a group 'to discern whether one is fit to teach' is ominous and raises fears that this may put in jeopardy the posts of some already teaching in Mennonite Brethren institutions. This implication, I am sure, could not have been missed by all the participants of the Conference. The ministry of teaching at Mennonite Brethren institutions, it seems then, is indoctrination in the Truth, not a questing after wider horizons and forever more adequate perspectives.

No criticism of the nature of the Conference convened at Fresno from the academics involved, nor others in Mennonite Brethren colleges and bible institutes, as far as I am aware, has been raised. Whether this is to be explained in terms of concepts such as 'intimidation' is a moot question. This does not mean, however, that criticism of Mennonite Brethren 'conditions' has been totally silenced. Although our official histories fail to advert to matters of the kind I have raised here[36] some criticism does from time to time appear in 'Mennonite Brethren print'. I refer the reader especially to the work of Delbert Wiens of Pacific College. Even though the concerns of Wiens are not directly those I have raised here, his fears do nevertheless relate to the closed character of the 'Mennonite Brethren mind'. Almost fifteen years ago in 'New Wineskins for Old Wine: A Study of the Mennonite Brethren Church' he perceptively and courageously wrote:

> Sometimes leaders know that they do not have many answers. And yet, bound by their understanding of the role of a leader, they feel the necessity of assuming a firm position. These are truly tragic figures. They are themselves unsure of answers which they preach with great conviction. They bear doubts in themselves to save us from hard questions. Having sacrificed their integrity, they also are finally rejected and are forced to bear the double fate of martyrs who cannot even respect themselves.[37]

And again:

> Because ministers do not understand their roles; because the official answers do not always apply; because we have lost our consensus; because we are not sure how our brothers think – we are afraid of each other, afraid to share even the truths we know. At a time when we need leadership as never before, we have made leadership almost impossible.[38]

Here and elsewhere[39] Wiens calls for an openness of thought *vis à vis* our 'established certainties' and calls for an openness to speak of our doubts. But his call, as the Fresno Conference seems to indicate, has gone unheeded.

Given the kind of mind-set I have been at pains to describe in the preceding argument of this essay, it is hardly surprising that 'the thinker' in the community is silenced, or ostracized; that there has been little in the way of creative and original intellectual productivity. The difficult task now, of course, is to account for this antiintellectualism. One might be tempted to see the causes behind this mentality to be of a psychological/sociological kind – an attempt, that is, to stave off acculturation/assimilation. Leo Driedger, for example, suggests that the 'ethnic village model' was a natural course for the urban settlement of Mennonites to take, for such development 'tends to hold the individual within an in-group orbit where much of his time and social interaction take place'.[40] Driedger laments the adoption of this model and sees it as entirely unnecessary.

> Individuals who feel secure in their social status, who are committed to an ideology which they believe is superior, and who have a sense of being a part of the God who acts in history, should be sufficiently flexible to intermingle with others without feeling threatened even though they are members of a minority.[41]

Nevertheless, the fear of assimilation is, I think, a major factor in the perpetuation of our anti-intellectualism not only amongst 'ordinary' members of the community but also amongst the leadership. The previous statements of this paper should leave little doubt about this. Certainly this is the dominant concern of Harold S. Bender's 'Outside Influences on Mennonite Thought':[42] or of Paul Peachy's 'Identity Crisis Among American Mennonites';[43] and of C. Norman Kraus's 'Re-examining Mennonite Reality: Shapes and Meaning of the Future'.[44] Even Driedger, contrary to the position taken in the above-mentioned article, takes a similar position in his 'The Anabaptist Identification Ladder: Plain Urbane Continuity in Diversity', in which he suggests that this identification ladder 'allows for identification with more urbanized groups of the same heritage, without assimilation'.[45] He argues for the maintenance of 'Plain-Urbane Continuity in Diversity' for it will 'in the long run resist assimilation best and it will enhance Anabaptist identification'.[46] Certainly such psychological/sociological factors have played an important part in the formation of the anti-intellectualism of much twentieth-century Mennonite thought. Other historical kinds of explanation that take into consideration political, economic, and other social factors would also, no doubt, help us to account for this phenomenon – perhaps even in an exhaustive fashion. Limitations of time and lack of training in this area, however, preclude further inquiries along this line. Nevertheless, the question as to the possible exhaustive empirical explanation of this phenomenon does require further discussion. The anti-intellectualism discussed in this paper is, I suggest, contrary to the opinion of C. Krahn noted above, endemic to Anabaptism/Mennonitism. And it may be that anti-intellectualism is an intrinsic aspect of 'the Anabaptist Vision'.

My discussion of Harold S. Bender above would seem to indicate that, according to Bender's interpretation of the essential character of the movement as practical and existential, anti-intellectualism is of the essence of Anabaptism. Robert Friedmann in an article on 'Anabaptism and Protestantism',[47] follows a similar train of thought, as does Walter Klaassen in a much more recent article on 'The Nature of the Anabaptist Protest'.[48] According to Klaassen the Anabaptist deliberately took a stand against what he calls 'the intellectualizing of the Christian faith'.[49] For the Anabaptist, he writes,

> Truth is … not abstract and ideological but existential in nature. It is not discovered in the universities but in the footsteps of Christ in everyday living. Thus the learned are not in the universities, courts, or bishops' palaces. In the school of discipleship God constantly reveals himself to the learned and unlearned alike. The measure of understanding is not relative to the level of intellectual ability, but to the measure of openness, of abandonment to God and his will.[50]

Given such a view it is not surprising that the life of the mind was not highly prized. In so far as our academic activities are concerned with the recovery of 'the Anabaptist Vision', therefore, the intellectuals are, paradoxically, involved in undermining the life of the mind. But more of paradox in what follows.

It seems to me that the emphasis placed upon the doctrine of the Church in Anabaptist theology is perhaps, in connection with the conception of discipleship as noted above, the most important factor in the anti-intellectualism of Anabaptism. The isolationism involved in that concept is effective not only politically but also intellectually. The Anabaptists formed a 'separated brotherhood' of believers who refused to compromise with the world and provided the possibility of a judgement upon the social order. (A possibility not always used, however, as the Mennonite experience in Russia illustrates.) But in the life of the mind the 'separated brotherhood' simply withdrew in fear from the world of mind. It led to the establishment of a peculiar hermeneutic that sealed itself off from all possibility of correction, development, and growth from the outside. John Howard Yoder brings this out in his summary of Anabaptism[51] when he points out the consequences of such a view of the Church for the interpretation of scripture. It implies the belief, he insists, that God leads people to an understanding of God's word only 'in the gathered congregation':

It was this conviction about the way in which the Holy Spirit leads in the congregation, which led the Anabaptists to reject any final authority of princes in the Church. Nor was this simply a confidence in the democratic process of majority rule; the spirit would overrule human weakness and allow the will of God to become known in the situation in which they met.... Unity in the knowledge of the will of God was not to be reached by political or intellectual authorities, nor by religiously gifted leaders enforcing a correct creed, but by the working of the Holy Spirit among the brethren as they gathered to study the scriptures.[52]

In this 'separatist' conception of the Church it seems to me that the Anabaptists not only gave over the state to 'the world' but that they also gave over the realm of the mind to 'the world'. We have here, I think, the 'birth' of an intellectual ghetto.

The 'reflections' in this chapter emerge largely out of a personal frustration in trying to live in two worlds simultaneously – within the world of thought and the Mennonite community. For long it has been a *feeling* that the legacy of our Mennonite heritage is unsuited to 'the thinker', to the intellectual. I have therefore attempted here to sketch why this is so. And I am persuaded that the problem stems from the very essence of the Anabaptist vision and that subsequent political, economic and social developments have only, in varying degrees, accentuated or exacerbated the basic problem. Obviously more research is required if these 'hunches' are to be verified.

The very thesis I have suggested may seem to some quite perverse in light of the tremendous educational activity in which Mennonites have been involved. There are Mennonite Bible Institutes, Colleges, and even Seminaries or Graduate Schools that would seem to indicate a healthy and vibrant life of the mind. This situation is, to say the least, paradoxical. But it can, I think, be explained because this situation is not peculiar to the Mennonites – it is characteristic of the Fundamentalist/Evangelical community more generally. G. M. Marsden in an article tracing the development of Evangelicalism from Fundamentalist roots certainly seems to indicate precisely this. He writes: 'Intellectually, evangelicals maintained their own colleges and seminaries that reflected their distinctive stance, yet they emphasized scholarship *sufficiently to put aside any image of anti-intellectualism*'.[53] I have placed the emphasis on the above quoted words in order to bring out what I think to be the motivating force behind not only the Fundamentalist/Evangelical educational drive but the Mennonite concern in education as well. James Barr in his *Fundamentalism*[54] also recognizes that in recent decades scholarship has become ever more important for conservative evangelicals[55] but he does not see in this a genuine concern for the intellectual life. Indeed, Barr sees the real problem of Fundamentalism to lie in its intellectual structures – intellectually, he argues, it is a sect for 'its doctrines, its literature, its biblical interpretation, its modes of speech, thought, and friendship mark out a clearly identifiable social organism'.[56] It is for this reason, of course, that one must question whether the scholarship of the Evangelical community, and of the Mennonites, is real or honest scholarship. They, as the sociologists point out, form a 'cognitive minority'.[57] Mouw, in his 'Evangelicals in Search of Maturity', simply refers to evangelical theological scholarship as 'for the most part' a wasteland.[58]

The growth of intellectual activity amongst Mennonites (and Evangelicals generally) reflects, I suggest, a growing alienation with their minority status. Having become, as church historian Martin E. Marty puts it, a social behavioural majority they have become increasingly discontented with their lack of 'cognitive prestige'. They are, however, unwilling or unable to pay the dues. Those dues are set out clearly by Barr:

> The longing of the conservative for recognition on an intellectual and scholarly level is a revenge of the intellect upon decisions of the religion. His annoyance at being alienated from the scholarly world is a long-range spiritual and cultural effect of the decision of his religion to unchurch those who believed differently and to treat their theology and their biblical work as if it was an enemy of God. He cannot undo this by pretending that his scholarly arguments are totally objective thinking on the basis of the facts alone and without any preconceptions whatever – an argument put forward most strenuously by those whose results are most exactly in accord with traditional fundamentalist doctrine. If he wants to undo his alienation, without leaving the world in which he is now embedded, he has to go back to his own religious people – their leaders, their simple believers – and tell them something more positive about the world of scholarship and theology in which he himself partly or wholly moves.[59]

I do not think the Mennonite intellectual community or church is yet ready to do this, for this would mean that, in taking account of the conflict between modern belief and tradition, one would have to be ready to reject the usual identification of orthodoxy with tradition. It would have to recognize that the real test of orthodoxy is truth rather than conformity with traditional formulation. Further, it would have to come to recognize that there is real value in the plurality of views – 'in a friendly clash of conflicting views'. This is how C. J. Cadoux put it a generation ago.[60] Cadoux rightly points out that 'the essence of the Gospel consists, not necessarily in what our Christian predecessors proclaimed, but in what the Spirit of the living God reveals to us as true, rejoicing the heart and enlightening the eyes.'[61] This does not, of course, mean that Mennonites would have to become liberals. But it does mean, as Barr insists, that Mennonites would 'have to recognize that the liberal quest is in principle a fully legitimate form of Christian obedience within the church, and one that has deep roots within the older Christian theological task and even within the Bible itself.'[62] There would have to be a recognition that in thought and scholarship there is not a 'conservative side' and a 'critical side' but rather merely thought and scholarship that recognizes both conservative and critical opinions. Unwillingness to move in this direction, I suggest, ought to require of us, for the sake of consistency, to abandon the realms of higher education altogether, as have done the Hutterian Brethren.[63]

The problem implicit throughout this paper is essentially that of 'rationality and identity'. Comprehensive analysis of these rather abstract notions cannot, unfortunately, be undertaken. Nevertheless some comment, however inadequate, does seem to be called for. What follows in this final section, therefore, is offered only as a stimulant to debate and discussion that might eventually provide us with a clearer insight into the nature of the problem hinted at in this chapter. If it contains the seeds of the resolution of our problem they will only come to fruition through critical debate.

Identity as Mennonites, or more generally as Christians, requires, it is claimed, an unquestioning commitment to certain specific distinguishing beliefs/characteristics whereas identity as rational and thoughtful persons seems to require the freedom to question one's commitments – to subject them to searching criticism. The difference of identity, that is, is not one that concerns the content of one's commitments, so to speak, but rather the 'way' in which those commitments are held. Neither is that difference one of commitment as opposed to non-commitment. The critical attitude of mind does not imply that no commitment can ever be made; rather it simply requires the *decision* made to be based on 'evidence and argument' and not merely on 'authority'. Consequently, the commitment of the 'rationalist' – a term I shall use here simply as a convenient locution for 'the critical inquirer' – is less than absolute; it is changeable in principle whereas that of the religious believer is not. The frame-of-mind of the believer, it appears therefore, is radically different from and in opposition to that of the 'rationalist'. Consequently it would appear, given this analysis, that one is bound to choose between one's identity as a Christian and one's claim to be a critical inquirer (i.e. a rationalist). To lay claim to both Christian identity and rational integrity, that is, does not seem possible.

The specific problem in this chapter is that this supposed irrationality of our 'Christian' (Anabaptist) 'identity' does not seem to bother us. Instead of grappling with the problem we attempt to evade it by 'fracturing' the very notion of rational thought; we invoke the *tu quoque* argument. The adoption of a 'rationalist stance', it is claimed, is also an irrational adoption of a 'lifestance'. A fine example of such argumentation, and in good measure representative of twentieth-century Mennonite thought, is to be found in John Redekop's article 'The Cult of Intellectualism':

> The cult of intellectualism includes a minimization of the role of faith, indeed, a built-in antipathy to faith. Paul tells us in Romans 10 that "faith cometh by hearing and hearing by the word of God". Intellectualists find it virtually impossible to accept the premise of this statement for it implies an inadequacy of self, of humanity, of the scientific method, of higher education, and of the entire natural realm. That is asking a lot. All of us should remember, of course, that we all live by faith of one kind or another; we all believe in something. Thus the ultimate question becomes, do we place ultimate faith in man or God?[64]

This kind of argument is not new to Christian thought. And it has been submitted to rather scathing criticism in W. W. Bartley's *Retreat to Commitment*.[65] Bartley sets out to rob the theologians, so to speak, of what he calls their rational excuse for irrational commitment and thereby to deny them their claim to both religious identity and intellectual or rationalist respectability. On the ground occupied by Redekop, I think Bartley's argument is successful. Bartley's development of a comprehensively critical version of the rationalist stance shows that rationalists need no longer take up their stance irrationally:

if my argument is sound, there can no longer be a general rational excuse of ultimate irrational commitments and those who continue to make them will really be irrationalists, in the sense that they will not be able to retain their protestant theological identity with the intellectual integrity which the argument about the limits of rationality afforded them, as long as it went unrefuted.[66]

As I have shown at length elsewhere,[67] the argument as stated by Bartley is not without flaw. It can be shown, that is, that Bartley's conception of 'Comprehensively Critical Rationalism' is somewhat inflated. And further analysis of the concept reveals that such rationalism need not preclude commitment from its account of rational procedure, not even the 'ultimate commitment' necessary to the religious (Christian) stance. Bartley makes the assumption that all 'ultimate commitment' is necessarily irrational commitment (i.e. absolute or unchangeable commitment). And it seems the Christian community adopts the same unexamined position. It is this failure to distinguish the kinds of ultimate commitments that are possible that leads Bartley to a rejection of a religious identity and the Christian (and the Mennonite, especially as reflected in Redekop's 'argument' against intellectualism) to an irrational espousal of such an identity. Both positions are false; neither is forced upon us.

There are at least two kinds of 'ultimate commitment'. The first kind is a commitment that is made 'once-for-all', never again to be opened to further assessment or criticism. Such ultimate commitment is irrational given Bartley's (correct, I think) understanding of the nature of rationality. The other kind of 'ultimate commitment' concerns a commitment which is 'ultimate' in the sense that it predominates and guides all subsequent decisions made by the one who holds it. Such a commitment is neither lightly made nor lightly rejected, but neither need it be made in such a fashion that it is never again reconsidered. One can be convinced, that is, that the principle or person to which commitment is made as a Christian is true and so maintain Christian identity, and yet maintain rational integrity in being willing to re-examine that conviction should new information or evidence come to light. To be ready to give up one's Christian faith with successful falsification of the 'Christian principle' is not in itself to give up one's Christian identity. It is difficult, therefore, to see why there exists such a profound fear of critical thought. Free critical inquiry is a threat to the Christian believer only if there is something inherently 'false' about Christian commitment. Recognition of this fact, I suggest, holds some promise of a resolution of our Anabaptist problem with the life of the mind. Fear of free and critical inquiry, and pressure to contain and to limit our intellectual activity – to build an intellectual ghetto – I suggest, is not indicative of a strong faith but rather reflects and helps to perpetuate weakness of faith.

12

Comprehensiveness: The Integrity of Anglican Theology

A colleague of mine recently said to me: "my wife is an atheist, but she wants to be an Anglican as well. Is there anything she can read?" "My dear fellow," I replied, "we've got plenty of books showing how the trick can be done."[1]

I

The Anglican Communion, it appears, is in trouble, and it is so, according to a number of observers and analysts, because of its theologians. More than fifteen years ago Ninian Smart, from whom the above epigraph derives, felt compelled to draw attention to 'the intellectual crisis of British Christianity which, oddly it seems, thrives unnoticed'.[2] Indeed, he found the entire situation 'shocking and ludicrous' and so to require the 'promotion of a little *odium theologicum* ... to bring some illumination into an area where all is sweetness and light'.[3] Ten years later John Bowden noted the signs of 'decline' in Anglican theological thought not only in the dwindling interest in, and productivity of, popular theological writing, but also in the deepening rift between academics and the laity.[4] More recently, and much more stridently, E. L. Mascal speaks out against the quiet '*Trahison des Clercs*', claiming 'that the theological activity of the Anglican Church is in a condition of extreme, though strangely complacent, confusion and that this is having a disastrously demoralizing effect upon the life and thought of the Church as a whole and of the pastoral clergy in particular'.[5] And according to Mascal, the fault is clearly to be laid at the door of the academics and professional theologians. Stephen W. Sykes in *The Integrity of Anglicanism* picks up

148

the same theme. Anglican theology, he claims, is threatened by the inroads of liberalism amongst Anglican theologians and the debilitating effects of the notion of 'comprehensiveness'.

I cannot help but feel, in reading the accounts of the various crises that allegedly plague Anglican theology, and in examining the (in appearance at least, reactionary) proposals put forward to 'rectify' the situation, an element of urgency about the 'future of Anglican theology debate' that almost borders on hysteria. The 'psychological distance' between Professor Smart's tongue-in-cheek 'attack' upon Anglican divines and Professor Mascal's '*Trahison des Clercs*' is worrisome. Like Bowden, I find it somewhat depressing to see much contemporary Anglican theology being 'greeted with horror, dismay, protest and abuse'.[6] My intention in this chapter is to show that it is also unwarranted. This chapter is, then, for the most part, a critique of Professor Sykes's analysis of the theological state of affairs in the Anglican Church, with special attention being given his attack on, and rejection of, the notion of comprehensiveness. And as critique the argument here is, unfortunately, largely negative, although I shall attempt to provide some grounds for an alternative interpretation of the meaning and value of the notion of comprehensiveness not only for Anglican theology, but for theology in general. I begin with a summary statement of Professor Sykes's position.

II

According to Professor Sykes, two main problems plague Anglican theological thought. The first is a lack of coherent identity, and the second, a lack of moral soundness. Both, however, seem to be connected to the even more fundamental problem of 'belief'. Anglican theology lacks identity, he argues, because of the notion of 'comprehensiveness':

> The major, and often recognized, problem which this tradition poses, is whether there are or could be any limits to the toleration extended to liberals within the Anglican Church.[7]

And integrity or moral soundness is lost if one, after hearing testimony to Christ, is unwilling 'to face up to the issues of belief':

The integrity of the communion is in question, because it appears to be offering the propositions of the Christian gospel as topics for debate and discussion, rather than to be witnessing to the mighty act of God in Christ.[8]

The problems so formulated, however, are hardly peculiar to Anglican theology and, although important, are not the central focus of attention. Questions of identity and integrity are of critical importance to all theology and for all theologians whereas Professor Sykes seems to be concerned with Anglican theology *qua* Anglican. A central concern in chapters 3, 4, and 5 of *The Integrity of Anglicanism*, for example, is the lack of a specific Anglican confessional position and chapter 6 discusses the lack of achievement by Anglican theologians in the field of systematic theology. Although the two sets of concerns overlap, I do not think they are simply identical. I am not entirely sure that Professor Sykes does not assume that they are. Further delineation of his position, therefore, may be helpful.

Professor Sykes argues that there is no clear 'Anglican standpoint', though once there was, whereby Anglicans are bound together as a distinctive community. Furthermore, he suggests, if this condition persists there will soon be no 'Church of England'. The causes of this condition are the peculiar notion of 'comprehensiveness' and the more general condition of a growing liberalism:

The case is rather that in response to the pressures initially of controversy and subsequently (and decisively) of biblical and historical criticism, the Anglican Church has progressively shed its distinctive confessional commitment, relatively broad though that always was.[9]

This is not the entire story, however. Professor Sykes does admit that there is, in fact, an Anglican method and an Anglican theology although they are not 'explicitly' available, so to speak. They are 'implicit' in that matrix provided for the 'growth of Christian character'; they lie 'embodied' in liturgy and canon law.

Professor Sykes's concern with the lack of productivity of Anglican theologians is not clearly delineated. He remarks in the Preface that systematic theology (understood as 'that constructive discipline which presents the substance of the Christian faith with a claim on the minds of men'[10]) cannot be safely ignored. Beyond that, however, his comments are confusing, for he seems to suggest that its

virtual non-existence is both cause and result of the lack of awareness of the Anglican theological stance. I quote two passages that
illustrate the tension:

> the lack of a history of major theological achievement has not a
> little to do with the failure of modern Anglicanism to foster any
> acute awareness of its own theological stance.[11]

> The Anglican Church has a standpoint, whether or not its theolo-
> gians are aware of it and are prepared to think carefully and criti-
> cally about it. But if and when they do so, they will write what
> can and should be called 'Anglican theology', which will be
> recognizably Anglican both as to content and to method.[12]

III

Disagreement with Professor Sykes might be raised on several
grounds. It is conceivable, for example, that his description of the
present state of affairs in Anglican theological thought needs further
clarification. The 'disparity' between traditional and contemporary
Anglican thought may not in fact be as great as he fears. And the
diversity of opinion within the contemporary Church may be
neither as profound nor as pervasive as he suggests. Furthermore,
questions might also be raised as to whether the 'diversity of theological opinion and belief' is any greater in the Anglican Church
today than ever it has been in the past. Matters of this kind are of
concern, however, to the historian and historical theologian.

Should there be general agreement of description of both past and
present 'theological states of affairs', there might still be disagreement as to the meaning or significance of either the diversity of
belief, past or present, or the change of belief. Whether doctrinal disagreement reflects a loss of integrity (wholeness) or increased love
(tolerance) or whether change of doctrinal belief constitutes degen-
eration of the Christian faith or a progressive elaboration and development of it cannot simply be read off the description itself. Such
decisions or assessments are tasks for the theologian and philosopher as much as they are for the historian.

Such questions of fact and significance, it is clear, are not
restricted simply to Professor Sykes's analysis of Anglican theology;
they can be asked of theology in general. Change of belief and a

growing diversity of belief has characterized the 'evolution' of theology in general and has not left any Christian community untouched. Assessing such developments in general, therefore, will have an important bearing on evaluating the significance of the occurrence within Anglican boundaries. Works such as R. Wilken's *The Myth of Christian Beginnings: History's Impact on Belief*[13] or V. A. Harvey's *The Historian and the Believer: The Morality of Historical Knowledge and Christian Belief*[14] are particularly helpful in this regard. However, it is not matters of this nature that occupy my interest here.

Even should there be agreement, not only upon historical description but also upon the assessment of the significance and meaning of particular (negative) theological 'developments', one might still find ground to disagree with Professor Sykes as to the best remedy, so to speak, for the degenerative state of affairs. The restriction of the intellectual freedom provided by the notion of comprehensiveness and a concomitant, if carefully selective, 'liberal bashing' (although this may be overstating the proposed measure somewhat), are, in my estimation, neither helpful nor intellectually or morally acceptable. The presumption that integrity – both as 'wholeness' and 'truthfulness' – can be achieved either by *fiat*, as seems at times to be implied in Professor Sykes's quest for an explicit confessional Anglican theology, or by ferreting out a systematic theology that lies implicit in the liturgy, and rules governing 'Anglican public performance' seems naive. The continued growth of 'alternative liturgies' in recent years seriously undermines this 'implicit theology' argument. Moreover, even if liturgical uniformity did exist and uniformity of confession were capable of being derived from it (or projected onto it), there would still be no guarantee that this would bring in its wake a uniformity of belief. Professor Sykes himself sets out, in an earlier work,[15] the reasons why this is so:

> even when all *say* that they believe the same thing by assenting to the identical form of words, it remains questionable whether all *understand* the same thing by that form of words. For example, in the creed we may say, 'I believe in one God, the Father Almighty, Maker of heaven and earth and of all things visible and invisible'. Whether all understand the same thing by this form of words is open to question, and is indeed only determinable, if at all by intense and laborious examination. The formidable Bishop Marsh (1757–1839) of Peterborough devised a set of eighty-seven questions for intending

clergy in his diocese by which he might detect whether their understanding of the Thirty-Nine Articles of the Church of England was open to an objectionable (Calvinistic) interpretation. The wretched clergy were being quizzed as to the meaning of their assent to the Articles; mere assent itself had not established, to the Bishop's satisfaction, a sufficient degree of uniformity of belief.[16]

It should be clear from the foregoing that my central concerns here with Professor Sykes's analysis of the Anglican community and proposal for the future of Anglican theology are primarily ones of 'assessment' and 'remedy'; they are, that is, philosophical rather than historical and are focused almost entirely upon his understanding of the notion of comprehensiveness. His claims that 'comprehensiveness', as an epistemic rule illegitimately wielded as a political tool, is responsible for the loss of coherent identity that once characterized the Anglican community, and that it undermines moral soundness in its theology are, it seems to me, unwarranted. There is no doubt that the notion of comprehensiveness 'permits' a diversity of belief that effects the identity of the community, but, I shall argue, the change involved is not such as to contribute to an erosion or loss of identity. Such diversity, I suggest, constitutes maturation in self-understanding and is inimical only to an 'identity by uniformity'. A proper understanding of the 'moral' character or quality of 'comprehensiveness' will show why this is so.

'Toleration of diversity itself', writes Professor Sykes, 'needs to be justified theologically if it is to be able to claim any kind of integrity'.[17] And he assumes, more than argues, it seems to me, that it cannot be so justified. It is difficult, however, to know what would constitute a 'theological justification'. If such justification is a matter of providing 'biblical' or 'traditional' warrants and backings, Professor Sykes might well be right since the notion of 'comprehensiveness' is – as is 'liberalism' – a peculiar modern phenomenon. Moreover, the notion is essentially epistemic and therefore requires an epistemic justification. And, strangely, I think Professor Sykes himself has provided the elements of such an argument in his earlier *Christian Theology Today* where he takes cognizance of the fact that modern theology, unlike traditional thought, 'takes place in a most rigorously critical environment'.[18]

The main thrust of Professor Sykes's argument in *Christian Theology Today* is that theology must be *pluriform*: that pluriformity of belief must not only be tolerated but rather seen to be 'a necessary condition of its essential activity'.[19] He also argues that the Enlightenment and subsequent growth of scientific knowledge force upon the theologian a relinquishing of the ideal of uniformity (of unanimous agreement), in the theological enterprise. Such developments provided sources of knowledge that either complemented or rivalled 'revealed knowledge':

> the Church no longer remained in sole control of the development of the Christian view of the world, as independent disciplines began to contribute new knowledge about the world and man.[20]

Although he does not believe the Christian theologian's view of humanity was superseded by modern anthropology, he does admit that the Christian cannot ignore the new developments and that the supposed 'eternal verities' of a previous age may well be put in doubt because of them:

> The point we are making is that because Christian theology is about the life of man, its origins and purpose, his destiny and his salvation, it is not possible for it to remain unaffected by what scientists may claim to be true about man's natural condition.... In as much as the 'eternal verities' were formulated at a time when such knowledge was not available, their proclamation in the contemporary world is bound to be influenced by it.... There can be no question but that the new knowledge upsets the deceptive simplicity of talk about the 'eternal verities'.[21]

A further, somewhat odd, defence of pluriformity is suggested in Professor Sykes's analysis of the 'conservative' claim that arguments are resolved by the hidden guidance of the Holy Spirit. He quite rightly raises questions as to whether it is to be believed that the Church invariably comes to a right decision in all matters of dispute, and he points out that uniformity of belief could only be imposed if the Church could establish, *a priori* it would seem, a specific (although reasonably brief) period of time within which such disputes would find their resolution. In the light of the difficulties that would pose he maintains that it would be inappropriate to require a convergence of belief amongst the faithful and argues, for the 'rights of error':

> there is real danger of coming to believe that whatever is, is right; that is, of depriving a protesting minority of its right to continue

opposition to a view which a majority has come to accept. The view that error has no rights has been one of the justifications of persecution offered by totalitarian regimes, both ecclesiastical and secular, for many centuries.[22]

However, the 'argument' for 'comprehensiveness' here appears to be a moral one and it ought, as I have suggested above, to have been an epistemological one. Some comments by Sykes about the fallibility of man (*sic*),[23] the decline of the role of authority in scientific matters,[24] and a discussion of the meaning for Christian theology of the re-emergence of world religions[25] show some, even if not wholly unambiguous, awareness of this.

What appears to be a radical change of heart in *The Integrity of Anglicanism* is not entirely precluded in the argument of the earlier work. Although Professor Sykes advocated a pluriformity of belief in the earlier work he nevertheless also argued that: '... theology requires a new understanding of the essence of Christianity if it is ever to attempt to resolve its doctrinal disagreements.'[26] And in chapter 3 of that work he maintains that plurality of belief does not mean that any and every theological view is tolerable.[27] 'Because Christianity is *about* Jesus,' he writes, 'about his birth, death and resurrection, its character is fundamentally shaped by the fact that Jesus actually existed'.[28]

This does not, however, spell out a specific set of beliefs that must be held, in respect of which 'deviation' is not permitted. Indeed, the very statement itself is open to some argument since it is obvious that Christianity could be about all the 'events' referred to even if it was only firmly believed that 'Jesus actually existed'. And firm belief that Jesus actually existed does not imply that he actually existed. Aware of such difficulties Professor Sykes proceeds:

> for the normative quest it is not a matter of identifying what, if anything, may be common to all who profess the name of Christian. It is the more difficult and adventurous task of trying to state what *ought* to characterize *true* Christianity.[29]

That task of providing a normative delineation, however, would involve, as he recognizes, assessment as to whether it accounts for the facts, is consistent exegesis of the Scriptures, and is true[30] – all matters open to dispute and upon which one can *reasonably* expect difference of opinion. Although Professor Sykes proceeds to discuss various doctrinal matters related to the person of Jesus, the nature of Christ, and God and creation, there is no sign of the emergence of an 'essential and indisputable core of beliefs' upon which all Christians *must* be agreed. And the claim in *The Integrity of Anglicanism* that such an indisputable core of beliefs exists implicitly in the liturgy and rules of order is not substantiated. The acceptance of a multiplicity of liturgical forms throws doubt upon such a claim as I have already intimated above. Furthermore, the belief that a 'doctrinal translation', so to speak, of the liturgy is likely to bring about a convergence of 'theological opinion' that can provide a wholeness presently lacking in the Church is about as convincing as the claim that a paraphrase of our most profound poetry will bring about complete agreement in our understanding of its meaning.

Two other matters of a logical character bear comment here: both concern the statement of purpose in the introduction to *Christian Theology Today*. Firstly, Professor Sykes's claim that theology requires a new understanding of the essence of Christianity if it is ever to resolve its doctrinal disagreement is tautological at best, if not entirely incoherent. A 'new understanding' of the essence of Christianity implies earlier and older understandings of that essence. Consequently it is obvious that the 'new understanding' of that essence is not necessarily identical with the essence of Christianity; it can but constitute yet another attempt to express doctrinally the essence of Christianity – an expression that stands alongside of, and in competition with, previous expressions. As such, it contributes to the pluriformity of belief and not to the resolution of doctrinal disagreement.

If Professor Sykes means to suggest in his statement of purpose that perceiving the essence of Christianity is necessary to resolving doctrinal disagreements, I suppose one can not help but agree. However, if the suggestion is meant to imply that that essence can be clearly perceived – in some way transcending the framework within which doctrinal dispute occurs – there would be, I think, ample grounds for disagreement with Professor Sykes over epistemological matters rather than *directly* theological ones. The danger in Professor Sykes's suggestions concerning a new understanding of the essence of Christianity is that a resolution of doctrinal disagreement, however it is achieved, might be taken as having perceived the essence of Christianity. To identify the essence of Christianity with doctrinal agreement is to invite 'persecution' of minorities. It also precludes further growth and development of theological understanding since 'difference of theological opinion' is read as 'deviation in theological belief'.[31] Consequently, *The Integrity of Anglicanism*, it seems to me, presents a danger to the theological enterprise rather than a foundation for the resolution of its problems.

The second comment required here concerns Professor Sykes's claim that pluriformity of belief is a *necessary* condition of the theological enterprise.[32] The claim, it seems, stands in contradiction with the expressed hope to achieve an understanding of the essence of Christianity which will, in turn, help bring about a resolution of doctrinal disagreement. Surely a necessary pluriformity of belief implies the impossibility of a resolution of doctrinal disagreement.

IV

As I have already pointed out above, I agree with Professor Sykes that 'comprehensiveness' requires justification. Moreover, I agree that matters of political expediency and the like do not constitute such a justification. (I am not convinced, however, that F. D. Maurice, Charles Gore, or William Temple are guilty of such reasoning as Sykes argues. Even if Sykes's analysis of their arguments were correct and their 'guilt' established beyond dispute, this would not imply that 'comprehensiveness' could not be justified on other grounds. Furthermore, I would suggest that on one reading of Sykes's *Christian Theology Today* his plea for the 'rights of error' could be taken as a move of political expediency. In any event it appears that Professor Sykes himself sees that plea as a kind of 'external justification' of pluriformity of belief: it is a moral justification for tolerance that, in my opinion, rightly proceeds on the basis of a distinction between a political right to believe and an epistemic right to believe. I shall have more to say of this below.) I part company with Professor Sykes, however, in his quest for a 'theological justification for comprehensiveness'. As I have suggested in the critique above, the notion of theological justification is, if not vague in the extreme, viciously circular. Furthermore, I suggest the notion of comprehensiveness (like pluriformity of belief) is an epistemic rather than a theological concept and therefore requires epistemic rather than theological justification.

It is obviously beyond the scope of this chapter to present an epistemological framework within which 'comprehensiveness' finds full justification. Nevertheless, some comments must be made that will show how such justification might be possible.

The first point that requires making here is that theology is a cognitively significant enterprise; theologians presume to tell us something about 'the world'. The theologian, like the scientist, therefore, is concerned with knowledge and, consequently, like the scientist *qua* scientist, is under primarily epistemic constraints. Further clarification may be helpful. The claim to knowledge, regardless of the field of study, requires justification; not just any claim has the 'right' to be designated 'knowledge'. Surely epistemology only makes sense if one can distinguish acceptable from unacceptable claims to knowledge on something like an 'objective' basis. And that is done by invoking various 'warrants and backings'[33] for the claims made by adducing evidence and logical support (for example, coherency, consistency, etc.) for the belief espoused.

The search for such a 'machinery of rational assessment'[34] is predicated upon the assumption of the correspondence theory of truth in which cognitive claims are true only if they 'mirror' the 'objective' state of affairs they presume to describe. Therefore, matters not germane to establishing the adequacy of 'description' to 'reality' ought not be given consideration when assessing the acceptability or unacceptability of knowledge claims. To do so would be to transgress the 'morality of knowledge' ('ethic of belief') – a morality internal to the enterprise of knowing itself.[35] (That 'internal morality of knowledge' may 'deny' one the right to hold a particular belief but one must recognize here that this is a denial of 'epistemic right', not 'political right'. Further, the question of the 'moral consequences' of a belief or set of beliefs is similarly external to the knowing process and must not, therefore, influence the outcome of epistemic deliberations.[36] The theologian, if she/he wishes to be *identified* as a participant of the 'epistemological community', so to speak, must, like all other members, abide by the epistemological rules.)

A critically important aspect of the generally accepted morality of (scientific) knowledge, I suggest, is its fallibilism – the recognition that no knowledge is ever absolutely certain. This in turn implies the *hypothetical* character of *all* our knowledge. To ask of theologians, therefore, an absolute commitment to particular theological claims on the basis of their membership in the Christian community would be, doubly so, to undermine the very morality of knowledge in terms of which their task is defined. Such a request makes identity as a Christian theologian *qua* Christian incompatible with identity as a Christian theologian *qua* theologian. Yet Professor Sykes, as I have already noted above, seems to require exactly this of Anglican theologians.

To refer to the hypothetical character of theological claims as offering 'the Christian gospel for debate and discussion' is to fail to see that 'hypothetical' is a technical term that does not have the same connotations as does its use in ordinary language. It does indeed mean that a claim so designated is less than certain, but it does not necessarily imply that no element of commitment can be made in light of the claim. It is, however an indication that should new information and evidence arise that places the original claim, and commitments made in light of the claim, in some doubt, that the claim will undergo re-examination. Theologians such as Wolfhart Pannenberg in his *Theology and the Philosophy of Science*[38] and Brian Hebblethwaite in his *The Problems of Theology*[39] have been concerned precisely with this aspect of theological thought that they consider to be of essential importance to it.

(I admit that there is less than unanimous agreement as to the nature of the 'internal morality of knowledge' referred to here. I suggest, however, that that morality will be seen not to be 'deontic', an ethic of absolute constraint that compels belief, but rather as a morality that requires an ethical modal logic involving the terms 'required', 'forbidden', and 'discretionary'. Given a proper clarification of this structure, it seems to me that the possibility of 'discretionary' epistemic choices, so to speak, will give the notion of comprehensiveness solid support – the kind of justification that I think Professor Sykes requests for it.)[40]

A second comment in support of the first concerns matters raised by Professor Sykes in *Christian Theology Today*, already adverted to above. I refer in particular to his recognition of the influence of the Enlightenment and the rise of science upon the theological enterprise, an influence that the theologian ought not attempt to evade. Professor Sykes, quite rightly I think, points out that the rise of science, since it has affected how we view the world, ought to influence our theological perspective on the world. He writes:

> progress in the understanding of experience and reality might be made irrespective of the religious belief of the enquirer.[41]... [And] if Christian theology is concerned with the true understanding of life, then it is bound to be affected by changes in our understanding of the natural conditions of life.[42]

He admits that such changes of belief upset talk of 'eternal verities' and yet maintains that this does not imply that science somehow supersedes Christianity. However, it is obvious that it has put the claims of the two communities at loggerheads, as the history of the warfare between Christian theology and science attests. Peace has been restored between the two communities by a reinterpretation of the 'Christian verities'. If such reinterpretation proves impossible in some future instance, then, presumably, either 'science' or 'Christianity' will be 'superseded' by the other. Unless such a possibility exists it is difficult to see in what sense the two enterprises are related – it would seem that theology would forfeit its claim to cognitive significance. Unwilling to admit this, theology's capacity to learn from science must imply the possibility of its being 'falsified' by science. The theologian *qua* theologian (and not simply as a member of a religious confessional community) therefore can never hold theological beliefs (or any others, for that matter) with absolute certainty.

One of the lessons of the Enlightenment and the rise of science, moreover, is of greater significance than the simple growth of knowledge. 'The Enlightenment' and 'science' were concerned not only with the substance of belief but with how beliefs were obtained and maintained. Acceptance of the new knowledge seems to imply the acceptance of the new epistemology upon which it is based. Professor Sykes recognizes, for example, that the new epistemology rejects the principle of truth transmissible by authority and the consequent rejection of the notion of revelation. Justification of theological claims would require, in order to 'count' as knowledge, a similar rejection of 'authority' (and revelation).[43]

A final comment must be made regarding epistemological issues in the theological enterprise. It is obvious that the 'subject matter' of theology is more complex by far than that treated by other disciplines. Consequently, one might well expect that conclusions drawn in theological argument would be more hesitant than in other disciplines and that, given the relative paucity of evidence in such matters, alternative interpretations of theological questions would exist; that is, pluriformity of belief in such a context would quite naturally be expected. 'Comprehensiveness', therefore (and quite contrary to Professor Sykes's suggestion in *The Integrity of Anglicanism*) is not the 'result of a poverty of thought and of sheer reluctance to attempt to come to grips with intractably difficult theological material'.[44] It is rather an appropriate response to the recognition of the 'intractable' character of the issues involved; a recognition that prevents drawing firm conclusions that are not warranted, or at least not exclusively warranted by the 'evidence'. To 'force' agreement here on anything other than epistemic grounds is simply not acceptable. Ambiguity of evidence in the face of intractably complex issues makes anything other than 'epistemic discretion' unacceptable. ('Epistemic discretion', it must be pointed out, means simply that where conclusions are not fully determined by the evidence, one may either choose to believe a conclusion not at odds with the available evidence or remain agnostic about the matter under discussion.)

V

It is not an easy matter to draw a firm conclusion on the basis of a not entirely complete and not wholly conclusive paper. Perhaps the most one would be warranted in saying here is that the nature of the theological enterprise has not yet been fully determined. That in itself would, however, provide sufficient ground I think for rejecting some of the suggestions concerning the future of Anglican theology put forward by Professor Sykes. However, if there is any merit whatsoever in the critique and comments set out above, other and more significant conclusions can be drawn, the most important of which concerns the notion of comprehensiveness. Not only is this notion not detrimental to Christian theology in general, or Anglican theology in particular, it is essential to it if theology is to be conceived as a cognitively significant enterprise. And far from implicating theology in immorality (intellectual deviousness), it is the very foundation of its proceeding in a morally responsible manner – both in respect of its moral responsibility to persons and with respect to the 'internal morality of knowledge'.

13

The Ambiguous Revolution: Kant on the Nature of Faith[1]

Kant, it has been said, brought a 'Copernican Revolution' to religion and theology no less so than he did to physics. According to Karl Barth, for example, Kant's theology diverges radically from tradition.[2] While rejecting the traditional proofs as a foundation for a knowledge of God (God's existence, etc.) as wholly inadequate, he nevertheless remained a theist. Unwilling to believe in God in the absence of good reasons for doing so, however, he offered an alternative justification for such belief. Religious belief, he insists, is based on practical considerations rather than on theoretical ones. Kant, therefore, did not consider it as necessarily irrational to hold a thing as true even though it be theoretically insufficient holding it to be true. According to him it is simply that in such a case the belief *that* 'something' is true does not constitute knowledge. And it is this displacement of knowledge in the religious sphere by faith that essentially constitutes the revolutionary change in theology.[3]

Contrary to this generally accepted view of Kant's thought. I shall in this chapter argue the essentially unrevolutionary character of his understanding of theology. There is, I shall maintain, a basic continuity in Kant's thoughts on religion with the theologies of the past. The faith of which Kant speaks, I shall attempt to show, is a *cognitive* faith – a source of beliefs that can quite legitimately, even if only in a weak sense, be referred to as religious knowledge.[4] His theology, therefore, is, like the theology of his predecessors, ultimately an inferential knowledge of the divine. I shall argue that although there is in Kant a move towards the establishment of a radically different theology he nevertheless failed to bring about the revolution in theology attributed to him.

II

It is Kant's emphasis on faith that characterizes his theological thought. In his understanding, faith is not only a rational enterprise, but also a necessary one because of the very nature of reason itself – its limitations and its grasp after infinity (completeness). In the 'Dialectic' of the first *Critique*,[5] Kant demonstrates the limitations of theoretical reason by means of an analysis of the fact that the human mind inevitably and repeatedly makes claims to knowledge of that which lies beyond the sphere of all sense experience. He shows that such claims achieve nothing stable, but rather plunge the mind into antinomies. Nevertheless, this move beyond 'the bounds of sense' is not simply arbitrary; it too shows up the nature of the human mind. In some sense such a move beyond sense is required to give humans completeness in their search after knowledge. That completeness is not obtained merely by adding empirical facts to other empirical facts *ad infinitum*. As Beck puts it, 'not more knowledge, but a different kind of knowledge is required if our knowledge is to be seen as a coherent, perfect and self-supporting whole'.[6]

This different kind of knowledge is, in Kantian terminology, 'pure rational knowledge' as opposed to 'empirical' or 'theoretical' knowledge. The latter kind is a knowledge which refers to that which is, whereas the former refers to that which must be in order for that which is, to be, and, therefore, only in that necessary sense 'is'. Pure rational knowledge refers therefore to an 'object' that transcends all our experience and whereby completeness in our empirical knowledge is obtained. As the passage referred to in the first *Critique* indicates, in so far as this knowledge transcends all our empirical knowledge it is strictly ideal and hence not theoretical knowledge of that which is, for such knowledge is only obtained, as we learn from the analytic of the first *Critique*, in the unity of intuition and concepts. And it is this strict ideality of pure rational knowledge which Kant wishes to make clear, because its indissoluble connection with empirical knowledge – as its completion – has led the mind into illusion, for the human mind inevitably adopts such pure rational knowledge as a genuine extension of its theoretical knowledge. 'The cause of this,' claims Kant, is that there are fundamental rules and maxims for the employment of our reason [subjectively regarded as a faculty of human knowledge], and that these have all the appearance of being objective principles. We therefore take the subjective necessity of a condition, for an objective necessity in the determination of things in themselves.[7]

The unconditioned – the ideas of reason whereby the unity of our conditioned knowledge is obtained – cannot be supported by any theoretical arguments without reason falling into conflict with itself. Nor would the possibility of substantiating such a claim even be desirable according to Kant, for as claims to theoretical knowledge they would be of relatively little value, since they could not be well founded; that is, they would be of a low level of probability compared to other theoretical claims – precisely where certainty is desired most. Thus Beck properly states the case against such a position when he claims that 'weighed as knowledge they would be found wanting; they would have to be declared chimerical and nugatory'.[8]

The denial of 'theoretical knowledge' as characterizing the unifying ideas of Reason, therefore, leaves a vacuum in the pursuit of a systematic knowledge, for the very apex of that pursuit – the unconditioned which brings the needed unity to all knowledge – is not itself knowledge; at least not theoretical knowledge. And the whole purpose of the *Critique of Pure Reason* is simply to keep speculative reason from presumptuously filling this cognitive vacuum with its ideas taken as theoretical knowledge. In doing this, however, Kant's aim is to point out, not simply the impossibility of traditional speculative metaphysics, but rather that that which is knowable is not all that is important; that the power of reason is not limited merely to the domain of the theoretical; that the 'rational' is not restricted in its scope to the purely 'cognitive'. But the question raised by recognition of the impotence of theoretical reason is: If theoretical reason cannot justify the belief in the unifying ideas of Reason, what can? Kant suggests an answer to the question in the preface to the second edition of the first *Critique*.[9] He writes:

On a cursory view of the present work it may seem that its results are merely negative, warning us that we must never venture with speculative reason beyond the limits of experience. Such is, in fact, its primary use. But such teaching at once acquires a *positive* value when we recognize that the principles with which speculative reason ventures out beyond its proper limits do not in effect *extend* the employment of reason, but, as we find on closer scrutiny, inevitably narrow it. These principles properly belong [not to reason but] to sensibility, and when thus employed they threaten to make the bounds of sensibility coextensive with the real, and so to supplant reason in its pure [practical] employment.[10]

What Kant is saying, in effect, is that Reason can neither hope to understand itself so long as it imagines itself complete merely in its theoretical capacities. He writes: 'We are convinced that there is an absolutely necessary practical employment of pure reason – the *moral* – in which it inevitably goes beyond the limits of sensibility.'[11] This practical reason is not a second reason functioning beside the theoretical reason; it is rather a practical function of the same reason. Kant points out, then, that even 'though (practical) reason, in thus proceeding, requires no assistance from speculative reason, it must yet be assured against its opposition that reason may not be brought into conflict with itself'.[12] That is, on knowing an object one must be able to prove its possibility, whether because it is actual in our experience or because reason shows it to be *a priori*. In contrast to this, however, one can think whatever one pleases, provided only that one does not contradict oneself. The possibility of the concept, that is, is assured even though one may never be able to prove that there is an object corresponding to it. 'But,' claims Kant,

> something more is required before he can ascribe to such a concept objective validity, that is, real possibility; the former possibility is merely logical. *This something more need not, however, be sought in the theoretical sources of knowledge, it may be in those that are practical.*[13]

Thus Kant obstinately denies knowledge of the unconditioned. The cognitive vacuum at the apex of our system of knowledge must remain theoretically or speculatively empty; *but not thereupon completely cognitively empty*. If reason in its theoretical use cannot fill the vacuum, perhaps reason in its practical use can. The ideas of reason, that is, if not capable of theoretical justification may be capable of a practical justification. According to Kant,

> when all progress in the field of the supersensible has thus been denied to speculative reason, it is still open to us to enquire whether in the practical knowledge of reason, data may not be

found sufficient to *determine reason's transcendent concept of the unconditioned*, and so to enable us, in accordance with the wish of metaphysics, and by means of knowledge that is possible *a priori*, though only from a *practical point of view*, to pass beyond the limits of all possible experience. Speculative reason has thus at least made room for such an extension; and if it must at the same time leave it empty, yet none the less we are at liberty, indeed we are summoned to take occupation of it, if we can, by practical data of reason.[14]

Therefore, according to Kant, if morality requires these ideas, then reason in its practical aspect, if we are to avoid moral absurdity (the *absurdum morale*, or *absurdum practicum*), requires that this cognitive vacuum in the system of our knowledge be filled with something more than mere logical possibilities. Certain assumptions must be made, that is, if moral experience is not to be denied as illusory or the moral law as invalid. Such assumptions or 'postulates', as Kant designates them,[15] can neither be affirmed nor denied but can be believed or disbelieved – they are 'mere things of faith', objects for concepts whose objective reality cannot be proved.[16] Thus Kant's conclusion is not at all surprising, when according to him,

even the *assumption* – as made on behalf of the necessary practical employment of ... reason ... is not permissible unless at the same time speculative reason be deprived of its pretensions to transcendent insight. For in order to arrive at such insight it must make use of principles which, in fact, extend only to objects of possible experience, and which, if also applied to what cannot be an object of experience, always really changes this into an appearance, thus rendering all *practical extension* of pure reason impossible. I have therefore found it necessary to deny knowledge, in order to make room for *faith*.[17]

It is therefore the 'things of faith' and not the 'things of fact' which, according to Kant, fit the cognitive vacuum in the system of our theoretical knowledge. They are rational – but they do not constitute theoretical or speculative knowledge. Acceptance of them is not justified on theoretical grounds but rather on practical grounds so that in some qualified sense at least, 'practical reason, without changing the theoretical picture in any way, is able to provide the needed justification for belief'.[18] The qualification is necessary, for in some sense, to be explained later, that which fills the cognitive vacuum in our system of knowledge must itself have a cognitive character. And it is for this reason that I think Barth correct in his claim that:

> The critique [of reason] is therefore meant to have brought honor, and not discredit, to knowledge by pure reason in particular. Kant does not think that in clarifying the relationship of pure reason to empirical perception he has destroyed metaphysics, but rather first and foremost that he made it possible as a science: metaphysics as knowledge by means of practical reason. That then is the true use of pure reason as it at last and finally emerged from the fire of Kant's critique of reason.[19]

It is in search of the specific character of that faith, that the practical metaphysical knowledge for which Kant made room requires analysis.

Kant at one point succinctly summarized the nature of faith in the following way:

> Faith ... is the moral attitude of reason as to belief in that which is unattainable by theoretical cognition. It is therefore the permanent principle of the mind to assume as true on account of the obligation in reference to it, that which is necessary to presuppose as condition of the highest final purpose, although its possibility or impossibility be alike impossible for us to see into.[20]

Kant, we see, therefore, does not at all abandon a rational basis for theology: he merely switches from the attempt to justify its beliefs by means of theoretical reason to practical reason.[21] The objects of faith, therefore, are, to be sure, not possible objects of theoretical knowledge, but yet are nevertheless objects of rational enquiry. Faith therefore is not the belief in things that are attainable by theoretical cognition but for which there is insufficient evidence. For Kant, such belief would not be faith (at least not pure religious faith) but rather credulity. Indeed, in some sense such belief would be immoral, for it would violate the rules of evidence. But since faith refers to objects that are not capable of cognition it is based on other than evidential grounds – although, to repeat, not other than rational grounds. F. Ferré I think correctly characterizes the Kantian faith as 'not in violation of the rule of evidence; and since it has sufficient grounds of a practical sort, faith is not proved guilty of arbitrariness, against which the rule of evidence functions as a barrier.'[22] Moreover, since practical reason refers to objects beyond the reach of theoretical reason, practical reason is not bounded by its limits.[23] It might appear, therefore, as if conflict between theoretical and practical reason is inevitable. Yet there is a hint here at the solution Kant eventually provides in the second *Critique*, namely, that theoretical reason can make no pronouncement as to what lies beyond the sphere of its activities (i.e. the sensuous sphere) whereas practical reason can. However, when practical reason does so, its pronouncements are not to be considered as the intuitive knowledge of theoretical reason, but rather as assumptions. However, when pure practical reason provides reality to these assumptions, transforming them into 'postulates', some entry into the theoretical sphere is gained, but not such as to allow us to call the postulates knowledge without some sort of qualification. Nevertheless, they are still more than mere assumptions.

Faith, therefore, in the Kantian view of things, is not outside the realm of reason, but is rather one aspect of reason, as is knowledge. Kant elucidates somewhat the nature of that faith in the third section of 'The Canon of Pure Reason' of the first *Critique*. Kant there distinguishes faith or belief from opinion on the one hand and knowledge on the other. It differs from opinion in that it involves a complete absence of doubt. 'Opining', writes Kant, 'is … insufficient not only objectively, but also subjectively', whereas believing is the holding of a judgement that is subjectively sufficient but 'at the same time taken as being objectively insufficient'.[24] Knowledge, unlike both opinion and faith, 'is sufficient both subjectively and objectively'.[25] Opinion therefore lacks both conviction (subjective sufficiency) and certainty (objective sufficiency); belief has conviction but no certainty and knowledge has both conviction and certainty. Belief then, in some sense at least, lies midway between opining and knowing. However, as I have indicated above, this does not at all suggest that faith is the adoption of a theoretical proposition on the basis of insufficient evidence; that is, of a proposition capable of greater evidential support than one presently has.

In another passage in the third *Critique* Kant also speaks of faith in terms of 'doubtful faith'.[26] Although it may appear at first sight as a contradiction of his description of faith in the first *Critique*, there is in fact no real contradiction. The adjective 'doubtful' attached to faith in the former work concerns, not the *conviction* of faith, its subjective sufficiency, but only the *certainty* of faith, its objective sufficiency. Faith, indeed, must be theoretically doubtful, 'for it is only from a *practical point of view* that the theoretically insufficient holding of a thing to be true can be termed believing.'[27] If it were not theoretically doubtful, it would then simply be knowledge or opinion.

Faith, moreover, is not for Kant all of the same quality. Kant speaks, for example, in terms of contingent and necessary belief in the first *Critique*. The former he entitled pragmatic belief which 'always exists in some specific degree, which, according to difference in the interests at stake, may be large or may be small'.[28] The latter type of faith is either doctrinal belief which 'refers only to the guidance which an idea gives me, and its subjective influence in that furthering of the activities of my reason which confirms me in the idea, and which yet does so, without my being in a position to give a speculative account of it,'[29] or moral belief. It is the last of these, namely moral faith (*moralischer Glaube*), which provides the content to fill the vacuum created by Kant's denial of knowledge discussed above.

The difference between doctrinal faith and moral faith is not extremely great but it is extremely significant. Doctrinal faith arises out of theoretical reason and moral faith out of practical reason. As to the differences Kant writes:

> The merely doctrinal belief is somewhat lacking in stability; we often lose hold of it, owing to the speculative difficulties which we encounter, although in the end we always inevitably return to it.
>
> It is quite otherwise with *moral belief*. For here it is absolutely necessary that something must happen, namely, that I must in all points conform to the moral law. The end is here irrefragably established, and according to such insight as I can have, there is only one possible condition under which this end can connect with all other ends, and thereby have practical validity, namely that there be a God and a future world ... [and] I am certain that nothing can shake this belief, since my moral principles would thereby be themselves overthrown, and I cannot disclaim them without becoming abhorrent in my own eyes.[30]

And again in his 'critique of all theology considered as speculative knowledge' he writes:

> Now since there are practical laws which are absolutely necessary, that is, the moral laws, it must follow that if these necessarily presuppose the existence of any being as the condition of the possibility of their *obligatory* power, this existence must be *postulated*;

and this for the sufficient reason that the conditioned, from which the inference is drawn to this determinate condition, is itself known *a priori* to be absolutely necessary.[31]

Faith thus rationally affirms on practical grounds a theoretical proposition which is not, as such, capable of demonstration. Thus there is conviction here although not certainty – and even the conviction is not logical but moral. Thus moral faith has an inescapable personal character about it; so much so that Kant claims that one 'must not even say "*It is* morally certain that there is a God, etc.", but "*I am* morally certain, etc."'[32] It would again seem then that Ferré's characterization of Kant's work comes very close to being correct when, as I pointed out above, he claims that for Kant 'practical reason, without changing the theoretical picture in any way, is able to provide the needed justification for belief'.[33] But this characterization I suggest here does not do *full* justice to Kant's position – it denies, I suggest, a very important aspect of Kant's characterization of the nature of moral faith – namely that through it we gain, in some small way, an *extension* of our theoretical knowledge.

On Ferré's (implied) account of the Kantian concept of moral faith it would seem that Kant makes no systematic distinction between *belief in* and *belief that*. This, more explicitly, is the claim of W. H. Walsh in his Dawes Hicks lecture, 'Kant's Moral Theology'.[34] Kant, suggests Walsh, is concerned with faith as *belief in*, as trust, rather than as *belief that*, which involves reference to some additional objects of theoretical cognition. Walsh claims that the Kantian concept of faith is:

> a form of belief which is intimately bound up with action and expresses itself in the adoption of a practical attitude; [so that] the inference may well be drawn that it is not *really* a truth of any kind. The words 'There is a God' ... do not express a proposition but a formula internal to a moral attitude: they have nothing to do with how things are, but get their meaning and force from deliberation about how things ought to be ... they have to do with the will and not with the understanding.[35]

Walsh concludes therefore that:

> it is entirely misleading to talk of moral theology resulting in an extension of the sphere of theoretical reason, even when this claim

is hedged about with the reservations with which Kant surrounds it. If we follow Kant's account of it to its logical conclusion, moral theology does not issue in any assertions proper; strictly speaking it is not even propositional.[36]

This conclusion, however, is, I think, highly questionable for at least two reasons. The first concerns the general consideration of the oddity of talk about *belief in* that is not in any way at all connected to some kind of *belief that*. The second concerns what I consider to be a rather dubious interpretation of Kant's claim to have extended the sphere of theoretical knowledge. As I shall point out, such an interpretation seems to *dichotomize* humans in a way that goes against the grain of Kant's philosophy. These two arguments, however, in the final analysis make essentially the same point.

The term 'faith', to be sure, can be used in both an epistemological and a non-epistemological sense. In accordance with common usage I shall refer to the former as *fides* and to the latter as *fiducia*. We often do claim to know that God exists, for example, and to speak of God in propositional terms. In such claims we use the term cognitively to refer to a procedure we consider to be similar to knowing. We speak for example of 'knowing this by faith'. Yet we also speak of faith as 'trust' – a trust, for example, in divine goodness which can in many respects be compared to the trust or confidence we have in other people. In the making of such a distinction, then, I have no quarrel with Walsh. Moreover one may even agree with Walsh that faith in the sense of *fiducia* is the primary sense of the word, even in Kant. Nevertheless it seems to me unreasonable to talk of *fiducia* without some at least implicit reference to *fides*. I think John Hick, for example, in his discussion of religious knowledge, comes much closer to the truth of the situation in his claim that:

> when the religious believer comes to reflect upon his religion, in the capacity of philosopher or theologian, he is obliged to concern himself with the noetic status of his faith; [and that] when he does so concern himself, it emerges that faith as trust [*fiducia*] presupposes faith [*fides*] as cognition of the object of that trust.[37]

Hick points out, for example, that a trust in God and a commitment of our lives to God's providential care certainly presupposes that we believe God to exist. John Baillie argues a similar point in his *Our Knowledge of God*. Although admitting that what practical reason gives to us is not theoretical knowledge but rather practical guidance and that what is asked in return is obedience and not mere intellectual assent, he nevertheless still claims that if we stop here we have only uttered a half truth. He continues:

> It is impossible to rest finally in this sharp dichotomy between knowledge and guidance, between understanding and obedience, since it is only by knowledge that we can be guided, and since we cannot obey what we do not understand. In the obligation that is revealed to us, some element of knowledge must be implicitly contained.[38]

Although Kant does not, as Walsh maintains, make a systematic distinction between *believing in* and *believing that,* and even though he may emphasize the former over the latter, the latter is, nevertheless, also present in Kant's thought. It seems to me, that is, that Kant attempts to make precisely the point made by Hick to which I referred above. It is to Kant's arguments concerning this matter that I now, therefore, turn attention.

Kant suggests this extension of theoretical knowledge through the practical reason as early as the first *Critique*. He there points out that all his interests, theoretical as well as speculative, can be summed up in the following questions: 'What can I know?'; 'What ought I to do?'; and 'What may I hope?' The first he claims is purely speculative and the second is purely practical, but of the third he writes:

> The third question – If I do what I ought to do what may I then hope? – is at once practical and theoretical, in such a fashion that the practical serves only as a clue that leads us to the theoretical question, and when this is followed out, to the speculative question. For all *hoping* is directed to happiness, and stands in the same relation to the practical and the law of morality as *knowing and the law of nature* to the theoretical knowledge of things. The former arrives finally at the conclusion that *something is* [which determines the ultimate possible end] *because something ought to happen*; the latter that *something is* [which operates as the supreme cause] *because something happens*.[39]

This is not at all to deny what Kant has been trying to say throughout the first *Critique*, as Walsh suggests. Indeed, in the second *Critique*, where Kant takes up this question more directly, he expressly points out that he does not consider the postulates of reason in any sense as theoretical dogmas.[40] To talk about God one must turn from theoretical to practical reason – 'God-talk', that is, makes sense only within the context of action. Yet by this he does not consider himself to be denying all connection of practical reason to theoretic reason, as if these were two entirely independent concerns of humankind. For Kant they are but two functions of the one faculty. And according to Kant, although the postulates

> do not extend speculative knowledge, they give objective reality to the ideas of speculative reason in general ... and they justify it in holding to concepts *even the possibility of which it would not otherwise venture to affirm.*[41]

And more specifically a little further on:

> By this, then, the *theoretical knowledge of pure reason does obtain an accession*, but it consists only in this – that those concepts which for it is otherwise problematical [merely thinkable] are now described assertorically as actually having objects, because practical reason inexorably requires the existence of these objects for the possibility of its practically and absolutely necessary object, the highest good. *Theoretical reason is, therefore, justified in assuming them.*[42]

It is true as well that for Kant this extension is 'only from a moral point of view'[43] and that as a consequence 'we can make no theoretical rational use' of them,[44] but this is not, I think, withdrawing with the left hand what Kant has given us with the right, as Walsh suggests. Surely there is here an *extension* of theoretical reason as distinct from simple speculation. In claiming such an extension of theoretical reason moreover, Kant is not at all suggesting a mode of knowledge which transcends the common understanding so that 'in regard to the essential ends of human nature the highest philosophy cannot advance further than is possible under the guidance which nature has bestowed even upon the most ordinary understanding'.[45] But, whereas theoretical reason could think the idea without contradiction, it could not assume any objective reality to it. Practical reason does give it that objective reality and hence extends theoretical reason. In so far as it does this for the idea of freedom in particular, claims Kant, it is:

> the keystone of the whole architecture of pure reason and even of speculative reason.... These concepts are founded upon the moral

use of reason, while speculation could not find sufficient guarantee even of their possibility.... Now practical reason itself, without any collusion with the speculative, provides reality to a supersensible object. This is a practical concept and as such is subject only to practical use; *but what in the speculative critique could only be thought is now confirmed by fact.*[46]

This moreover is the whole point of Kant's argument on the primacy of the pure practical reason in its association with speculative reason. To be sure, neither one must yield to the other as if they were in conflict with each other, as I have already intimated above. It is simply that if practical reason requires the cognitive vacuum in our system of knowledge to be filled on pain of involving ourselves in an *absurdum morale*, and if the postulates of practical reason do not conflict with the principles set out by theoretical reason, then practical reason has primacy over theoretical reason. Kant puts this claim of his succinctly in the second *Critique*:

If pure reason of itself can be and really is practical as the consciousness of the moral law shows it to be, it is only one and the same reason which judges *a priori* by principle, whether for theoretical or for practical purposes. Then it is clear, that, if its capacity in the former is not sufficient to establish certain propositions positively (which however do not contradict it), it must assume these propositions just as soon as they are sufficiently certified as belonging imprescriptibly to the practical interests of pure reason. It must assume them indeed as something offered from the outside and not grown in its own soil, and it must seek to compare and connect them with everything which it has in its power as speculative reason. It must remember that they are not its own insights but extensions of its use, in some other respect, viz., the practical; and this is not in the least opposed to its interests which lie in the restriction of speculative folly.[47]

III

Kant's attempt to move beyond a theology based upon speculative principles of reason, as I have noted above, has been taken to constitute a revolutionary change in the character of the theological enterprise. And the substitution of 'faith' for 'knowledge' in his discussion of the nature of the religious experience (of religion) seems to substantiate that judgement to some extent. It appears, that is, that Kant has rejected all possibility of an inferential move from world to God and has thereby turned the methodological assumptions of medieval theology upside down. Some, indeed, have seen in this rejection of speculative theology the glimmer of a notion of faith as a 'direct interior persuasion' in matters of religious truth. John Baillie, for example, considered Kant to have moved in this direction, although only in a 'sadly curtailed and impoverished form'.[48] The denial of knowledge in favour of faith, according to Baillie, was the 'recovery of the fundamental truth that Absolute Reality, instead of being reached speculatively by means of deduction from the data of sense, is revealed to us directly in the form of Absolute Obligation'.[49]

The analysis of Kant's view of faith that I have provided here rules out such a 'revolutionary' interpretation of his theological proposals. Kant, as I have shown, does not reject logical argument in the theological enterprise. (Whether Baillie is right or wrong to criticize him for not having done so is not a matter which I wish to pursue here.[50]) Kant's rejection of the traditional proofs of God's existence is not a rejection of argumentation but only of 'bad argumentation'. In Kant's scheme of things, I have argued, 'knowledge' of God can be had – a 'knowledge', however, that is gained by inference based not upon empirical data but rather upon moral data. Although the *grounds* of the argument have changed the *procedure* has remained the same. God, even if God is the first in the order of being is still, as in medieval theologizing, last in the order of knowing. The moral data, so to speak, are known first – just as in earlier theology, for example with Aquinas and the *analogia entis*, the sensible things are known first and from them one can conclude to the existence of God.[51]

A recent critical discussion of 'Kant's Moral Proof of the Existence of God' by Peter Byrne, already adverted to above, in a rather strange fashion supports the analysis undertaken here. Although Byrne admits that Kant's argument is not strictly a proof he maintains that it is, nonetheless, subject to the criteria we would normally apply to proofs because 'informal reasoning of that sort still retains a connection with the extension of knowledge'.[52] Byrne believes Kant's argument is fundamentally incoherent, however, since 'if one rules out knowledge of God as impossible in principle then one also rules out the possibility of faith, where this entails believing or thinking that God exists'.[53] Byrne is quite right to insist that Kant argues the impossibility of knowing that God exists but he does not emphasize that the impossibility exists only when that knowledge is based upon the *speculative principles* of Reason. For Byrne to claim that Kant argues that 'we never could have reasons of any sort for making such a claim,'[54] is simply not borne out in the text as the passages quoted above indicate. It seems to me highly improbable that so simple an error can be laid to Kant's charge. However a detailed discussion of this matter is not required here. My concern in the present chapter has not been primarily with the validity or soundness of Kant's argument but rather with the interpretation of the significance of that argument for the theological enterprise.

14

The 'Centripetal Theology' of *The Great Code*

If Frye's disclaimer is taken seriously the theologian *qua* theologian will have little interest in *The Great Code*.[1] This book, as he put it, 'is not a work of Biblical scholarship, much less [one] of theology'.[2] It has, he insists. none of the system – historical, scientific, or metaphysical – that characterizes theology but is, rather, a work of *bricolage*, as is the Bible itself.[3] The 'putting together of bits and pieces of whatever comes to hand,' whether in the Bible or in his book, he suggests, however, yields a deeper comprehension of reality than does abstract, scientific and rational thought. And that suggestion, his disclaimer notwithstanding, I shall argue here, indicates that *The Great Code* is very much a theological, or at least a metatheological, exercise and that it should, therefore, be of considerable interest to theologians. Frye's acknowledgement of the 'emotionally explosive' character of the thesis he presents indicates, moreover, the radical, and therefore important, nature of his (hidden) theological agenda.[4]

Stated bluntly, Frye 'proposes' a rejection of the traditional theological interpretation of the Bible on the ground that it constitutes a mode of thought wholly incompatible with the mythological thought forms of the Bible and substitutes for it a literary-critical interpretation. Traditional theology, based as it is on the 'centrifugal' language of science, constitutes 'thought *about* God' and presents us with a reasoned, objective account of God neatly packaged in a system of doctrines which, however, inevitably fall prey to the superior cognitive power of the sciences.[5] Frye contends, therefore, that theology should 'think God', and that such a theology can only emerge if, like the literary critic, the theologian conforms to the predominantly 'centripetal' patterns of thought of the Bible itself, which in 'thinking God' creates God. Theology, that is, should not be concerned with the extra-biblical world, physical or metaphysical, but rather with the world concerned with the meaning of human life that is created in the Bible, for, as Frye puts it, 'the Bible deliberately subordinates its referential or centrifugal meaning to its primary syntactical, centripetal meaning.'[6] The task of the theologian, therefore, is not the scientific one of providing us with a proof for the existence of God or a set of cognitive claims about God but rather, like that of the literary critic, 'to make us more aware of our mythological conditioning.'[7]

Very little of the theological agenda I have attributed to Frye can be found explicitly espoused by him. It is implicit, however, in his understanding of the nature and purpose of the 'language' of the Bible as I shall now attempt to show.

According to Frye, three distinct stages characterize the development of language – the metaphorical, metonymic and demotic.[8] The first is the concrete language of 'the primitive mind', lacking true verbal abstraction, and is wholly free of the subject/object distinction of the latter two stages. It is poetic language; a language of feeling and expression and so a language of immediacy and immanence; a language of magic, spell and charm. Metonymic language, however, is not wholly immanent and autonomous for it involves a significant degree of conceptualization wherein words 'stand for' things. The sense of identity between persons and 'nature' present in metaphorical language is here replaced, to a degree, by a sense of relatedness to something not the self in a language of analogy. Metonymy, therefore, is a language of transcendence. It 'parallels' metaphorical with conceptual language but it does so, Frye maintains, in such a way that the conceptual has the primary authority. What is interesting, he writes, 'is that when a metaphorical tradition conflicts with the metonymic need for conceptual and moral models, it is the tradition that has to give way.'[9]

Demotic language completes the move away from metaphor begun in metonymic language. It clearly distinguishes subject from object and is primarily a conceptual and descriptive language concerned with the objective world – 'the order of nature' which is essentially an order of 'necessity'.[10] It is the language of reason and science.

Despite the three-stage analysis Frye provides, it is obvious that he perceives in the development of language only two modes of thought, and that the two are, in a very significant sense, incompatible: 'it seems to me' he writes, 'useful to separate both the language of immanence, which is founded on metaphor, and the language of transcendence, which is founded on metonymy in my sense, from descriptive language.'[11] He admits that each of these 'modes of thought' has its own benefits and limitations but points out, nevertheless, that the growth of the latter is destructive of the former. The growth of scientific language is based on the assumption that 'objective' means 'real' so that '[t]he bigger the objective world becomes, the smaller in range and significance the subjective world seems'.[12] Consequently, argues Frye, '[t]he "subject" is subjected to the objective world, and not only subjected but almost crushed under it'.[13] And for Frye, the traditional language of theology in assessing the credibility of the 'God-talk' to be found in the Bible in terms of the objective criteria of the 'scientific universe' constitutes a mode of thought, therefore, that utterly destroys what the religious mind, a very different kind of mentation, has produced. Traditional theology, therefore, must be rejected by those who would understand the Bible, or we must jettison God-talk altogether, as Frye clearly sets out in the following passage:

> In the first, or metaphorical, phase of language, the unifying element of verbal expression is the 'god,' or personal nature-spirit. In the second phase the conception of a transcendent 'God' moves into the center of the order of words. In the third phase the criterion of reality is the source of sense experience in the order of nature, where 'God' is not to be found, and where 'gods' are no longer believed in. Hence for the third phase of language the word 'God' becomes linguistically dysfunctional, except when confined to special areas outside its jurisdiction. Mythological space became separated from scientific space with the new astronomy of the seventeenth century, and mythological time from scientific time with nineteenth-century geology and biology. Both developments helped to push the conception of God out of the world of time and space, even as a hypothesis. The charge of 'God-building' is a most damaging one to a third-phase writer, and the subject that used to be called natural theology does not now make much cultural impact, with the remarkable exception of Teilhard de Chardin.[14]

The rejection of traditional theology is not for Frye, however, the end of critical reflection on the Bible. Its demise seems to call for the creation of a new kind of theology – a theology that recognizes the literary (non-argumentative) character of the Bible, and the importance of the function of literature in recreating the metaphorical style of language suppressed by the demotic. Only a 'theology' that takes on the very character of the Bible itself will do, for, as the quotation above suggests, only the 'literary' can keep 'God' alive since it created 'God' in the first place, and it alone can 'recreate.' This is clearly evident in Frye's understanding of the Bible, (his apologetic statements regarding the title of the book notwithstanding), as literature – or, at least, as predominantly literary in character.

It is true that Frye claims he does not view the Bible as literature but neither does he see it as non-literary – it is, he insists, 'as literary as it can well be without actually being literature.'[15] Its 'mode of thought', that is, is that of literature and not that of the sciences. Consequently, even though not wholly metaphorical in style it is closer to the metaphorical than to the demotic. Like the metaphorical it is 'obsessively concrete' and makes no functional use of abstraction and presents no rational argumentation.[16] Indeed, at times it appears to go against reason entirely.[17] Its concern is not to present information either of the natural world or of historical events.[18] Nor is its thinking concerned with the causal thinking of the sciences.[19] The Bible, it is true, finds itself situated in the natural world and in history, and it draws upon them, in one respect or another, in weaving its story; but, unlike science or history, owes its 'allegiance' not to scientific or historical truths but rather to the spiritual truth of the 'story' it contains. That 'story' is not 'caused' by its situation but rather is a creative and imaginative construction whose purpose it is 'to draw a circumference around a human community and to look inward toward that community',[20] and so to assist it to live in its situation and to triumph over the merely natural world. The priority of meaning, then, is given to the mythical structure or outline of the story and not to its content,[21] and Frye refers to this as its centripetal or poetic meaning.[22] The wisdom of the Bible is centred in human concern rather than in the exploration of the world and thus gives the Bible a focus and cohesiveness that the multiplicity of demotic concerns could not possibly provide it.[23] Such wisdom is 'knowledge' of a sort but not of nature or of history;[24] it is *vision* rather than cosmology,[25] and must therefore be linked with the concepts of revelation[26] and faith[27] rather than with science. Only that reflective treatment of the Bible that recognizes all this, is then, for Frye, an adequate theology, and his work here, from a literary-critical point of view, he maintains, does just that: 'Traditionally, the Bible's narrative has been regarded as "literally" historical and its meaning as "literally" doctrinal or didactic: the present book takes myth and metaphor to be the true literal bases.'[28] In a later, clarifying, passage Frye writes: 'The Bible includes an immense variety of material and the unifying forces that hold it together cannot be the rigid forces of doctrinal consistency or logic, which would soon collapse under cultural stress, but the more flexible ones of imaginative unity, which is founded on metaphor.'[29]

Thus far I have only looked at Frye's metatheology – his assessment of the character and meaning of traditional theology in relationship to the Bible. His theology lies implicit in that discussion, however, even though it is not highly visible. He expresses it explicitly in pointing out that the 'theology' of the Bible emerges on the basis of the 'Feuerbach principle', namely, that human persons create their gods in their own image.[30] In this sense, as Frye stated it in an interview, the Bible is 'a book which has no outside.'[31] When asked whether he thought there is a divinity (God) separate from the human imagination he, after admitting that, in theory, that possibility exists, remarked: '... but that is a theory that would take me beyond human experience, and I can't go beyond human experience.'[32] On further questioning as to whether this position was not itself a theory (a theology of the traditional variety?) Frye concluded: 'As far as man is concerned, it seems to me, there is no reality in the conception of God outside human consciousness.'[33]

Frye's concern with the meaning of the 'story' of the Bible, with its focus on the life of the individual and the community, rather than with extra-Biblical physical, historical, or metaphysical states of affairs, constitutes what I have referred to in the title of the essay as Frye's 'centripetal theology'. The model for that kind of theological thought, obviously, is literary criticism rather than science and metaphysics as in the past. And in this, if not in the 'results' of that activity, Frye presents an important proposal for consideration by the community of traditional theologians. In a time when history and the sciences have eschewed the use of the God-hypothesis and so have given birth, as Jüngel has put it, to 'an age of the verbal placelessness of God',[34] a 'centripetal theology' that refuses to seek a meaning for God outside the language-context – the story/myth – in which it is found may be the only adequate theology to be had. It may in fact be true, that is, and paradoxically so it would seem, that only in denying the importance of the question of the extra-mythological (extra-biblical) existence of God may the reality of God be found and kept alive.[35]

15

An Unholy Alliance? The Creationists' Quest for Scientific Legitimation

An evolutionary account of the origin and nature of life seems, to most of us, highly likely. We cannot be absolutely certain about such a theory, but given our present state of knowledge it must be taken as being beyond reasonable doubt. This is not to say that in its present form it provides us with a wholly adequate account and explanation of all biological phenomena.[1] Hardly anyone, especially biologists and philosophers of biology, would want to make that claim. Phenomena not yet accounted for by evolutionary theory, however, do not automatically constitute counter-instances to it. They are, to be sure, anomalies, but may well be accounted for on further elaboration of the theory. Just how and when anomalies become genuine counter-instances, in Thomas Kuhn's sense of the word,[2] has never really been satisfactorily explained by the philosophers of science. However, this much most philosophers are agreed upon: unless an alternative framework of interpretation is provided that can account for the biological data explained by the reigning (evolutionary) theory, and for the apparent anomalies as well, they remain mere anomalies. And according to biologists and philosophers of biology, no credible alternative to evolutionary theory in biology presently exists.

I DARWINISM AND SCIENTIFIC-CREATIONISM

Shrill dissent accompanied the publication of Darwin's evolutionary theory, even though the winds of evolutionary thought had been blowing for some time. Darwinism, it seemed to many, required denial of a biblical truth that witnessed to the exalted status of human beings over the rest of the animal domain. Evolutionary theory was seen to be supplanting divine purpose and design in the universe with the meaninglessness of random mutation and natural selection that reduced human nature to mere animality. In 'naturalizing' the person, evolutionary theory challenged the dignity and worth of humankind as portrayed in Christianity.

By most accounts, Darwin triumphed in that battle against a creationist understanding of life, and modern evolutionary theory has increased the explanatory power and scope of Darwin's original insight. But modern evolutionary theory still has its shrill dissenters – heirs in a direct line of descent from Darwin's detractors. However, what draws our attention is not that creationism, in some new and powerful guise, has provided a paradigm for biological thought that can account for the anomalies to the reigning theory. Scientific confidence in evolutionary theory, as I have just stated, has not been shaken by some alternative non-evolutionary framework of interpretation. It is, rather, the *non-scientific* activity of today's dissenters that has called the academic community to arms – to restructure and restate the case against scientific-creationism. Scientific-creationists have skilfully cultivated an extraordinary popular sympathy and are creating a powerful lobby in the political arena in order to gain official status for their beliefs in the educational systems of our society. Although meeting with defeat in some communities, they have achieved success in many others and are not likely to give up their struggle for what they see as the right to disseminate their beliefs as part of the publicly funded school curriculum.[3]

The academic community, however, seems to be agreed that a political triumph by the scientific-creationists in gaining such a right would not simply affect the teaching of biology in the schools but would also seriously undermine all the earth sciences, as well as astronomy and even physics, and so would put in question the integrity of the entire educational system. In its disregard for theory construction and the empirical testing of theories as presently deemed reasonable, scientific-creationism, in effect, asks for a 'surrender' from all of science and not just from evolutionary theory.[4]

The academic community has, in recent years, gradually become aware of the radical intellectual and educational implications of scientific-creationism activity and thought.[5] Rather than striking back simply on the political level, however, they have entered into a debate with their scientific-creationist opponents in an attempt both to expose the weaknesses of scientific-creationist 'theory' and to substantiate the claims for an evolutionary interpretative framework for the biological sciences. And the academic community has, in my opinion, marshalled a considerable case against the scientific-creationists, and that on several grounds – scientific,[6] philosophical,[7] legal,[8] moral,[9] and even religious.[10] Scientific-creationists, nevertheless, have not been persuaded of the truth of that argument in any of its several aspects.

I am convinced, however, that scientific-creationism is not a rationally justifiable view of the development of forms of life in this world. I will not concern myself, though, with attempting yet again to ferret out the errors and weaknesses of the scientific-creationist 'theory' of the progress of life on earth, or with attempting to establish the soundness and fruitfulness of some form or other of evolutionary theory that will dissuade them from their present beliefs. Rather, it is my intention to assess the *religious* significance of their stance and to show it wanting in that regard. It seems to me, that is, that their concern to achieve scientific legitimation for their creationist beliefs shows a profoundly significant lack of faith in what they themselves refer to as 'the revealed word of God' (the Bible) on these matters. That is, in seeking scientific legitimation for their 'creation claims' they subject religion (Christianity) to adjudication in terms foreign to itself – they seek an 'alliance' with that to which the creationist view of life is, it would seem, essentially opposed. To be able to show, even if only indirectly, that that kind of rationalistic theological structure constitutes an 'unholy alliance,' I suggest, would provide the grounds necessary to establish a genuinely 'religious argument' against scientific-creationism. It would, moreover, be the kind of argument the scientific-creationist might be open to hearing, since it comes from within an orthodox religious community of thought rather than from a liberal religious context or a hostile scientific one.

II POETIC-CREATIONISM

As I have just now intimated, a 'religious argument' has already been raised against scientific-creationism in recent articles and debate. That argument can be of considerable help in establishing my claim here, but not, I am afraid, in any direct kind of way. Ironically, as the remainder of this essay will show, it is a critique of that argument that will constitute a genuinely religious case against scientific-creationism, for, as I shall demonstrate, the 'religious argument' does not, in its original form, so much undermine the (deviant) rationalism[11] of scientific-creationism as recapitulate it in a less blatant, more sophisticated form. There are, moreover, distinct advantages to such an indirect argument. The obliqueness of the approach might well gain a hearing from the scientific-creationist, which a direct, frontal assault so far has not. Furthermore, this critique clearly shows the anxiety[12] that characterizes the scientific-creationist to be much more pervasive within the (Christian) religious community than might at first appear to be the case.

It is common knowledge, I think, that those opposed to scientific-creationism are not all anti-religious or irreligious persons. The court action taken against the Arkansas law requiring that creation-science be given equal time with evolution in the curriculum of the Arkansas public school system was initiated by the Reverend William McLean, the principal official of the Presbyterian Church in that state. Moreover, McLean was officially joined in the complaint by leaders of other Christian denominations, as well as of several Jewish organizations, indicating the existence of a kind of 'ecumenical consensus' rejecting creation-science on biblical and, more generally, religious grounds.[13]

The cornerstone of the religious argument against the scientific-creationists rests on the claim that they fail to recognize the true nature of the Bible and, therefore, of the biblical story of creation as religious literature. The Bible (and other myths of origins, one presumes), it is argued, never intended to provide us with the kind of knowledge about objective nature that can be acquired through science. It is not the purport of the Bible, that is, to deal with the speculative questions concerning the origins and genesis of the earth and all that it contains, but rather to deal only with the *meaning* of human existence – our existence – in the world. Its intent, therefore, is 'symbolic' and not scientific – its concern is meaning rather than knowledge. Consequently, no conflict between science and religion, properly understood, can arise. I shall refer to this 'symbolic' view of creation stories in religious texts as 'poetic-creationism'.[14]

Poetic-creationism, it must be noted, can take either a strong or a weak form. Proponents of the strong view – which I shall refer to as 'poetic-creationism proper' – maintain that the concerns in the present debate involving the scientific-creationists would simply go unrecognized by the authors and earliest readers of Genesis or of other creation accounts.[15] The specific cognitive intentionality of the scientific enterprise, they insist, was unknown to such early communities of thinkers. The creation story was not *intended* by them to provide knowledge but rather attempted to express deep-seated truths about human personhood. The creation account, that is, objectified for them what would otherwise have been an inexpressible mystery concerning their being – the reason for their existence – rather than objectively describing and explaining a physical reality distinct from themselves, but of which they formed a constituent element.

Of course, in eschewing any and all claims to cognitive status – that is, in denying that it is making any claim at all about a mind-independent reality – poetic-creationism proper does indeed avoid any possible conflict with evolutionary theory, both doctrinally and methodologically. And, unlike scientific-creationism, it avoids all charge of anachronism, for it does not attempt to read into the texts of religious traditions, intentions and aims that could not have been present in the original authors. Poetic-creationism does not unconsciously reconstruct religious traditions to fit the modern age, but rather, quite consciously, attempts to disengage from such traditions what will be of value in the new ideology it fashions in order to make sense of human existence here and now.

Although admirable in many respects, such ideological reconstruction and appropriation of religious texts seem to be in conflict with religion's (not fully conscious) perception of itself. It may be true that the religious *intention* in the 'construction' of its myths is not a cognitive one. But this does not imply that the authors and earliest readers of those myths did not, in and through the myths, *know* 'the world' in which they lived. In the act of structuring a meaningful existence, the myth emerges as a response to recognized structures in the universe and so constitutes an *implicit knowledge* of the world. And refusing to acknowledge that 'epistemic quality' of the myth, unconscious though it be, as does poetic-creationism proper, constitutes an outright rejection of the religious tradition.[16]

III METAPHYSICAL-CREATIONISM

Religious scholars, unwilling to adopt the creation-science interpretation of the 'implicit knowledge' of the creation story as 'scientific', but equally unwilling to reject the cognitive character or value of myth – and in particular, the creation myth – espouse a modified form of poetic-creationism that I shall here dub 'metaphysical-creationism'.[17] Knowledge of creation, its proponents claim, can only come from a non-scientific source and therefore cannot be a rival to scientific knowledge, but, rather, complements it. And it is in that extra-scientific yet cognitive complement to scientific knowledge about life that the meaningfulness and significance of life is revealed, for it relates life here to an external and ultimate 'life-principle' as its source and end. In laying claim to extra-scientific knowledge, then, metaphysical-creationism sees itself as religiously acceptable, unlike poetic-creationism proper, and scientifically unobjectionable, unlike scientific-creationism. Metaphysical-creationism, therefore, seems to see itself as having provided a framework of thought within which one might retain traditional religious identity, without having to forego rational/scientific integrity – a framework of thought within which one can be a creationist and an evolutionist at one and the same moment. Hence the surprise expressed by some at the apparently widespread belief that this is not possible. Langdon Gilkey, in writing on the creationist controversy, for example, exclaims: 'Many people still assume that to believe in God or the Bible one must reject the notion of evolution.' He continues: 'Many scientists share with the fundamentalists the confused notion that so-called religious knowledge and scientific knowledge exist on the same level and that, as science advances, scientific knowledge simply replaces and dissolves religious myth.'[18] 'Recognizing' a distinction between scientific and other forms of knowledge undermines all this, claims Gilkey, so that 'historians of science now recognize that the image of warfare between science and religion was not even true in the nineteenth century.'[19]

The claim that the imagery of warfare is inappropriately used in describing the relationship of science to religion – and especially with respect to the relationship of evolutionary biology to the Bible – is a bold one, but it is also, I think, false, if not preposterous.[20] This is obviously so at the superficial level of historical description. Historians concerned with relating the state of affairs that has existed between the scientific and religious communities since the rise of modern Western science with Copernicus and Galileo are entirely justified in using such imagery. Indeed, it is obviously applicable to the present relationship between the community of biologists and teachers of biology and the religious community espousing scientific-creationism.[21] Religion and science, even if they were not logically mutually exclusive, would be in conflict with each other – and Gilkey himself has been embroiled in just such a conflict. Obviously, then, Gilkey's claim must be that had religious devotees and theologians been more perceptive, a different history would have occurred, one allowing an account of the relationship between the two communities without invoking the imagery of warfare. However, this also, and equally obviously, depends on the cogency of Gilkey's own form of creationism – that is, metaphysical-creationism.

Metaphysical-creationism, unlike scientific-creationism, it is claimed, does not interfere with science; rather, it transcends science (and evolutionary theory) by providing a knowledge about 'life' not available to science. But to maintain that this is not interference seems ludicrous. It is not the *direct* interference of the scientific-creationist, but it does, *indirectly*, interfere by suggesting that the assumption made by scientists (the scientific community) that they can adequately account for phenomena is unacceptable. Scientists set out to provide explanations – not partial explanations. Denying that their present explanations are exhaustive, which as I suggest in the introduction is, in fact, the case, does not imply that they see themselves as incapable in principle of explaining fully, but rather reveals a humility in the face of their present ignorance. Science is operational, then, so to speak, only if the world as 'insoluble mystery' is excluded, *a priori* – that is, excluded on *methodological* considerations. Science can only 'explain' events if they are part of a discoverable causal order. To see presently unexplained events as outside that causal nexus is to assume, on equally *a priori* grounds, that the world is, ultimately, an 'insoluble mystery'. Contrary to the claims of the metaphysical-creationists, therefore, it would appear that science and religion – not just scientists and religious devotees – are in conflict; that they are two mutually exclusive *perspectives* from which to view 'the world'; two contrasting and conflicting modes of explaining or making sense of 'the world'.[22]

One further comment. It seems to me that metaphysical-creationism, although somewhat more sophisticated than scientific-creationism, makes the same error as the latter in its 'understanding' of religious texts (myths). Poetic-creationists proper are right to accuse the scientific-creationists of anachronistic thinking in their assumption of a scientific intention in the myth. But to assume a metaphysically cognitive intention on the part of the authors of the creation stories is, I suggest, similarly anachronistic. Such an 'understanding' of the myth also ascribes meanings to the text that the authors could not have entertained. Structurally, therefore, scientific-creationism and metaphysical-creationism appear indistinguishable.

IV   THE SHIFT FROM A THEOLOGICAL TO A POSITIVE 'EPISTEME'

A close analysis of the emergence and success of evolutionary theory in biology will reveal, I would maintain, that evolutionary thought is both the product of a new episteme in Western culture and a causal factor in the ascendancy of that episteme – an 'episteme' being a communal definition of what constitutes knowledge and of what is knowable. This fact is clearly established, I think, by N. C. Gillespie in his *Charles Darwin and the Problem of Creation.*[23] The point of this new episteme, however, will require further clarification.

An episteme is not a full-blown world-view with a well-developed metaphysic, although it may encourage or discourage certain kinds of metaphysical/ontological commitments; but neither is it merely an important empirical or theoretical scientific discovery that provides a central paradigm, *à la* Thomas Kuhn, for further scientific research in the relevant discipline. An episteme is, rather, a formal aspect of thought, an *a priori*, that for any given period of history defines the conditions of possibility of all knowledge.

The episteme in biology that precedes the rise of evolutionary theory is one hospitable to creationism. But that episteme can not simply be complemented – it has either to reign, and thereby undergird creationism, or to be replaced, for it is immediately obvious from the definition just given that there cannot be two epistemes at any one time. Consequently, Gillespie introduced his thesis on Darwin and creation as follows:

> Those who argue that there was no real warfare between science and religion in the nineteenth century ignore the presence of these two sciences. The old science was theologically grounded; the new was positive. The old had reached the limits of its development. The new was asking questions that the old could neither frame nor answer. The new had to break with theology, or render it a neutral factor in its understanding of the cosmos, in order to construct a science that could answer questions about nature in methodologically uniform terms. Uniformity of law, of operation, of method were its watchwords. The old science invoked divine will as an explanation of the unknown; the new postulated yet-to-be-discovered laws. The one inhibited growth because such mysteries were unlikely ever to be clarified; the other held open the hope that they would.[24]

In order to clarify the analysis I have thus far undertaken here, I shall elaborate, briefly, upon Gillespie's argument. Gillespie's reference to creationism as the old theologically grounded *science* is, I think, entirely appropriate despite the claim of the poetic-creationists discussed above. This is not a failure on his part to recognize that religion (and therefore Christianity) is symbolic and not a cognitively oriented enterprise. It is rather a judgement, on the basis of sound historical evidence, that the implicit knowledge claims of the Christian tradition were developed – whether rightly or wrongly is beside the point for the moment – as a science. Indeed, it is generally agreed that from the time of Linnaeus to Charles Darwin, the doctrine of special creation provided the only coherent framework for understanding the rapidly accumulating body of facts of the sciences of geology, biology and palaeontology, among others. 'Special creation', whether viewed as miraculous or nomothetic, was commonly recognized to have strong empirical evidence.[25] And though Darwin opposed all variations of the 'special creation' theory, even he did not, at least in *The Origin of Species*, reject divine creation per se. The *Origin*, as is well known, contains a variety of passages that refer to, and in a sense invoke as an explanatory device, the deity.[26] Moreover, it has been argued, that Darwin in that volume condemns the 'special creation' theory on *theological* grounds.[27] Darwin's early opposition to creationism, therefore, was directed only against those views of creation that invoked a belief in the stability of species and invoked the direct, volitional and purposeful intervention of God in the course of nature. Darwin was deeply suspicious, however, of modes of thought that relied on the notion of design. As a kind of 'mental explanation' of phenomena, it seemed to him, design precluded the need for finding their physical causes and therefore posed a threat to science, which is founded on the assumption of the existence of such a causal nexus.

Although special creation, involving God's direct and miraculous intervention, had virtually outlived its usefulness after the publication of the *Origin*, it grew in strength in its nomothetic character thereafter. In its nomothetic form, the ends once achieved by the direct, miraculous, creative acts of God were now seen to be the result of God's 'miraculous' manipulation of the natural laws of the universe. As Gillespie puts it, this view, for Darwin, began almost immediately to spread with an appalling swiftness.[28] Special creation in its nomothetic forms shrouded in mystery the question of the succession of species as much as did the miraculous view and so, like the latter, inhibited further inquiry.

Even though Darwin had given up adherence to any form of orthodox Christianity, he did not give up religion entirely. It seems that Darwin espoused a form of theism, for he could not bring himself to believe that nature was not, ultimately, benevolent. He had dropped theology from his science but not, as Gillespie puts it, from his world-view.[29] Thus, the *Origin* was, in a very important sense, a manifesto for a positive science, but it also fell short of a complete positivism. Nevertheless, Gillespie concludes, and I think correctly so, that 'the end of special creation as a plausible scientific idea was also the beginning of the end of significant obstacles to a completely positive biology.'[30] And this would include the demise of Darwin's theism, as is suggested in Darwin's own negative response to the non-miraculous nomothetic creationism proposed by Asa Gray.[31] Non-miraculous nomothetic creationism presupposes a body of laws, established by God from the beginning of the world, through the operation of which new species evolved. In such a view, new species are seen to be 'divinely created' but without involving any *special intervention* by God. It amounts, in effect, to a view of 'providential evolution'. Gray developed it to explain the lack of a causal account of variation in individual organisms. However, the theory, and all such theories, involved a belief in double causation that Darwin, despite being haunted by the question of design, refused to accept. Such a causal view of the world contradicted a basic principle of positive science, namely, that when sufficient natural or physical causes are not known they must be presumed to exist. The possibility of a divine origin, even if indirectly so, of variations clearly threatened Darwin's theory of natural selection and so also his hope for a positive biology. As Gillespie puts it: 'The touchstone of positive biology, at bottom, was not law or natural causes, but the absence of conscious contrivance or purpose, however these might be conceived.... For the positivists, miracle was not the only source of obscurantism. A theological understanding of admittedly natural causes, in the final reckoning, required theological explanations.'[32]

Given Gillespie's account, I shall now attempt to delineate the primary characteristics of the two epistemes underlying evolutionism and creationism. A positive and empirical understanding of science, as underlying evolutionism, is not a social prescription but, rather, a way of practising science, whereas that which underlies creationism, in whatever form, is in the first instance a framework of human action and existence and only secondarily a source of (or method for obtaining) knowledge about the world. Whereas the 'positive understanding of science' deals with science as a system of empirically verifiable facts and processes, the ground of creationism leaves room for facts and processes that are not open to empirical verification or falsification. The positive outlook, therefore, constructs theories to link the facts but does so on the basis of patterns of causes known to exist and whose operations are observable; but creationism either leaves room for miraculous interventions in an otherwise causal nexus of events or invokes the existence of undiscovered divine causal relationships that once existed but do so no longer. Consequently, science – especially evolutionary science – was determined to remain open, at all levels, to investigation, whereas creationism retreated to mysteries that must, so to speak, remain inviolable. The theological scientist or creationist can, therefore, describe the operation of processes of nature but cannot explain them, except teleologically – that is, by means of (spurious) purposeful explanations that blunt the need to search further for causal explanations.[33] Thus, even though the creationist did, and still does, speak of causes, he or she invokes primary and secondary causes, with the latter being subordinated to the former, so that 'mental explanations' preclude the need for physical explanations. Teleological explanations it seems, then, leave room for caprice in the universe, whereas the essence of science in the positive episteme is accountability. In fact, it is precisely such accountability that characterizes science in the positive episteme as heuristically valuable – a guide to observation and theorizing that can lead to new discoveries. Creationism and the theological episteme can but patiently await the self-revealing divine activity in the universe; the mystery of divine activity cannot be accounted for, providing little or no guidance for the construction of research paradigms.

Given such an array of contrasts between the creationists, including the providential evolutionists, and the evolutionists proper, in the middle of the nineteenth century, it is obvious that we have here a radical epistemic shift among scientists. Furthermore, that epistemic shift amounts, in the final analysis, to a conflict between science and religion, unless religion, that is, creationism, gives up any and all epistemic/cognitive pretensions. And that, as I have already argued, constitutes a radical revolution in religion. On this point I think Gillespie summarizes the matter very neatly: 'The shift from one episteme to another,' he writes, 'required not the surrender of religion as such, but rather its replacement by positivism as the epistemological standard in science. And this eventually took God out of nature (if not out of reality) as effectively as atheism.'[34]

V   RELIGIOUS-CREATIONISM

The strangeness of the creationists' quest for scientific legitimation should by now be obvious. The espousal of science as generally practised in our educational institutions – whether directly as with the scientific-creationists, or indirectly as with the metaphysical-creationists – seems to constitute an implicit rejection of creationism. It appears, that is, as if religion is seeking legitimation from that which can only destroy it. Though paradoxical, if not simply contradictory, this move by the creationists is not entirely 'un-understandable'. The question of origins has been central in traditional/religious cultures to understanding the meaning of human existence; indeed, to guaranteeing meaningfulness to human existence. The creationist is loath, therefore, simply to give up the question to the scientists. Even though the scientists may not speak of 'absolute origins' in their scientific capacity, there seem to be 'metaphysical' implications in the purely scientific discoveries that run contrary to traditional religious belief.[35] On this score, the Victorian dissenters were, I think, entirely correct.

Further, given the prestige and authority of science and the sciences in modern society, this quest for scientific legitimation is understandable on several counts, for not only is science a powerful tool that provides benefits we should not like to forgo, it is also the criterion by which our modern society measures intellectual respectability in cognitive matters, and, hence, the criterion of rational identity. And if creationism is not rationally acceptable it would seem that, in the eyes of the creationists at least, the 'question of origins' has, in fact, been surrendered to the scientists. Consequently, the creationists strive for a 'compatibility system'[36] that would allow them to retain both their religious identity and rationalist identity (that is, intellectual integrity). The scientific-creationists seek that legitimation directly by boldly claiming for themselves the status of scientists, and metaphysical-creationists seek it indirectly by a hermeneutical device that would allow them to hold to the cognitive significance of myth without running foul of science, while the poetic-creationists proper, cognitively speaking, capitulate to science. In all three cases I suggest, therefore, that religion submits itself to a principle of adjudication foreign to its own nature and so forges 'an unholy alliance', that can only be detrimental to religion *and* science. Taken as scientific language, the mythic narratives of creation are simply false, and to understand science in the broader framework of religious myth as an implicit epistemology is to destroy science. The integrity of each requires that neither be subordinated to the other.[37]

The only appropriate understanding of the myth, then, it seems to me, is that it is 'revealed truth' and as such stands opposed to scientific understanding both methodologically and doctrinally. This is 'religious-creationism'. It admits that the authors of the creation myths were not primarily concerned with knowledge *per se* and that, consequently, on the level of intention, science and religion – creationism and evolutionism – are incommensurables. But religious-creationism also acknowledges that in the framework that it created in order to make life meaningful, a knowledge of the world is implied and that such implicit knowledge is commensurable with the consciously achieved knowledge of the sciences *and in conflict with it*. Consequently, one must choose between science and religion and not seek to legitimate religion by invoking science. To try to have both destroys both and so leaves one with neither.

Lev Shestov, a Russian philosopher much concerned with the relation of science to religion in general – that is, with the negative effect of science on religion – adopts such a religious-creationism. And I close this paper with the opening paragraph of his comment on 'Darwin and the Bible' indicative of a truly religious-creationism unwilling, like its 'competitors', 'to bend the knee', so to speak, to science: 'The Bible recounts to us the fall of our progenitor Adam, the first man. You believe that this is only an invention of ignorant Jews? You believe the discovery of an English scientist is closer to the truth and that man is descended from the ape. Well, permit me to tell you that the Jews were closer to the truth, that they were indeed very close to it.'[38]

Notes

1 COMPREHENSIVELY CRITICAL RATIONALISM

1. S. Hook, *The Quest for Being*, (New York: St. Martin's Press, 1961), p. 76.
2. Ibid., p. 74.
3. M. Polanyi, *Logic of Liberty: Reflections and Rejoinders*, (London: Routledge & Paul, 1951), p. 10.
4. Polanyi, *Personal Knowledge: Towards a Post-Critical Philosophy*, (London: Routledge & Kegan Paul, 1958), p. 286.
5. Ibid., p. 381.
6. Ibid., p. 286.
7. W. W. Bartley, *The Retreat to Commitment*, (New York: A. Knopf, 1962), p. 89.
8. Ibid., p. 90.
9. Ibid., p. 96.
10. Ibid., p. 94.
11. Ibid., p. 90.
12. Ibid., p. 144.
13. Ibid., pp. 147, 148.
14. Ibid., p. 2, 83.
15. Ibid., p. 150.
16. J. W. N. Watkins, however, has not accepted CCR as even logically tenable as an adequate characterization of rationality. Cf. 'Comprehensively Critical Rationalism', *Philosophy*, 44, (1969): 57–62. Although the *reductio ad absurdum* achieved by Watkin's criticism of Bartley's argument is correct, I nevertheless believe that it is not a telling criticism of CCR. Cf. J. Agassi, I. C. Jarvie and T. W. Settle, 'The Grounds of Reason', *Philosophy*, 46 (1971): 43–9.
17. K. Popper, *Conjectures and Refutations: The Growth of Scientific Knowledge*, (New York: Basic Books, 1962), p. 47.
18. Although advocating the substitution of the 'critical attitude' for the 'dogmatic attitude' of justificationary programmes, Popper nonetheless does not wish to dispose with dogmatism altogether. Indeed he cannot, as he points out: 'The critical attitude is not so much opposed to the dogmatic attitude as superimposed upon it: criticism must be directed against existing and influential beliefs in need of critical revision, in other words, dogmatic beliefs. A critical attitude needs for its raw material, as it were, theories or beliefs which are held more or less dogmatically' (Popper, op. cit., 1962, p. 50).
19. Although I agree with Popper that the inductivists are unable to establish the existence of a logical relationship between our observational experience and our theories or hypotheses, I nevertheless

disagree with his further claim that our theories are 'psychologically or genetically *a priori*, i.e., to all observational experience' (Popper, op. cit., 1962, p. 47). Whereas Popper claims the expectation of finding a regularity as an 'inborn propensity to look out for regularities, or with a *need* to *find* regularities', Polanyi claims that it is 'only by our common acquaintance with facts, which either persist for a while on a single occasion, or keep recurring at different places and times, that we can appreciate what is meant by Uniformity or limited Variety in Nature and that these conceptions would be quite unintelligible to us if we lived in a gaseous universe in which no circumscribed or recurrent facts could ever be discerned' (Polanyi, op. cit., 1958, p. 162). Polanyi, I suggest, attempts to solve the problem concerning the origin of our theories through attempting to find a logic of discovery while Popper proceeds to dissolve the problem by fiat.

Although Polanyi does not consider such a logic of discovery to consist of a structure which can be extracted and written down and used again he nevertheless maintains that a logic of discovery is to be found in the structure of 'tacit knowing'. 'It is the *function* of a subsidiary item that counts in classing it as subsidiary. We may call it its *logical function*. When I see visual clues as a coherent object, the relationship between my awareness of the clues to the knowledge derived from them is similar to that between premisses and conclusions derived from them: it is a logical relationship. The clues enter here into a procedure of *tacit inference*, with integration replacing deduction' (Polanyi, 'Sense-Giving and Sense-Reading', in T. A. Langford and W. H. Poteat (eds) *Intellect and Hope: Essays in the Thought of Michael Polanyi*, [Durham, NC: Duke University Press, 1968], p. 417).

20. This distinction between what Reichenbach has called 'the context of discovery' and 'the context of justification' of a theory, is, I suggest, both *ad hoc* and obscurantist. It solves no problem. Instead it blocks research that might yield important data for the development of an adequate epistemology. It serves no other purpose, as far as I can see, than to shore-up a sadly inadequate and sagging account of our knowledge in objectivist terms. Recognizing the *personal* nature of discovery, but holding fast to an objectivist conception of knowledge as impersonal, the objectivists insist on such a distinction, for only then, they assume, can our knowledge be kept free from utter subjectivity and relativism. R. J. Blackwell expresses my sentiments to this objectivist procedure most precisely: 'Many who deny a logic of discovery dismiss it with the remark that discovery is a matter of individual psychology and not of philosophical analysis. One sometimes gets the impression that the real impact of such remarks is that it is better not to try to discuss the problem at all, and that psychology is a convenient *refugium peccatorum* to dispose of the issue' (A. L. Fisher and G. B. Murray (eds), *Philosophy and Science as Modes of Knowing: Selected Essays*, [New York: Appleton-Century-Croft, 1969], p. 67).

21. Polanyi, 'Problem Solving', *British Journal for the Philosophy of Science*, 8, (1957), p. 89.

22. Popper, op. cit., 1962, p. 57.
23. Popper, *The Logic of Scientific Discovery*, (New York: Harper & Row, 1968), p. 86 and op. cit., 1962, p. 41.
24. Popper, op. cit., 1968, p. 11.
25. Ibid., p. 42.
26. Ibid., p. 108 and op. cit., 1962, p. 228.
27. A. Koestler, *Sleepwalkers: A History of Man's Changing Vision of the Universe*, (London: Hutchinson, 1959), pp. 51, 52.
28. Polanyi, op. cit., 1951, p. 18.
29. C. Friedrich, 'A Review of Personal Knowledge', *Natural Law Forum*, 7 (1962): 148.
30. Polanyi, op. cit., 1958, p. 214.
31. Bartley, op. cit., p. 215.
32. Ibid., p. 54.
33. B. Mitchell, 'The University Debate', in A. Flew and A. MacIntyre (eds), *New Essays in Philosophical Theology*, (London: SCM Press, 1955), p. 105.
34. Cf. for example, W. Hordern, *New Directions in Theology Today*, Vol. 1 (Philadelphia; Westminster Press, 1966): '... God's revelation [for Christians] includes a historical event, in this case the life of Jesus.... This understanding of revelation involves Christian faith in a complex relation to history ... such that if historical study should demonstrate that Jesus never lived, it would destroy Christian faith since Christian faith is not a collection of truths that could be true apart from Jesus', (p. 56).
35. Bartley, op. cit., p. 89.
36. T. Kuhn, *The Structure of Scientific Revolutions*, (Chicago: University of Chicago Press, 1962), p. 151. Cornford perhaps put the case most succinctly years ago: 'Almost all philosophic arguments are invented afterwards to recommend, or defend from attack, conclusions which the philosopher was from the outset, bent upon believing, before he could think of an argument at all. That is why philosophical reasonings are so bad, so artificial, and so unconvincing. *To mistake them for the cause which led to a belief in the conclusion, is generally to fall into a naive error.* The claims of the early Greek philosophers lie in the fact that to a large extent, they did not trouble to invent bad arguments at all, but simply stated their belief dogmatically. They produced a system as an artist produces a work of art' (F. M. Cornford, *From Religion to Philosophy: A Study in the Origins of Western Speculation*, [New York: Harper & Row, 1957], p. 138. The italics are mine).
37. Such a distinction between the *message* and *the statement of the message* Bartley implies is illegitimate – simply an escape mechanism. This criticism holds however only upon accepting the traditional critical assumption that knowledge is wholly explicit. Polanyi, I think, presents a sound case for accepting knowledge as both tacit and explicit. Cf. Polanyi's *Personal Knowledge*. For the positive theological implications of such a view of knowledge see J. Baillie, *The Sense of the Presence of God*, (London: Oxford University Press, 1962).
38. Bartley, op. cit., p. 165. Italics mine.

39.   Polanyi, op. cit., 1958, p. 286.
40.   Bartley, op. cit., p. 151.
41.   Polanyi, *The Study of Man* (Chicago: University of Chicago Press, 1959), pp. 26, 27.
42.   Polanyi, op. cit., 1958, p. 267.
43.   Polanyi, op. cit., 1951, p. 31.

2   IS RELIGIOUS BELIEF PROBLEMATIC?

1.   On this score see R. J. Ackermann, *Belief and Knowledge* (New York: Macmillan, 1972), chapter 2. Particularly interesting problems arise here for the theologian. The utterance 'God is love' may be less a proposition requiring 'notional assent' (in Newman's sense) than the revelation of an attitude or disposition to behave in certain ways on the part of the one who utters it, *à la* R. B. Braithwaite in his *An Empiricist's View of the Nature of Religious Belief* (New York: Cambridge University Press, 1955). By the same token one may adopt the same disposition without ever uttering the phrase at all. And if all moral actions imply a framework or world-view within which they fit as rational responses, and by the 'principle' that actions speak louder than words, there might be many more 'religious (Christian) believers' than theologians are often willing to countenance. See here, for example, the story of the sheep and the goats in Matthew 25 as illustrative of the principle 'by their fruits ye shall know them' as well as Baillie's reference to Bertrand Russell as an atheist at the top of his head but a Christian in the depth of his heart: John Baillie, *Our Knowledge of God* (New York: Oxford University Press, 1939). See also Ignace Lepp's last chapter, 'The Unbelief of Believers' in his *Atheism in Our Time* (New York: Macmillan, 1963); and Martin E. Marty's *Varieties of Unbelief* (New York: Holt, Rinehart & Winston, 1964), especially chapter 9.
2.   H. H. Farmer, *Towards Belief in God* (London: SCM, 1942), p. 176.
3.   A. Boyce Gibson, *Theism and Empiricism* (London: SCM, 1970), p. 12. See also pp. 32, 33. In the same regard see Dorothy Emmet's *The Nature of Metaphysical Thinking* (London: Macmillan, 1966), p. 7. In the realm of Christian religious thought there are at least two other strong contenders to this view: the first is to see religious belief simply or only as a regulative moral principle (a view that stems from Kant's work in the first two *Critiques* and is found clearly expressed in Braithwaite referred to in note 1 above) which as I have already pointed out has a good deal in its favour (note 1 above); and the second is to take religious belief as immediate awareness of the Divine; a direct *I–thou* acquaintance (which flows largely from Buber's influence on Protestant theologians such as, for example, Bultmann). There is no space, however, to submit these proposals to analysis here. For further discussion on these and other alternatives see Paul Helm's *The Varieties of Belief* (London: Routledge & Kegan Paul, 1973). For

further support of the position I have adopted here see Wolfhart Pannenberg's 'The Nature of Theological Statement', *Zygon*, 7 (1972): 6–19; see especially p. 9.

4. See here, for example, Peter L. Berger's *The Sacred Canopy: Elements of a Sociological Theory of Religion* (Garden City: Doubleday, 1967) and G. Lenski's *The Religious Factor* (Garden City: Doubleday, 1963).

5. The phrase 'a morality of knowledge' may appear not only new but awkward and clumsy – a fusing of two distinct fields of intellectual investigation, namely epistemology and ethics. The concept however is not new (being coined by W. Clifford in the latter half of the nineteenth century – see his 'The Ethics of Belief', in G. Mavrodes [ed.] *The Rationality of Belief in God* [Englewood Cliffs, New Jersey: Prentice-Hall, 1970] and has recently come into vogue. See, amongst others, the contributions of Van Harvey in his *The Historian and the Believer: The Morality of Historical Knowledge and Christian Belief* (New York: Macmillan, 1966), and James C. Livingstone in his *The Ethics of Belief* (Missoula, Montana: The Scholars Press, 1975).

6. At least this is how the problem is set up by W. W. Bartley in his *Retreat to Commitment* (New York: A. P. Knopf, 1962). There are difficulties with Bartley's analysis, however, which I have attempted to set out in my '"Comprehensively Critical Rationalism" and Commitment', *Philosophical Studies*, 21 (1973): 186–201, which is reprinted in this volume (Chapter 1).

7. The terms are Harvey's, op. cit.

8. I. Scheffler, *Science and Subjectivity* (Indianapolis: Bobbs-Merrill, 1967), p. v.

9. S. Hook, *The Quest for Being* (New York: St. Martin's Press, 1961), p. 76.

10. See, amongst others, T. R. Miles, *Religion and the Scientific Outlook* (London: Allen & Unwin, 1959); W. F. Zuurdeeg, *An Analytical Philosophy of Religion* (London: Allen & Unwin, 1959); Donald Evans, *The Logic of Self-Involvement* (London: SCM, 1963), and his 'Differences Between Scientific and Religious Assertions', in I. G. Barbour, *Science and Religion* (New York: Harper & Row, 1968): 101–33; Alastair McKinnon, *Falsification and Belief* (New York: Humanities Press, 1970); Ronald Hepburn, 'From World to God', in Basil Mitchell (ed.) *The Philosophy of Religion* (Oxford: Oxford University Press, 1971): 168–78; Emerson Shideler, *Believing and Knowing: The Meaning of Truth in Biblical Religion and in Science* (Ames, Iowa: Iowa State University Press, 1966), although the account is, here, confused and confusing; and R. B. Braithwaite, op. cit.

11. As Van Harvey has put it in his 'Is There an Ethics of Belief?' *Journal of Religion*, 49 (1969): 41–58, one has no more right to hold a belief without reason than one has to drink a pint of beer for which one has not paid; the same can be said of the injunctions spoken of here.

12. I have subjected the non-cognitivist tradition in the interpretation of the meaning of religion to closer criticism in my 'Truth and the Study of Religion', in *Philosophical Studies* 25 (1977): 7–47.

13. I shall not here subject any particular religious belief to minute examination. Religious belief exhibits a complex structure. I have suggested

that such belief is at least in part cognitive in character, that it is concerned to tell us something about the world. Religious concepts, that is, are often invoked to explain specific states of affairs in the world just as are scientific concepts, and the interpretation of those concepts is, generally speaking, a realist one for both the religious devotee and the scientist. I have discussed this at greater length in my 'Explanation and Theological Method', in *Zygon*, 11 (1976): 35–49, which is reprinted in this volume (Chapter 4). Since my concern is one with the cognitive facet of religious belief there is no need to discuss any particular religious beliefs in detail here.

14. This seems to me to be particularly so of the positivist philosophers of science in their attempt to account for knowledge and its growth in a logical step-by-step fashion. E. Nagel, for example, sees the fruits of science as an institutionalized art of inquiry as 'the achievement of generalized theoretical knowledge concerning fundamental determining conditions for the occurrence of various types of events and processes; [and] the emancipation of men's minds from ancient superstitions ... [and] the undermining of the intellectual foundations for moral and religious dogmas, with a resultant weakening in the protective cover that the hard crust of unreasoned custom provides for the continuation of social injustices ...' (*The Structure of Science* [London: Routledge & Kegan Paul, 1961], p. vii). According to H. Reichenbach, religion is 'abundant in pictures that stimulate our imagination but [is] devoid of the power of clarification that issues from scientific explanation' (*The Rise of Scientific Philosophy* [Berkeley: University of California Press, 1951], p. 9). Sydney Hook, already quoted above, contrasts even more emphatically the two modes of thought, asking the philosopher to 'counterpose the public and self-critical absolute of reflective intelligence or scientific method ... [to the] tom-tom of theology and the bagpipes of transcendental metaphysics' (Hook, op. cit., p. 44). Similar contrasts can be found in I. Scheffler's *Science and Subjectivity* op. cit.; H. Feigl, 'Is Science Relevant to Theology?', *Zygon*, 1 (1966): 191–9; and Carl R. Kordig, *The Justification of Scientific Change*, (Hingham, Mass.: Reidel, 1971).

This assumption seems to pervade even Professor Karl R. Popper's philosophy of 'conjectures and refutations' (in his volume by that title [New York: Harper & Row, 1962] as is pointed out by M. Grene in her *The Knower and the Known* (London: Faber & Faber, 1966), p. 33. See also the conclusions of such Popperians as W. W. Bartley, op. cit., and J. Agassi, 'Can Religion Go Beyond Reason?', *Zygon*, 4 (1969): 128–68.

15. Objections could be made to the distinctions I have drawn here. W. V. O. Quine's criticism of the synthetic/analytic distinction, is a case in point, (see his *From a Logical Point of View* [New York: Harper & Row, 1961]). Such objections are not, however, critical to the point I make here. If sense-statements are not, in fact, privileged information about inner mental states, then neither do they have the absolute certainty so often attributed to them. With respect to the 'tautologies', I do not think talk of 'synthetic *a priori*' assertions at all acceptable. If the objections to the distinctions I have drawn here

stand, then both sense-statements and 'tautologies' are actually informative or fact-stating propositions and so subject to the analysis of those propositions given below.

16. See here, however, the qualifications Popper adds to this claim in his *The Logic of Scientific Discovery* (New York: Harper & Row, 1959).

17. See Popper, op. cit., 1963.

18. The basic intention of J. Piaget's book *Insights and Illusions of Philosophy* (New York: New American Library, 1971) is to argue against the falsifiability or testability of such claims and hence to establish their non-cognitivist character. The same point however was made by Popper sometime earlier in his *Conjectures and Refutations*, pp. 257 ff.

19. Popper, op. cit., 1962.

20. See in this respect R. S. Heimbeck's *Theology and Meaning* (London: Allen & Unwin, 1969).

21. N. R. Hanson, *Patterns of Discovery, An Inquiry into the Conceptual Foundations of Science* (New York: Cambridge University Press, 1965), p. 67.

22. Popper, op. cit., 1959; p. 65.

23. 'Falsification and the Methodology of Scientific Research Programmes', in I. Lakatos and A. Musgrave (eds) *Criticism and the Growth of Knowledge* (Cambridge: Cambridge University Press, 1970), p. 97.

24. Ibid., p. 99.

25. I refer here to discussions by Malcolm in his 'The Verification Argument', and 'Knowledge and Belief', both in N. Malcolm, *Knowledge and Certainty: Essays and Lectures* (Englewood Cliffs: Prentice Hall, 1963), pp. 1–57, 58–72; and in his 'Certainty and Empirical Statements', in John Hospers (ed.) *Readings in Philosophical Analysis* (London: Routledge & Kegan Paul, 1969). No detailed analysis of Malcolm's argument is possible here.

26. What one must look for here then is not knock-down proofs but rather, as Mitchell points out (op. cit.) a 'cumulative argument'.

27. Joseph Pieper, *Belief and Faith, A Philosophical Tract* (London: Faber & Faber, 1964), p. 34.

28. H. H. Price, *Belief* (London: Allen and Unwin, 1969), p. 72.

29. Ibid., p. 78.

30. Ibid., p. 85.

31. Ibid., p. 269.

32. Ibid., p. 86.

33. J. L. Austin, 'Other Minds', in *Philosophical Papers*, J. O. Urmson and G. J. Warnock (eds) (New York: Oxford University Press, 1970), pp. 76–116.

34. The problems raised by W. H. F. Barnes, 'Knowing', *Philosophical Review*, 72 (1963): 3–16, and Maxwell Wright, '"I Know" and Performative Utterances', *Australasian Journal of Philosophy*, 43 (1965): 35–47, are not, I think, critical. Unfortunately space does not allow an analysis of their critiques here.

35. See here F. Ferré's 'Science and the Death of God', in I. G. Barbour (ed.) *Science and Religion: New Perspectives on the Dialogue*, (New York: Harper & Row, 1968), pp. 134–56.

36.   I have carried out a detailed analysis of several such proposals in my *Science, Religion, and Rationality: Questions of Method in Science and Theology*, (unpublished doctoral dissertation, University of Lancaster, England); see especially chapter four: 'Verification, Confirmation and Rationality in Science and Theology'.

37.   See M. Polanyi, *Personal Knowledge* (New York: Harper & Row, 1958); Thomas Kuhn, *The Structure of Scientific Revolutions* (Chicago: University of Chicago Press, 1962); E. Harris, *Hypothesis and Perception, the Root of Scientific Method* (London: Allen & Unwin, 1970); P. Feyerabend, *Against Method: Outline of an Anarchistic Theory of Knowledge*, in M. Radner and S. Winoker (eds) Minnesota Studies in the Philosophy of Science, Vol. 4 (Minneapolis: University of Minnesota Press, 1970); R. Nash, *The Nature of the Natural Sciences* (Boston: Little, Brown, 1963).

38.   By William Christian in his 'Domains of Truth', in the *American Philosophical Quarterly*, 12 (1975): 61–8.

39.   See Van Harvey, op. cit.

40.   See, for example, Basil Mitchell's *The Justification of Religious Belief* (New York: Macmillan, 1973).

41.   See here Polanyi, op. cit., 1958.

42.   Where such claims are made it generally involves the claim that religious discourse is meaningless. See, for example, Kai Nielsen's 'The Intelligibility of God-Talk', *Religious Studies*, 6 (1970): 1–21, Bernard Williams' 'Has "God" a Meaning?' *Question*, Vol. 1 (1968), or Paul Edwards' 'Difficulties in the Idea of God', in E. H. Madden and M. Farber (eds) *The Idea of God: Philosophical Perspectives* (Springfield, Illinois: Charles C. Thomas, 1968), pp. 43–77. I assume here, for lack of space, the inadequacy of the 'meaningless' indictment (I have carried out a critique of Nielsen's argument elsewhere; see note 35 above.)

43.   See Basil Mitchell, op. cit., and J. Wisdom, *Paradox and Discovery* (Oxford: Blackwell, 1965). I have discussed Wisdom at length in 'Positivism and the Cognitive Status of Religious Assertions', (a paper read to the philosophy colloquium, University of Manitoba, 1975, and subsequently heavily revised and published in *Sophia*, 24, 1984, 4–21, and is reprinted in this volume as Chapter 3).

44.   See J. Hick, *Faith and Knowledge* (Ithaca, New York: Cornell University Press, 1966), pp. 127, 135, et passim.

45.   See, for example, Heinrich Vogel, *Consider Your Calling* (Edinburgh: Oliver & Boyd, 1962), chapter 3, 'Truth'.

3   THE COGNITIVE STATUS OF RELIGIOUS BELIEF

1.   M. L. Diamond, 'Wisdom's Gods', *Sophia* 22 (1983): 2–12.
2.   Ibid., pp. 2, 3.
3.   Ibid., p. 3.
4.   Ibid., p. 12.

5. Ibid., p. 10.
6. Ibid., p. 12.
7. Ibid., p. 9.
8. See D. Z. Phillips, 'Wisdom's Gods' in the *Philosophical Quarterly* 19 (1969): 15–32, which is reprinted in his *Faith and Philosophical Enquiry*, (London: Routledge & Kegan Paul, 1970), pp. 170–203.
9. Diamond, op. cit., p. 2.
10. From the introduction of J. Wisdom, *Paradox and Discovery*, (Oxford: Blackwell, 1965).
11. Wisdom, op. cit., 1965, p. 7.
12. R. M. Hare, 'Theology and Falsification' in *New Essays in Philosophical Theology*, A. Flew and A. MacIntyre (eds), (London: SCM Press, 1955), pp. 99–103.
13. R. S. Heimbeck, in *Theology and Meaning*, (London: Allen & Unwin, 1969), sees this as a serious misreading of Hare, claiming that although Hare does sharply demarcate assertions from *bliks*, he also 'everywhere hints that *bliks* have cognitive import' (p. 100, n. 1). It seems to me, however, that Passmore's judgement to the effect that 'Hare's reasoning in this passage is distinctly odd' (in 'Christianity and Positivism' in the *Australasian Journal of Philosophy*, 35 [1957], p. 130) is much more sound. It is interesting to note here that in one passage in his *Our Experience of God* (London: Fontana, 1959), p. 65, H. D. Lewis comes close to accepting a *blik*-type position.
14. The point here is simply this: a religious expression may well be performative, but not on that account be totally devoid of cognitive import. Performative utterances, that is, presuppose the existence of appropriate conditions for their proper use; they 'misfire' if such conditions do not obtain.
15. J. Wisdom, *Philosophy and Psycho-Analysis*, (Oxford: Blackwell, 1953), p. 154.
16. Wisdom, op. cit., 1965; pp. 53, 54.
17. Ibid., p. 56.
18. Ibid., p. 6.
19. Ibid., p. 156.
20. This is certainly true of such a Christian assertion as 'God is three in one and one in three', but not all Christian theological utterances are of this sort either. There are many that have what might be referred to as empirical entailments such as 'Jesus of Nazareth is the son of God,' or 'Jesus died for our sins', etc. See on this matter, R. S. Heimbeck, op. cit.
21. Wisdom, op. cit., 1953, p. 149.
22. Ibid., p. 156.
23. Ibid., p. 157.
24. The illustration is Wisdom's, cf. op. cit., 1965, p. 9.
25. Such a defence, I would argue, would also require a critique of Kuhn's understanding of the role of anomalies in relation to 'extraordinary' science. Kuhn's view of anomalies appears to be primarily negative in the sense that they create the pressure on the scientist to search for a new paradigm. Kuhn seems to suggest therefore that they play no

positive role in the formulation or justification of the new paradigm. Although I have no hard evidence to offer here, it seems to me that, since it is not the solitary anomaly to a reigning paradigm but rather a number of critically important anomalies that force a theory's abandonment, a pattern perceived, either consciously or unconsciously, in the anomalies themselves provide 'clues' for the development of alternative theories/paradigms and could also provide the initial ground of justificatory argument for the successful, new theory/ paradigm. That 'move' in extraordinary science, I suggest therefore, is less arbitrary and radical than Kuhn perceives it to be.

26. Thomas Kuhn, *The Structure of Scientific Revolutions*, (Chicago: University of Chicago Press, 1962), p. 34.

27. Wisdom, op. cit., 1965; p. 7.

28. Ibid., p. 152. Arguments, he insists are relevant to the persuasion of scientists.

29. Not all interpreters of Wisdom would agree with my understanding here. Besides Phillips and Diamond, one would have to include James Kellenberger who, for example, claims Wisdom in support of his thesis that religious knowledge is really non-hypothetical or non-experimental in nature. He refers to religious knowledge then as non-hypothetical discovery (see his *Religious Discovery, Faith and Knowledge*, [Englewood Cliffs, NJ: Prentice-Hall, 1972], especially chapter 1, and p. 12). However, it seems to me that when Kellenberger sees the acceptance of the evolutionary hypothesis in biological research as an example of non-hypothetical discovery (p. 19), he in fact supports the case being made out here.

30. See John Hick, *Faith and Knowledge*, (Ithaca, NY: Cornell University Press, 1966). I shall not attempt a defence of Hick here. Although he has come under severe criticism (see for example, W. Bean's 'Eschatological Verification ... Fortress or Fairyland?' in *Methodos*, 16 [1962]), his position has, I think, been ably defended by T. Penelhum in his *Religious Knowledge*, (New York: Macmillan Press, 1971).

31. John Hick, op. cit., 1966, pp. 114, 115.

32. John Hick, 'Theology and Verification', in *The Existence of God*, (New York: Macmillan, 1964), pp. 257, 258, 259.

33. Wisdom, op. cit., 1953; p. 150.

34. Wisdom, op. cit., 1965, p. 16. Again, not all interpreters of Wisdom would agree with me on this point. R. Jenson, for example, (in *The Knowledge of Things Hoped For*, [London: Oxford University Press, 1969]) takes these remarks, together with some of Wisdom's remarks in 'The Meaning of Life' (op. cit., 1965, and develops a Wisdomian conception of verification akin to drama (or novel) interpretation. Macquarrie in 'On Gods and Gardeners' (in *Contemporary Philosophic Thought*, Vol. 3: *Perspectives in Education, Religion and the Arts*, [ed.] H. E. Kiefer), insists that Wisdom's main point is that sophisticated believers and non-believers no longer debate the now spurious question of whether there is a reality called 'God' or not (see p. 107). The debate now is rather one about the character of the world. However, I think K. Nielsen's claim that the disputes can be about both simulta-

neously is well taken. (See his 'On Waste and Wastelands' in the same volume, especially p. 118).

35. Ibid., p. 50–4.

36. Antony Flew, in the 'University Discussion', in *New Essays in Philosophical Theology,* op. cit., p. 96.

37. Ibid., p. 97.

38. It might just be pointed out here that Flew's parable does not so much prove religious assertions to be meaningless as it tends to show them to be false. That is, signals of the divine are so meagre and weak in his picture of the world that one would be forced to conclude that God does not exist. And it is a moot point as to whether his parable parallels the situation in the real world.

39. J. A. Passmore in writing on Christianity and positivism some years ago remarked: 'The deadness of logical positivism is more like the deadness of a dead metaphor than it is like the deadness of phlogiston theory.... [A] dead metaphor can spring into renewed life in a particular context; positivism is most alive where it touches religion' ('Christianity and Positivism', in the *Australasian Journal of Philosophy,* 35 [1957], p. 128). R. S. Laura much more recently claims that 'the remnants of positivist doctrine still exert considerable influence in the philosophical world, and theologians in particular are acutely aware of the perennial polemics bandied about in many theological discussions' ('The Positivist Poltergeist and Some Difficulties with Wittgensteinian Liberation', in the *International Journal for the Philosophy of Religion,* 2 [1971]: p. 186). Whereas Laura claims that influence to be oppressive and illegitimate (resting on an uncritical acceptance of the synthetic/analytic distinction), W. H. Austin sees it as neither oppressive nor illegitimate (in 'Religious Commitment and the Logical Status of Doctrines', in *Religious Studies,* 9 [1973]: p. 39). Diamond stands in the tradition of Laura while I fall in with Austin, but we both agree with Passmore that positivism's influence, positively or negatively, is not yet over.

40. The problems here have been clearly delineated by the positivists themselves. See C. G. Hempel's 'Empiricist Criteria of Cognitive Significance: Problems and Changes', in his *Aspects of Scientific Explanation,* (New York: Macmillan, 1965), pp. 101–19.

41. See here, for example, the claim of K. Nielsen in his *Contemporary Critiques of Religion* (New York: Macmillan, 1971), p. 56. It is clear, however, that I do not agree with Nielsen's further claim (on the same page) that those terms of verification need be observable, empirical terms. This issue cannot be taken up here. I refer the reader to three discussions of that issue: E. L. Mascal's *Christian Theology and Natural Science,* (London: Ronald Press, 1956), especially pp. 81 ff.; M. Polyani's Terry Lectures published as *The Tacit Dimension,* (Garden City: Doubleday, 1967), especially chapter 1; and Jean Ladriere's *Language and Belief,* (New York: Macmillan, 1972).

42. J. A. Martin, *The New Dialogue Between Theology and Philosophy,* (London: A. & C. Black, 1966), p. 64.

43. I have treated this issue at length elsewhere. See my 'Comprehensively Critical Rationalism and Commitment', in *Philosophical Studies,*

21 (1973): 186–201; 'Explanation and Theological Method', in *Zygon*, 11 (1976): 35–49; and 'Is Religious Belief Problematic?' in *Christian Scholar's Review*, 7 (1977): 22-35. All three papers are reprinted in this present volume (Chapters 1, 4, and 2 respectively).

44. R. Jenson, op. cit., p. 133. See also on this score H. Owen, *The Christian Knowledge of God*, (London: Athlone Press, 1969), especially pp. 16, 17.

45. R. M. Hare, op. cit., p. 99.

46. B. Mitchell, 'Theology and Falsification', in *New Essays in Philosophical Theology*, op. cit., pp. 103, 104.

47. This is brought out even more clearly by W. Austin in his comparison of central religious beliefs to the inner core beliefs of Lakatosian 'research programmes.' See his 'Religious Commitment and the Logical Status of Doctrines', op. cit.

48. B. Mitchell, op. cit., p. 105.

4 EXPLANATION AND THEOLOGICAL METHOD

1. Hans Reichenbach, *The Rise of Scientific Philosophy* (Berkeley: University of California Press, 1951).

2. The phrase is G. F. Woods'; see his *Theological Explanation* (Welwyn, Hertfordshire: James Nisbet, 1958).

3. Carl G. Hempel, *Aspects of Scientific Explanation* (New York: Crowell Collier & Macmillan, 1965).

4. Woods appears to have taken it as such: 'The acid test of any explanation is whether it explains.... [If] a steady scrutiny of a proffered explanation shows that matters remain obscure, we cannot escape from the obscurity by calling what is offered an "explanation" of the problem' (Woods, op. cit., p. 38). This lack of interest in non-psychological criteria characterizes his book. Although a serious flaw, it nevertheless does draw attention to the oversight of the importance of the psychological element in explanation.

5. Michael Scriven, 'Explanations, Predictions and Laws,' in *Readings in the Philosophy of Science*, (ed.), B. A. Brody (Englewood Cliffs, NJ: Prentice-Hall, 1970), pp. 88–104. The deductive model seems to imply a symmetry of explanation and prediction, as is particularly clear in R. B. Braithwaite, *Scientific Explanation* (New York: Harper, 1953), pp. 335, 337. Such a thesis is clearly undermined, I think, by the analyses offered by Stephen Toulmin, *Foresight and Understanding* (New York: Harper & Row, 1961), pp. 38, 60, and by N. R. Hanson, 'On the Symmetry between Explanation and Prediction', *Philosophical Review* 68 (1959): 349–58.

6. Scriven, op. cit., p. 97.

7. Ibid., p. 99. Indeed, according to Scriven, not even Hempel's own paradigm of a good, physical science explanation (Cf. Hempel, op. cit., p. 246) truly fits the deductive-nomologlcal pattern.

8. Scriven, op. cit., p. 90.

9. Reichenbach, op. cit., p. 9.

10. See Dietrich Bonhoeffer, *Letters and Papers from Prison* (London: William Collins, 1967), pp. 103–4.

11. Braithwaite, op. cit., p. 347.

12. Ian Ramsey, *Religion and Science: Conflict and Synthesis* (London: SPCK, 1964), p. 79.

13. See, e.g., A. Flew, *God and Philosophy* (New York: Dell Publishing, 1969), p. 194; and P. J. McGrath, 'Professor Flew and the Stratonician Presumption', *Philosophical Studies* 1 (1969): 150–9.

14. As quoted in *The Encyclopedia of Philosophy*, Paul Edwards (ed.), 8 vols. (New York: Macmillan, 1967), 8:299.

15. John Baillie, *The Sense of the Presence of God* (London: Oxford University Press, 1962), pp. 52–3.

16. Ibid., p. 100.

17. Ibid., p. 8.

18. C. B. Martin, 'A Religious Way of Knowing', in *New Essays in Philosophical Theology*, A. Flew and A. MacIntyre (eds), (New York: Macmillan, 1955), pp. 212–26.

19. C. J. Ducasse, *A Philosophical Scrutiny of Religion* (New York: Ronald Press, 1953), p. 148.

20. See D. M. MacKay, 'Christianity in a Mechanistic Universe', in *Christianity in a Mechanistic Universe and Other Essays* (London: Inter-Varsity Fellowship, 1965), pp. 11–48; and '"Complementarity" in Scientific and Theological Thinking', *Zygon* 9 (1974): 225–44.

21. John Baillie, *Our Knowledge of God* (London: Oxford University Press, 1939).

22. This thesis has seen some significant disagreement; however see P. T. Mora, 'Urge and Molecular Biology', *Nature* 199 (1963): 212–19.

23. James Richmond, *Theology and Metaphysics* (London: SCM Press, 1970), p. 108.

24. Ibid., p. 2.

25. Edwards, op. cit., p. 301.

26. Ibid. M. Heidegger is quite right, therefore, in claiming that Christians cannot ask the question he himself considers the fundamental philosophical question, namely, 'Why is there anything at all rather than nothing?' (Cf. *Introduction to Metaphysics* [New Haven, Conn.: Yale University Press, 1959], pp. 6–8). But what sense that question makes is altogether another matter.

27. R. S. Heimbeck, *Theology and Meaning: A Critique of Metatheological Scepticism* (London: George Allen & Unwin, 1969), p. 53.

28. Richmond, op. cit., pp. 130–1.

29. Ibid., p. 133.

5   SCIENCE AND RELIGION: IS COMPATIBILITY POSSIBLE?

1. Cf. Eric L. Mascal, *Christian Theology and Natural Science: Some Questions in Their Relations*, (Hamden, Conn.: Archon Books, 1965), p. 31, 32.

2. See I. Scheffler, *Science and Subjectivity* (Indianapolis: Bobbs-Merrill, 1967); and W. W. Bartley, *Retreat to Commitment* (New York: A. Knopf, 1962).
3. The concept of a morality of knowledge is not new. It was first used in the last century by William Clifford ('The Ethics of Belief', in G. Mavrodes [ed.], *The Rationality of Belief in God*, [Prentice-Hall, 1970], pp. 152–60). The idea refers both to the intimate connection between belief and action and to the act of believing in itself. It is argued, that is, that there is a moral demand upon us, in all the claims we make, to be as clear as possible about what we are or are not saying, and that we hold all such claims open to *criticism*. The scientists, then, are asking the theologians to be as clear in these regards as they are themselves. See also R. N. Chisholm, 'Epistemic Statements and the Ethics of Belief', *Philosophy and Phenomenological Research*, 16 (1956): 442–60; V. A. Harvey, *The Historian and the Believer: The Morality of Historical Knowledge and Christian Belief*, (New York: Macmillan, 1966); and I. Lakatos, 'Falsification and the Methodology of Scientific Research Programmes', in I. Lakatos and R. Musgrave (eds), *Criticism and the Growth of Knowledge*, (Cambridge: Cambridge University Press, 1970), pp. 91–196.
4. The concept is from N. Smart, *The Science of Religion and the Sociology of Knowledge*, (Princeton: Princeton University Press, 1973), pp. 82, 83.
5. There is no suggestion here that the typology is exhaustive. There may be other different and more fruitful ways of interpreting the vast literature on the subject. I have found this particular classification helpful here.
6. See R. B. Braithwaite, *An Empiricist's View of the Nature of Religious Belief*, (Cambridge: Cambridge University Press, 1955).
7. See T. R. Miles, *Religion and the Scientific Outlook*, (London: Allen & Unwin, 1959).
8. See D. Evans, *The Logic of Self-Involvement*, (London: SCM Press, 1963); and his 'Differences Between Scientific and Religious Assertions' in I. G. Barbour (ed.), *Science and Religion*, (New York: Harper & Row, 1968), pp. 101–33.
9. See Wm. F. Zuurdeeg, *An Analytical Philosophy of Religion*, (London: Allen & Unwin, 1959).
10. See J. H. Randall, *The Role of Knowledge in Western Religion*, (Boston: Starr King Press, 1958).
11. Miles, op. cit., pp. 217, 218, 219.
12. K Heim, *Christian Faith and the Natural Science*, (New York: Harper, 1953).
13. Ibid., pp. 190–1.
14. Ibid., p. 170.
15. Ibid., p. 192.
16. M. Diamond, *Contemporary Philosophy and Religious Thought*, (New York: McGraw Hill, 1974), p. 303.
17. S. Kierkegaard, *Concluding Unscientific Postscript*, (Princeton: Princeton University Press, 1941).
18. L. Gilkey, *Religion and the Scientific Future*, (New York: Harper & Row, 1970).

19. L. Gilkey, *Naming the Whirlwind*, (Indianapolis: Bobbs-Merrill, 1969).
20. For a similar analysis consult A. Greeley, *Unsecular Man: The Persistence of Religion*, (New York: Dell, 1974).
21. Gilkey, op. cit., 1970; p. 60, 61.
22. Ibid., p. 77.
23. K. Cauthen argues the same case in his *Science, Secularization and God*, (Nashville: Abingdon Press, 1969), pp. 13–15, et passim.
24. Gilkey, op. cit., 1970; pp. 92, 95.
25. Ibid., p. 99.
26. R. Burhoe, 'The Concepts of God and Soul in a Scientific View of Human Purpose', *Zygon* 8 (1973): 412–42.
27. Harvey, op. cit.
28. Scheffler, op. cit.
29. Ibid., p. v.
30. By 'justify', I mean here 'to make acceptable'. In this sense I regard K. Popper's talk of falsification as a procedure for making some claims (tentatively) acceptable. Space does not permit an analysis of Popper's claims here. I refer the reader to, *inter alia*, P. Achinstein, 'Review of K. R. Popper's *Conjectures and Refutations*', *British Journal for the Philosophy of Science* 19 (1968): 159–68; S. C. Thakur, 'Popper on Scientific Method,' *Philosophical Studies*, 18 (1970); and W. Kneale, 'Scientific Revolutions for Ever?' *British Journal for the Philosophy of Science*, 19 (1967): 22–42.
31. It is assumed here that knowledge can be radically distinguished from belief – only the former having certitude. I have subjected this assumption to critical analysis elsewhere and will not repeat the argument here. Suffice it to say that I see this distinction to be philosophically unsound; belief and knowledge exist on the same continuum. See my 'Is Religious Belief Problematic?', *Christian Scholar's Review*, 7 (1977): 23–35, – reprinted in this volume (Chapter 2).
32. See F. C. S. Schiller, 'Scientific Discovery and Logical Proof', in Charles Singer (ed.), *Studies in the History and the Methods of the Sciences*, (London: Wm. Dawson, 1955), pp. 235–89.
33. This is the burden of M. Polanyi's argument throughout his *Personal Knowledge: Towards a Post-Critical Philosophy*, (New York: Harper & Row, 1958) as well as of his other writings.
34. H. K. Schilling, *Science and Religion: An Interpretation of Two Communities*, (London: Allen & Unwin, 1963).
35. Ibid. Similar theses are maintained by C. Coulson, *Science and Christian Belief*, (London: Collins Fontana, 1961), and in his 'The Similarity of Science and Religion', in I. G. Barbour (ed.), *Science and Religion*, (New York: Harper & Row, 1969); I. T. Ramsey, *Religion and Science: Conflict and Synthesis*, (London: SPCK, 1964); I. G. Barbour, *Issues in Science and Religion*, (Englewood Cliffs, NJ: Prentice-Hall, 1966); as well as by a host of others.
36. Th. van Baaren and H. Drijvers (eds), *Religion, Culture, and Methodology*, (The Hague: Mouton, 1973).
37. P. L. Berger, *The Sacred Canopy: Elements of a Sociology of Religion*, (Garden City: Doubleday, 1967).

38.　M. Yinger, *The Scientific Study of Religion*, (New York: Macmillan, 1970), p. 531.
39.　E. Durkheim, *Elementary Forms of the Religious Life*, (London: Allen & Unwin, 1971), p. 430.
40.　Yinger, op. cit., p. 61; see also pp. 93, 94.
41.　Cf. N. Smart, *The Religious Experience of Mankind*, (London: Collins Fontana, 1969).
42.　I have dealt with the issue of religious explanation in my 'Explanation and Theological Method', *Zygon*, 11 (1976): 35–49, reprinted in this volume (Chapter 4).
43　The assumption of methodological atheism arises in a variety of works by Berger: *The Precarious Vision: An Essay on Social Perception and Christian Faith*, (Garden City: Doubleday, 1961); *The Sacred Canopy: Elements of a Sociology of Religion*, (Garden City: Doubleday, 1967); *A Rumour of Angels*, (Harmondsworth: Penguin, 1969); and with T. Luckmann, *The Social Construction of Reality*, (Harmondsworth: Penguin, 1971).
44.　For further discussion of this issue see my 'Is A Science of Religion Possible?' *Studies in Religion*, 7 (1978): 5–17.
45.　Smart, op. cit., 1973; p. 22, 23.
46.　A thesis similar to Gilkey's is to be found in the works of J. Ellul, especially in his *The Technological Society*, (New York: Random House, 1964), as well as in P. Slater's *The Pursuit of Loneliness* (Boston: Beacon Press, 1970), his *Earthwalk* (New York: Doubleday, 1974), and also in A. Wheelis's *The End of the Modern Age*, (New York: Harper & Row, 1971), and his *The Moralist*, (Harmondsworth: Penguin, 1973). I do not, however, find myself in full agreement with the thesis as Gilkey frames it. According to Gilkey, the myth asserts that humans become human and can control their destiny if they become properly educated, providing knowledge which can change what had previously been a blind determining force over humanity into its instrument. But this is not what such advocates of the 'myth' in fact proclaim. Such a picture of the new 'myth-makers,' applied indescriminately to all philosophers of science, is extremely crude. What the 'secular person' says, it seems to me, is not that people can control their destiny, but that since there is no one else (i.e. some great magician or divinity of whom we are aware as controlling our destinies for our benefit) to look after them, humans must, if they are to survive, do this themselves. And the best way of proceeding in this task is to know as much as possible about the nature of the physical and social worlds we encounter. As Karl Popper has put it, to suggest that people cannot and must not make changes and must not attempt to 'remake' the world is to offer a very poor solution, or none at all, to the problems they face (see Popper's *The Poverty of Historicism*, [London: Routledge & Kegan Paul, 1957] and *The Open Society and its Enemies*, 2 vols. [New York: Harper & Row, 1962]). It is due to advice such as this that so many cry out against a return to theology (e.g., S. Hook, *The Quest for Being*, [New York: St. Martin's Press, 1961], and E. Nagel, *The Structure of Science*, [London: Routledge & Kegan Paul, 1961] and others). To be

sure, control must be wielded over the 'controllers', as Gilkey puts it, But that control also is a human control. (See here particularly the section entitled 'The Principle of Leadership' in chapter seven of Popper, op. cit., 1962.) Thus Popper, among others, in direct contrast to Gilkey, claims on behalf of the rationalist the lofty aim of bringing about a more reasonable world – a society that aims at humaneness and reasonableness; at a reduction of war, strife, etc.; at equality and freedom; a world in which one day people 'may even become the conscious creators of an open society, and thereby of a greater part of their fate' (Popper, op. cit., 1962; Vol. 2, p. 94). Neither the intention nor the result of rationalist action then is, as Gilkey has depicted it, necessarily tyrannical. Its intention, and possibly the result as well, is to lead people from a 'closed society' in which their fate is almost totally controlled by others, to the 'open society' in which the individual comes increasingly to direct his or her own fate.

47. F. Shuon, *The Transcendent Unity of Religions*, (New York: Harper & Row, 1975), p. 8.
48. See Mascal, op. cit.
49. See M. Polanyi, op. cit.; T. Kuhn, *The Structure of Scientific Revolutions*, (Chicago: University of Chicago Press, 1962); and P. Feyerabend, *Against Method: Outline of an Anarchistic Theory of Knowledge*, in M. Radner and S. Winoker (eds), *Minnesota Studies in the Philosophy of Science*, Vol. 4 (Minneapolis: University of Minnesota Press, 1970). Similar suggestions are to be found in R. Nash, *The Nature of the Natural Sciences*, (New York: Little, Brown, 1963); J. M. Ziman, *Public Knowledge*, (Cambridge: Cambridge University Press, 1968); and Errol Harris, *Hypothesis and Perception: The Root of Scientific Method*, (London: Allen & Unwin, 1970).

6 RELIGION TRANSCENDING SCIENCE TRANSCENDING RELIGION …

1. See Robert W. Friedrichs, 'Social Research and Theology: End of Detente?' *Review of Religious Research*, 15 (1974): 113–27.
2. I have surveyed this literature to some extent in my essay 'Science and Religion: Is Compatibility Possible?' *Journal of the American Scientific Affiliation*, 30 (1978): 169–76, reprinted in this volume (Chapter 5).
3. See especially James R. Moore's *The Post-Darwinian Controversies: A Study of the Protestant Struggle to Come to Terms with Darwin in Great Britain and America, 1870–1900* (Cambridge: Cambridge University Press, 1979).
4. My account of Shestov's position here draws, with permission, on my critical note on Shestov entitled, 'Being Faithful and Being Reasonable as Mutually Exclusive,' to be found in *Ultimate Reality and Meaning* 7 (1984): 166–9.
5. Shestov, *Potestas Clavium*, (Chicago: Henry Regnery Company, 1968).
6. Ibid., p. 3.

7. Ibid., p. 29.
8. Ibid., p. 11. This formulation reminds one of the thesis put forward by
    Thorlieff Boman in his *Hebrew Thought Compared with Greek*, (London:
    SCM, 1950). That thesis has been under heavy fire for some time (see, for
    example, James Barr's *The Semantics of Biblical Language*, [London:
    Oxford University Press, 1961]) and alternative readings of the differ-
    ence between the two cultures have been offered: e.g., D. M. Macdonald,
    The Hebrew Philosophic Genius, (Russell and Russell, 1965); Claude
    Tresmontant, *A Study of Hebrew Thought*, (New York: Desclée, 1960); and
    his *The Origins of Christian Philosophy*, (New York: Hawthorne Books,
    1963). Nevertheless, there is some life left in Boman's suggestions, I
    think, especially in his reference to the Lévy-Bruhlian notion of Hebrew
    thought as a kind of prelogical thought (Boman, op. cit., p. 195). How-
    ever, I gave that whole matter, including discussions of the nature of the
    thought-life throughout the ancient Near East, close attention in my
    book *The Irony of Theology and the Nature of Religious Thought*, (Montreal:
    McGill-Queen's Press, 1991).
9. Shestov, *Kierkegaard and the Existential Philosophy*, (Athens: Ohio
    University Press, 1969).
10. Ibid., pp. 264–5.
11. Ibid., p. 235.
12. Shestov, op. cit., 1968; pp. 154–5.
13. Shestov, op. cit., 1969a; p. 308.
14. Shestov, op. cit., 1968: p. 257.
15. Shestov, *Athens and Jerusalem*, (Athens: Ohio University Press, 1969),
    pp. 70 and 98.
16. Shestov, op. cit., 1969; p. 185.
17. Ibid., p. 306.
18. Ibid., p. 295. Of relevance to this point is Shestov's critique of Plato in
    Athens and Jerusalem. Plato erred, he insists, in seeking proofs to con-
    vince others of 'his' revelation: 'But it is precisely because and inas-
    much as Plato wished to make his revelation a truth that constrains, a
    truth obligatory for all ...' (op. cit., 1969; p. 109) that he leaves himself
    open to 'the fall'; '... Plato did not succeed in bringing back to men
    what he had found beyond the limits of all possible knowledge. When
    he tried to show men what he had seen, the thing changed itself mys-
    teriously under his eyes into its contrary' (p. 116).
        Although the revelation of God, then, has no justification, neither
    does reason, for it provides the framework for all justifications (see
    p. 164). On this point Shestov and Gellner, as I shall soon indicate, are
    in entire agreement.
        For a somewhat similar interpretation, although not evaluation, see
    J. C. S. Wernham's *Two Russian Thinkers: An Essay in Berdyaev and
    Shestov*, (Toronto: University of Toronto Press, 1968), especially pp. 63ff.
19. Shestov, op. cit., 1969; p. 282.
20. Ibid. p. 305. Shestov maintains that this was done first by Philo for
    Judaism: 'Philo praised Holy Scripture to the skies but in praising it he
    delivered it into the hands of Greek philosophy' (op. cit., 1969, p. 42).
    Shestov argues in *Kierkegaard* that Hegel did the same to Christianity

much later. This theme is repeatedly raised by Shestov as well in his *Potestas Clavium*. The Catholics, he argues here, are obviously the most 'hellenized' (p. 48), but so also, he insists, are the Protestants (p. 101).

21. Ibid., p. 299–300.
22. Ibid., p. 299. That it is not an appropriate bridge was certainly sensed by some medievals like St Bernard. See, for example. J. Leclerc's *The Love of Learning and the Desire for God*, (New York: New American Library, 1962), especially chapter 9 on monastic theology; and several essays by B. Nelson in his *On the Roads to Modernity: Conscience, Science and Civilization*, (Totowa, NJ: Rowman & Littlefield, 1981). A recent but weak counter-proposal is offered by A. Louth in *Discerning the Mystery: An Essay on the Nature of Theology*, (Oxford: Clarendon Press, 1983). Indeed, Louth's thesis seems to call for a return to Bernard's way of doing theology rather than Abelard's way of doing it. This matter, however, is the focus of another argument and cannot be pursued here.
23. Ibid., p. 321. See also Shestov, op. cit., 1969; p. 27.
24. Ibid., p. 307.
25. Shestov, op. cit., 1969; pp. 76 and 135.
26. Ibid., p. 94. Shestov here describes faith as the loss of reason in order to find God. See also Shestov, op. cit., 1969; p. 323.
27. Shestov, op. cit., 1969; p. 325.
28. The assumption of rational argument would, of course, pinch the real nonrationalist and Shestov does not feel bound to adopt it. The reason is obvious, for to assume rational argument to destroy it one must originally be bound by the accepted criteria of reasoning. Further, to assume the criteria to undermine the criteria is not itself a coherent project and so seems to preclude adopting the original assumption. The conundrums involved here are not new. And Shestov's relation to them seems to foreshadow much in contemporary literary criticism, particularly in respect of the deconstructionist literature of authors such as Barthes, Foucault and especially Derrida. The problems this presents for theology have only recently been explored in a rather superficial manner: see, for example, M. C. Taylor's *Deconstructing Theology*, (Atlanta, Ga: Scholars Press, 1982) and the volume of essays, (eds, T. J. J. Altizer. et al.) *De-construction and Theology*, (New York: Crossroad Press, 1982).
29. Shestov, op. cit., 1969b, p. 288.
30. Many see such a recognition of the inadequacy of philosophy to salvation as the point at which Christian revelation can be added to philosophy as its necessary complement. Obviously, as I point out immediately below, it is precisely that kind of thesis against which Shestov sets himself here as being seductive and dangerous. Louis J. Shein commits such an error of interpretation in his 'The Philosophy of Infinite Possibility: An Examination of Lev Shestov's Weltanschauung,' in *Ultimate Reality and Meaning*, 2 (1979).
31. E. Gellner, 'The Savage and the Modern Mind', in R. Horton and R. Finnegan (eds) *Modes of Thought: Essays on Thinking in Western and Non-Western Societies*, (London: Faber & Faber, 1973a), pp. 162–81.

32. E. Gellner, *Legitimation of Belief*, (Cambridge: Cambridge University Press, 1974), p. 170.
33. Ibid., p. 29.
34. E. Gellner, *Spectacles and Predicaments: Essays in Social Theory*, (Cambridge: Cambridge University Press, 1979), p. 1.
35. Gellner, op. cit., 1974, p. 174.
36. Gellner, op. cit., 1979, p. 175.
37. Ibid., p. 182.
38. Gellner, op. cit., 1974, p. 127.
39. I have developed this theme in an as yet unpublished paper, 'In Two Minds: Religion and Philosophy in Ancient Greece', read at the American Academy of Religion's Mid-West Regional Meeting meeting, April 1990.
40. Gellner, op. cit., 1974, p. 189.
41. Ibid., pp. 106 and 132.
42. Gellner, op. cit., 1979, pp. 7–8. See also Gellner, 1974, pp. 99, 107, and 151.
43. Gellner, op. cit., 1974, p. 127.
44. This seems to be the kind of counsel offered by J. Ellul in his analysis of modern technological society, (in, for example, his *The Technological Society*, [New York: Vintage Books, 1961], and elsewhere) but the 'sentiments' are radically different. Ellul 'rejects' knowledge and affirms faith in a fashion not dissimilar to Shestov (See especially Ellul's *Living Faith*, [New York: Harper & Row, 1980]). A more popular response of the same kind can be found in A. Wheelis's persuasive *The End of the Modern Age*, (New York: Harper & Row, 1971). See also F. J. Moreno's *Between Faith and Reason*, (New York: Harper & Row, 1977). From a psychological point of view similar problems are raised by E. Becker, especially in his *The Denial of Death*, (New York: Free Press, 1973).
45. See Gellner, op. cit., 1979, p. 205.
46. E. Gellner, *Cause and Meaning in the Social Sciences*, (London: Routledge & Kegan Paul, 1973b), p. 50.
47. For further elaboration see Gellner, op. cit., 1979, pp. 177–8 and Gellner, op. cit., 1973b, p. 69.
48. This does not, however, commit the scientist/rationalist to assuming that science will be, as it is often stated, the saviour of humanity. It does mean, however, that there is no longer a passive dependence on some agency other than human persons, on whom the world, so to speak, rests. To survive, persons must act and such action, it is claimed by the rationalists, is more successful the more accurate and complete the knowledge on which it rests. Consequently the scientific response to life is not one of offering some absolute solution to life's problems but does urge an active, informed reaction to the problems and therefore it *transcends* religion/theology that, in the final analysis, counsels dependence and passivity. See on this score, for example, S. Hook's *Quest for Being*, (New York: St. Martin's Press, 1969); E. Nagel's *The Structure of Science*, (London: Routledge & Kegan Paul, 1961); and K. R. Popper's *The Poverty of Historicism*, (London: Routledge & Kegan Paul, 1957) and also *The Open Society and Its Enemies*, 2 vols, (New York: Harper & Row, 1962).

49. Gellner, op. cit., 1974, pp. 111–22.
50. Gellner, op. cit., 1973b, p. 73.
51. Gellner, op. cit., 1979, p. 6. See also his 1974, p. 101.
52. A strong case for such 'idealism' in anthropology, however, is set out by Malcolm Crick in his *Explorations in Language and Meaning: Towards a Semantic Anthropology*, (London: Malaby Press, 1976). A critique of Crick's argument, however, cannot be undertaken here.

7   IS SCIENCE REALLY AN IMPLICIT RELIGION ?

1. This chapter was originally a paper prepared for the tenth annual 'Implicit Religion Consultation' held at Denton Hall, Ilkley, 9 May 1987. It combines aspects of two earlier papers, 'Science and Religion: Is Compatibility Possible?' *Journal of the American Scientific Affiliation*, 30 (1978): 169–76 and 'Incommensurable and Incompatible: Some Programmatic Comments on the Nature of the Relationship Between Scientific and Religious Thought' (read to the Triangle Club, Cambridge University, 6 March 1987 – unpublished). The position taken here and in the last-mentioned paper controverts the thesis of the 1978 essay. I wish to thank the members of the Triangle Club and participants at the Denton Consultation for their critical comments. Even though I have not incorporated their points of view here, I have been much assisted by them in reformulating various aspects of the argument for publication. My thanks also to the anonymous *Studies in Religion* assessor for suggestions that helped clarify the central thrust of the argument and its mode of expression.
2. See here my 'Religion Transcending Science Transcending Religion ...', *Dalhousie Review*, 65 (1986): 196–7; reprinted in this volume (Chapter 6). Since writing this essay, *God and Nature: Historical Essays on the Encounter Between Christianity and Science*, edited by David C. Lindberg and Ronald L. Numbers (Berkeley: University of California Press, 1986), has come to my attention. Though conceived as an exercise in correcting the historical record with respect to the relationship of the scientific and religious communities, it is unpersuasive in the claims it makes. A close analysis of many of the essays included in the volume reveals a reliance upon, or assumption of, the very conflict thesis they were meant to undermine. Unfortunately analyses of those essays cannot be undertaken here.
3. Langdon Gilkey, *Naming the Whirlwind* (Indianapolis: Bobbs-Merrill, 1969).
4. Gilkey, *Religion and the Scientific Future* (New York: Harper & Row, 1970), pp. 60–1.
5. Ibid., p. 77.
6. Ibid., p. 99.
7. See, for example, Karl R. Popper, *The Poverty of Historicism* (London: Routledge & Kegan Paul, 1957), and his *The Open Society and Its Enemies*, 2 vols. (New York: Harper & Row, 1962).

8. See here particularly the section entitled 'The Principle of Leadership' in chapter 7 of Popper's *The Open Society*. It is because of advice like Gilkey's that so many react vehemently to the call for a return to theology. See, for example, Sydney Hook, *The Quest for Being* (New York: St. Martin's Press, 1961).

9. Popper, op. cit., 1962, Vol 2., p. 94.

10. See, for example, T. R. Miles, *Religion and the Scientific Outlook* (London: Allen & Unwin, 1959), or, more recently, the position implicitly adopted by N. Frye in his *The Great Code: The Bible and Literature*, (Toronto: Academic Press Canada, 1982).

11. See, for example, Karl Heim, *Christian Faith and Natural Science* (New York: Harper, 1953).

12. Such traditional apologetics can be found in the past (for example, in William Paley) and in the present (in the work of contemporary scientific creationists).

13. In my own earlier work I, like many others, attempted to work along these lines as can be seen especially in my '"Comprehensively Critical Rationalism" and Commitment', *Philosophical Studies*, 21 (1973): 186–201; 'Explanation and Theological Method', *Zygon*, 11 (1976): 35–49; and 'Is Religious Belief Problematic?', *Christian Scholars Review*, 7 (1977): 23–35 – all of which are reprinted in this volume (Chapters 1, 4, and 2 respectively).

14. N. Frye, I think, would have no problem with this as I make clear in my 'The "Centripetal Theology" of *The Great Code*', *Toronto Journal of Theology*, 1 (1985): 122–7, reprinted in this volume (Chapter 14). T. R. Miles, it seems to me, would not find this palatable.

15. D. Wiebe, 'The Prelogical Mentality Revisited', *Religion*, 17 (1987): 29–61.

16. This essay, together with that referred to in the previous note, constitute the foundation of a larger work (in progress) that attempts to show the essentially mythopoeic character of religious thought. [Subsequently published as *The Irony of Theology and the Nature of Religious Thought*, (Montreal and Kingston: McGill-Queen's Press, 1991).]

17. This phrase is borrowed from Peter Munz, *Our Knowledge of the Growth of Knowledge: Popper or Wittgenstein?* (London: Routledge & Kegan Paul, 1985).

18. It also needs saying, I think, that the value of catechismic beliefs does not seem to depend on their being true since religious beliefs that most of us think false are still of value to those who still believe them to be true. I do not here follow Munz who argues that such beliefs must be false if they are to fulfil their function. On the everyday, material object level of existence, of course, there is near universal consensus concerning knowledge of certain aspects of the physical world, acquired early in infancy (or even earlier through genetic inheritance) but it is not belief at this level that operates catechismically. And there does not seem to be a second-order theoretical interest in the primitive mind with respect to this order of reality.

19. See E. Gellner, 'Concepts and Society', in D. Emmet and A. MacIntyre (eds), *Sociological Theory and Philosophical Analysis* (New York: Macmillan, 1970), pp. 115–49.

20. See here Gellner, 'The Savage and the Modern Mind', in Robin Horton and Ruth Finnegan (eds) *Modes of Thought: Essays on Thinking in Western and Non-Western Societies* (London: Faber & Faber, 1973), pp. 162–87.
21. I. C. Jarvie, *Rationality and Relativism: In Search of a Philosophy and History of Anthropology* (London: Routledge & Kegan Paul, 1984), p. 34.
22. Ibid., p. 105.
23. Compare here views dominated by a 'Wittgensteinian fideism'.
24. See here the essay referred to in note 2 above.
25. This work is undertaken in the book referred to in note 15 above: *The Irony of Theology and the Nature of Religious Thought*.

8 RELIGION, SCIENCE, AND THE TRANSFORMATION OF 'KNOWLEDGE'

1. I have in mind here historians like James F. Moore who argues that the use of warfare imagery in discussions of the relationship of religion to science is wholly inappropriate. See here especially his *The Post-Darwinian Controversies: A Study of the Protestant Struggle to Come to Terms with Darwin in Great Britain and America, 1870–1900*, (Cambridge: Cambridge University Press, 1979). See also the introduction by David C. Lindberg and Ronald L. Numbers to their *God and Nature: Historical Essays on the Encounter Between Christianity and Science*, (Berkeley: University of California Press, 1986).
2. I have developed this argument at greater length in my book *The Irony of Theology and the Nature of Religious Thought*, (Montreal: McGill-Queen's University Press, 1991).
3. See here my 'Science and Religion: Is Compatibility Possible?' *Journal of the American Scientific Affiliation*, 30 (1978): 169–76, reprinted in this volume (Chapter 5).
4. On the matter of the religious nature of science, or lack of it, see my 'Is Science Really an Implicit Religion?' *Studies in Religion*, 18 (1989): 171–83, reprinted in this volume (Chapter 7).
5. Max Weber, 'Science as a Vocation', in Peter Lassman and Irving Velody (eds), *Max Weber's 'Science as a Vocation'*, (London: Unwin Hyman, 1989), p. 17. Italics are in the original.
6. Care must be taken in the use of the word *knowledge* for it has a different reference range, so to speak, in different contexts. The word is appropriately used to refer to the frameworks of understanding of the world in which archaic/primitive persons exist, even though much of what they took (take) to be knowledge would not constitute knowledge in the sense of 'scientific' knowledge. In this essay I shall use the word knowledge free of quotation marks to refer to scientific knowledge, and knowledge within quotation marks to designate 'the framework of understanding' in archaic cultures which constituted their 'knowledge'. Though aspects of the 'knowledge' of other cultures is isomorphic with modern scientific knowledge of the world, much

more is inconsistent with scientific knowledge. 'Knowledge', that is, is much broader in scope than is scientific knowledge.

7. Clifford Geertz, *Local Knowledge: Further Essays in Interpretive Anthropology,* (New York: Basic Books, 1983), p. 4. It seems to me that Geertz might more appropriately have entitled the book 'Local Knowledges' since there will be as many 'knowledges' as there are cultural systems.

8. Fredrik Barth, *Cosmologies in the Making: A Generative Approach to Cultural Variation in Inner New Guinea,* (Cambridge: Cambridge University Press, 1987), p. 19.

9. Ibid., p. 46.

10. Ibid., p. 66.

11. Ibid., p. 72.

12. Ibid., p. 73.

13. Ibid., p. 84.

14. A more nuanced and qualified picture of this development can be found in my *The Irony of Theology;* see n. 3 above.

15. *Phaedo* in *Plato, Five Dialogues,* G. M. A. Grube (trans.), (Indianapolis: Hackett, 1981), 96b.

16. Ibid., 97c.

17. Ibid., 98b.

18. Ibid., 98b.

19. Stanley Jeyaraja Tambiah, *Magic, Science, Religion, and the Scope of Rationality,* (Cambridge: Cambridge University Press, 1990), p. 108, emphasis added.

20. Ibid., p. 137, emphasis added.

21. Barth, op cit., p. 73.

22. I have in mind here the kinds of complaints to be found, for example, in Allen Wheelis's *The End of the Modern Age,* (New York: Harper & Row, 1971) or Morris Berman's *The Reenchantment of the World,* (Ithaca NY: Cornell University Press, 1981).

23. Paul Feyerabend, 'Notes on Relativism', in his *Farewell to Reason,* (London: Verso, 1987), p. 31.

24. Ibid., p. 72.

25. Ibid., p. 65.

26. Ibid., p. 73.

27. E. Gellner, 'The Savage and the Modern Mind', in Robin Horton and Ruth Finnegan (eds), *Modes of Thought: Essays on Thinking in Western and Non-Western Societies,* (London: Faber & Faber, 1973), p. 178.

28. E. Gellner, *Plough, Sword, and Book: The Structure of Human History,* (London: Collins Harvill, 1988), p. 214.

9   HAS PHILOSOPHY OF RELIGION A PLACE IN THE AGENDA OF THEOLOGY?

1. This essay was originally read at the Canadian Theological Society meeting held in Windsor, Ontario, 1988.

2. See Harry Austryn Wolfson, *The Philosophy of the Church Fathers: Faith Trinity, Incarnation* 3rd edn (Cambridge: Harvard University Press, 1976).

3. Diogenes Allen, *Philosophy for Understanding Theology*, (Atlanta: John Knox Press, 1985), p. iii.

4. Ibid., p. iv.

5. D. Wiebe, *The Irony of Theology and the Nature of Religious Thought*, (Montreal: McGill-Queen's Press, 1991). A central theme of that book, however, has been presented in my essay 'The Prelogical Mentality Revisited', *Religion* 18 (1988): 29–61.

6. See Edwin Hatch, *The Influence of Greek Ideas and Usages Upon the Christian Church*, (London: Williams & Norgate, 1888).

7. Ibid., p. 349.

8. Wolfson, op. cit., pp. 11–14.

9. Eric Osborn, *The Beginning of Christian Philosophy*, (Cambridge: Cambridge University Press, 1981).

10. Ibid., p. 4.

11. Ibid.

12. See A. H. Armstrong and R. A. Markus, *Christian Faith and Greek Philosophy* (London: Darton, Longman & Todd, 1960).

13. Osborn, op. cit., p. 4. Emphasis mine.

14. Michel Despland, *The Education of Desire: Plato and the Philosophy of Religion* (Toronto: University of Toronto Press, 1985), p. 203.

15. For a further discussion on this theme see the critique of Despland's thesis in my 'From the Open to the Closed Society? Michel Despland on the Philosophy of Religion', *Scottish Journal for Religious Studies* 9 (1988): 19–28.

16. E. Durkheim, *The Evolution of Educational Thought* (London: Routledge & Kegan Paul, 1977).

17. Ibid., p. 73.

18. Etienne Gilson, *The Philosopher and Theology*, (New York: Random House, 1962).

19. Ibid., p. 100.

20. Ibid., p. 101.

10 POSTULATIONS FOR SAFEGUARDIND PRECONCEPTIONS

1. Although I refer to the 'discipline' of 'Religious Studies' in this essay, I do so only because of the commonness of the locution. I have argued elsewhere that Religious Studies is not a discipline but rather a field of studies; see my 'Is a Science of Religion Possible?', *Studies in Religion*, vol. 7, 1978.

2. The philosophy of religion is not held in high esteem today. It receives little attention either in departments of philosophy or in departments of Religious Studies. The former seldom hire philosophers with primary expertise in this area and the latter see philosophy, like theology,

to be outside the boundaries of their 'discipline'. In part the intention of this chapter is to show the relevance and importance that this 'sub-discipline' can and ought to have.

3. Willard Van Orman Quine, *The Time of My Life*, (Boston: MIT Press, 1985).

4. See my 'The Failure of Nerve in the Academic Study of Religion', *Studies in Religion*, vol. 13, 1984.

5. Laurence J. O'Connell, 'Religious Studies, Theology and the Undergraduate Curriculum', *The Council on the Study of Religion Bulletin*, vol. 15, 1984; p. 146.

6. Ibid.; emphasis is mine. It is obvious, or so it would appear, that even the apparently 'predominantly religious studies' identity of the first-year course would also be, at bottom, essentially theological.

7. See W. H. Capps, 'Religious Studies/Theological Studies: The St. Louis Project'; L. J. O'Connell, 'Religious Studies, Theology and the Humanities Curriculum'; J. Neusner, 'Why Religious Studies in America? Why Now?'; P. J. Cahill, 'Theological Studies, Where Are You?'; and W. F. May, 'Why Theology and Religious Studies Need Each Other'. All are to be found in the *Journal of the American Academy of Religion*, vol. 52, 1984, pp. 727–57. The essay by Neusner seems 'out of step' with the otherwise common call for retheologizing of religious studies in the university.

8. See note 4 above.

9. Claude Welch, 'Identity Crisis in the Study of Religion? A First Report from the ACLS Study', *Journal of the American Academy of Religion*, vol. 39, 1971.

10. Some discussion of a number of such papers can be found in the 'Failure of Nerve' essay referred to in note 4 above.

11. C. A. Holbrook, 'Why an Academy of Religion?', *Journal of Bible and Religion*, vol. 32, 1964; see especially p. 100.

12. The report is also to be found in the volume containing Holbrook's above mentioned AAR Presidential Address.

13. Langdon Gilkey, 'The AAR and the Anxiety of Nonbeing: An Analysis of Our Present Cultural Situation', *Journal of the American Academy of Religion*, vol. 48, 1980, p. 17. This, by the way, is something Van A. Harvey, ten years earlier, predicted would happen, namely, the development of a *theology* in the context of graduate departments of religion – although he thought they would be non-Christian, more strictly philosophical, and *not* servants of the Church or Tradition. See on this score his 'Reflections on the Teaching of Religion in America', *Journal of the American Academy of Religion*, vol. 38, 1970.

14. Gordon Kaufman, 'Nuclear Eschatology and the Study of Religion', *Journal of the American Academy of Religion*, vol. 51, 1983, p. 13.

15. Ibid.

16. Wilfred Cantwell Smith, 'The Modern West in the History of Religions', *Journal of the American Academy of Religion*, vol. 52, 1984.

17. Ibid. p. 18.

18. I do not mean here simply to ignore the critiques of 'objectivity' by Polanyi, Kuhn, Feyerabend, and others. I am well aware that any simple espousal of 'objectivity' can become unacceptable 'objectivism'.

Nevertheless, it does seem to me that a kind of 'intersubjectivity' characterizes the claims we make/espouse in the sciences and it ought also to characterize claims made by the academic/scientific student of religion when making claims about religions or religion. We may never be able to construct a wholly value-free/bias-free study of any subject matter, but that fact does not constitute grounds for espousing any and every value-framework as equally acceptable for doing our science. As someone has put it, because a completely aseptic condition can never be obtained in the operating room is no reason for surgery to be done in a sewer.

19. See here the thesis of the above-mentioned 'Failure of Nerve' article (especially note 7), as well as the preface and introduction to my *Religion and Truth: Toward an Alternative Paradigm for the Study of Religion,* (Leiden: Mouton, 1981).

20. William Clebsch, 'Religious Studies Now: Not Why Not? But Why Not Not?', *Religious Education,* 1975. See also his AAR presidential address – somewhat of an anomaly amongst such addresses as one might guess, 'Apples, Oranges, and Manna: Comparative Religion Revisited', *Journal of the American Academy of Religion,* vol. 49, 1981.

11 PHILOSOPHICAL REFLECTIONS ON TWENTIETH-CENTURY MENNONITE THOUGHT

1. *The Mennonite Encyclopedia, A Comprehensive Reference Work on the Anabaptist/Mennonite Movement.* 4 vols. (Scottdale, Pa., Mennonite Publishing House, 1955–59), IV, 704–07.

2. J. B. Toews, 'Cultural and Intellectual Aspects of the Mennonite Experience In Russia', *Mennonite Quarterly Review* (henceforth *MQR*), 53 (1979): 137–59.

3. Ibid., p. 142.

4. Ibid., p. 140.

5. Ibid., p. 157.

6. I refer here, of course. to that constellation of belief, attitude, and practice that Harold S. Bender referred to as 'the Anabaptist vision'. Bender's article by that title was first published in *Church History* 13 (1944): 3–24, and has been reprinted numerous times. My reference to it here is to its reprinting in Guy F. Hershberger (ed.), *The Recovery of the Anabaptist Vision,* (Scottdale, Pa., Herald Press, 1957), pp. 29–54. Although Bender's paper is generally taken as authoritative, different views as to the essential character of Anabaptism have been raised. See, for example, Walter Klaassen, 'The Nature of the Anabaptist Protest', *MQR,* 45 (1974): 291–311; and J. A. Oosterbaan, 'The Reformation of the Reformation: Fundamentals of Anabaptist Theology', *MQR,* 51 (1977): 171–95.

7. Certainly this is true of Russian Mennonites as reference to J. B. Toews' research (op. cit.) indicates. Further historical research would be required, of course, to fully substantiate this more general claim.

8. C. Krahn, 'Prolegomena to an Anabaptist Theology', *MQR*, 24 (1950): 5–11.
9. Bender, op. cit., 1957, p. 40.
10. Ibid., p. 43.
11. Jarold Knox Zeman, 'Anabaptism: A Replay of Medieval Theses or a Prelude to the Modern Age?' *MQR*, 50 (1976): 259–71.
12. Zeman, op. cit., p. 270, suggests that unhindered critical inquiry is a criterion of modernity applicable only in the nineteenth and twentieth century and therefore not properly involved in assessing early Anabaptism. This appears rather naive in light of the philosophy of Descartes or Kant. Surely unhindered critical thought is of the essence of modernity at its birth.
13. I make particular reference to the Mennonite Brethren community since I am [was] a member of it. The events of relevance here are more familiar to me and I have in my possession some documentation that is not, as yet, available elsewhere.
14. John Braun, 'Manifesto of the Radical Mennonite Community', unpublished, 1969. This document is not in the Mennonite Brethren archives.
15. Ibid., p. 1.
16. Ibid., p. 2.
17. John Braun, 'A Radical Confession of Faith', unpublished, 1969. This document is not in the Mennonite Brethren archives.
18. Since no documentation about this group exists in the archives I have been unable to chart its destiny. From inquiries made it would appear that it has all but slipped from memory.
19. Donald Wiebe, 'This Way to an Exciting Christian Life', *Mennonite Brethren Herald* (henceforth *M. B. Herald*) 3 May 1968. Reprinted in George David Pries, *A Place Called Peniel: Winkler Bible Institute, 1925–75*, (Winkler Bible Institute, 1975). Reference here is made to it in the Pries volume: see p. 141.
20. The Winkler Bible Institute Committee or Executive was elected from a larger body, The Board of Christian Education for the M. B. Conference of Manitoba to whom they were directly responsible.
21. These phrases appear in the 'Winkler Bible Institute Bulletin,' sent out to all the churches of Manitoba as part of a public relations and fund-raising programme. This together with the other documents relating to this matter have been copied and placed in the M. B. archives at the M. B. College.
22. Board Minutes, 22 November 1968, p. 1.
23. Board Minutes, 16 December 1968, p. 1.
24. Letter of 'protest' of resigning faculty members to the Board of Reference and Counsel; 7 February 1969, p. 1.
25. Pries, op. cit., p. 143.
26. *Alumni Newsletter*, 2, 2 (undated): 1, 4.
27. 'Study Conference on the Bible', noted in the *M. B. Herald* (17 September 1976).
28. Ibid., p. 11.
29. 'Editorial' by Harold Jantz, *M. B. Herald* (17 September 1976).

30. Harold Jantz, 'Bible Teachers Test Their Views', *M. B. Herald* (7 January 1977), p. 12.
31. Ibid., p. 14.
32. John A. Toews, 'Introductory Message', *Direction*, 6 (1977): p. 4. The claim here seems somewhat naive. It assumes that clearing our minds of philosophical sophistication will save us from corruption. This is precisely the programme I attempt to expose here. Furthermore, it appears, at least in some respects historically wrong. See, for example, H. S. Bender's 'Outside Influences on Mennonite Thought', *Mennonite Life*, 10 (1955): p. 48.
33. Jantz, op. cit., p. 14.
34. Ibid., p. 11. Ironic, of course, because the very Conference seems to be an attempt to hide it.
35. Ibid., p. 14.
36. Unfortunately, our denominational histories are too often 'hagiography' rather than history; more a work of filial piety than critical, analytical history.
37. Delbert Wiens, *New Wineskins for Old Wine: A Study of The Mennonite Brethren Church*, (Kansas: Mennonite Brethren Publishing House, 1965), p. 14.
38. Ibid., p. 14.
39. See, for example, Delbert Wiens, 'Incarnation and Ideal: The Story of a Truth Becoming Heresy', in Paul Toews (ed.), *Pilgrims and Strangers. Essays in Mennonite Brethren History* (Fresno, California, 1977), pp. 28–51.
40. Leo Driedger, 'Canadian Mennonite Urbanism: Ethnic Villagers or Metropolitan Remnant?' *MQR*, 49 (1975): p. 232.
41. Ibid., p. 237.
42. Bender, op. cit., 1955.
43. Paul Peachy, 'Identity Crisis Among American Mennonites', *MQR*, 42 (1968): 243–59.
44. C. Norman Kraus, 'Re-examining Mennonite Reality: Shapes and Meanings of the Future', *MQR*, 52 (1978): 156–64. The same theme can be found in J. Howard Kauffman and Leland Harder, *Anabaptists Four Centuries Later*, (Scottdale, Pa: Herald Press, 1975) and in several contributions to *Call to Faithfulness: Essays in Canadian Mennonite Studies* Henry Poettcker and Rudy A. Regehr (eds), (Winnipeg: Canadian Mennonite Bible College, 1972).
45. Leo Driedger, 'The Anabaptist Identification Ladder: Plain-Urbane Continuity in Diversity,' *MQR*, 51 (1978): p. 291.
46. Ibid., p. 291.
47. Robert Friedmann, 'Anabaptism and Protestantism', *MQR*, 24 (1950): 12–24. Indeed, it is because of this perception of the Anabaptists/ Mennonites that Friedmann became a Christian: see Walter Klaassen, 'Robert Friedmann as Historian', *MQR*, 48 (1974): pp. 127–8; and Robert Friedmann, 'My Way to the Mennonites', *Mennonite Life*, 17 (1962): 136–9.
48. Walter Klaassen. 'The Nature of the Anabaptist Protest', *MQR*, 45 (1971): 291–311.
49. Ibid., p. 296.

50. Ibid, pp. 296–7.
51. John Howard Yoder, 'A Summary of the Anabaptist Vision', chapter 8 in Cornelius J. Dyck (ed.), *An Introduction to Mennonite History* (Scottdale, Pa., Herald Press, 1967), pp. 103–11.
52. Ibid., pp. 104–5.
53. George M. Marsden, 'From Fundamentalism to Evangelicalism: A Historical Analysis,' in David F. Wells and John W. Woodbridge (eds), *The Evangelicals* (Nashville: Abingdon Press, 1975), pp. 122–42.
54. James Barr, *Fundamentalism* (London: SCM Press, 1977).
55. Ibid. See especially 'Conservative Biblical Scholarship', (chapter 5).
56. Ibid., p. 342.
57. See Martin E. Marty 'Tensions within Contemporary Evangelicalism: A Critical Appraisal', in Wells and Woodbridge, op. cit. See also Gerhard Lenski's *The Religious Factor: A Sociologist's Inquiry* (Garden City: Doubleday, 1963). Lenski there defends his views on Catholic education against Andrew M. Greeley. Lenski maintains that Catholic education is not anti-intellectualist but goes on to claim that Catholics have adopted a 'variant form of intellectualism'. I think his thesis weak and would suggest it is both variant and deviant. The discussion in the remainder of this chapter will begin to show some of the reasons why.
58. Richard J. Mouw, 'Evangelicals in Search of Maturity', *Theology Today*, 35 (1978), p. 44. Mouw, however, does not think that this need necessarily be the case.
59. Barr, op. cit., p. 343.
60. C. J. Cadoux, *The Case for Evangelical Modernism* (London: Hodder & Stoughton, 1938). There is much to be learned from the spirit in which this little book is written.
61. Ibid., p. 17.
62. Barr, op. cit., p. 344.
63. See, for example, Victor Peters, *All Things Common: The Hutterian Way of Life* (New York: Harper & Row, 1965), p. 130.
64. J. H. Redekop, 'The Cult of Intellectualism', *M. B. Herald*, 3 October (1969).
65. W. W. Bartley, *The Retreat to Commitment* (New York: Alfred A. Knopf, 1962).
66. Ibid., p. 215.
67. D. Wiebe, '"Comprehensively Critical Rationalism" and Commitment,' *Philosophical Studies*, 21 (1973): 186–201. See also my 'Is Religious Belief Problematic?' *Christian Scholar's Review*, 7 (1977): 22–35. Both essays are reprinted in this volume (Chapters 1 and 2 respectively).

12   COMPREHENSIVENESS: THE INTEGRITY OF ANGLICAN THEOLOGY

1. Ninian Smart, 'The Intellectual Crisis of British Christianity', in M. E. Marty and Dean G. Peerman (eds), *New Theology*, 3 (1966): 20–9.

2. Ibid., p. 20.
3. Ibid.
4. John Bowden, 'The Future Shape of Popular Theology', in R. H. Preston (ed.), *Theology and Change: Essays in Memory of Alan Richardson*, (London: SCM, 1975), p. 16.
5. E. L. Mascal, *Theology and the Gospel of Christ: An Essay in Reorientation*, (London: SPCK, 1977), p. 1.
6. Bowden, op. cit., p. 23.
7. Stephen W. Sykes, *The Integrity of Anglicanism*, (London: Mowbray, 1978), p. 5.
8. Ibid., p. 44.
9. Ibid., pp. 42–3.
10. Ibid., p. ix.
11. Ibid., p. 78.
12. Ibid., p. 74.
13. Robert L. Wilken, *The Myth of Christian Beginnings: History's Impact on Belief*, (Garden City: Doubleday, 1972).
14. Van A. Harvey, *The Historian and the Believer: The Morality of Historical Knowledge and Christian Belief*, (New York: Macmillan, 1966).
15. Stephen W. Sykes, *Christian Theology Today*, (London: Mowbray, 1971).
16. Ibid., p. 34.
17. Ibid., pp. 6–7.
18. Ibid., p. 7.
19. Ibid., p. 8.
20. Ibid., p. 20.
21. Ibid., 23–4.
22. Ibid., p. 50.
23. Ibid., p. 17.
24. Ibid., p. 18.
25. Ibid., pp. 111–18.
26. Ibid., p. 8.
27. Ibid., p. 44.
28. Ibid., p. 52.
29. Ibid., p. 54.
30. Ibid.
31. Ibid., p. 8.
32. Ibid.
33. The terminology used here is that of Stephen Toulmin, *The Uses of Argument*, (Cambridge: Cambridge University Press, 1969).
34. This terminology is Harvey's, op. cit.
35. I use the phrase 'internal morality of knowledge' in the sense that Lon Fuller talks of the 'internal morality of the law'. See Lon Fuller, *The Morality of Law*, New Haven: Yale University Press, 1964).
36. The question as to whether there are moral values that supersede that of knowledge, however, is another matter. See, for example, Allen Wheelis, *The End of the Modern Age*, (New York: Harper & Row, 1971).
37. Sykes, op. cit., 1978, p. 44.
38. Wolfhart Pannenberg, *Theology and the Philosophy of Science*, (London: Longman, Darton & Todd, 1976).

39. Brian Hebblethwaite, *The Problems of Theology*, Cambridge: Cambridge University Press, 1980).
40. I have suggested elsewhere that an epistemology that allows such 'discretionary choice' is possible. See my '"Comprehensively Critical Rationalism" and Commitment', *Philosophical Studies* 21 (1973): 186–201 and 'Is Religious Belief Problematic?' *Christian Scholar's Review* 7 (1977): 22–35 – both of which are reprinted in this volume (Chapters 1 and 2 respectively). Further discussion of these matters with Dr R. Sykes has been immensely beneficial.
41. Sykes, op. cit., 1971, p. 18.
42. Ibid. p. 23.
43. Harvey points out, and I think correctly so, that the theologian since the Enlightenment is as much a doubter as a believer. Theologians cannot rest on the old authorities but neither can they rid themselves entirely of 'former beliefs' or, perhaps better, 'the beliefs of a former age'. See his 'The Alienated Theologian', in R. A. Evans (ed.), *The Future of Philosophical Theology*, (Philadelphia: Westminster Press, 1971).
44. Sykes, op. cit., 1978, pp. 14–15.

13   THE AMBIGUOUS REVOLUTION: KANT ON THE NATURE OF FAITH

1.   I wish to acknowledge here the critical and helpful comments on an earlier draft of this paper by the editors of the *Scottish Journal of Theology*.
2.   Karl Barth, *Protestant Thought: From Rousseau to Ritschl*, (New York: Simon & Schuster, 1969), p. 151.
3.   This claim appears odd in light of Kant's remarks, in his 'What is Enlightenment?', with regard to the autonomy of reason and his comment in the *Critique of Pure Reason* that 'Our age is, in especial degree, the age of criticism, and to criticism everything must submit'. (*Kant on History*, ed. by L. W. Beck, [Indianapolis: Bobbs-Merrill, 1963], p. 3, and I. Kant, *Critique of Pure Reason*, [New York: Macmillan, 1965], AXIa.) Kant's displacement of theoretical knowledge by faith, however, is not a displacement of the rational by the irrational for, as Barth points out (Barth, op. cit., p. 156), this move to faith is the result of reason's perception of its own limitations. Religion for Kant, that is, is seen, as Barth puts it, 'as a necessary phenomenon of reason' (ibid., p. 188).
4.   I have argued elsewhere that the generally assumed distinction between belief and knowledge in Western philosophy is not tenable. See my 'Is Religious Belief Problematic?', *Christian Scholar's Review*, 7 (1977): 22–35 – reprinted in this volume (Chapter 2). I shall be assuming throughout the critical sections of this paper, therefore, that *knowledge* and *justified belief* are indistinguishable.

5.   Cf. Kant, op. cit., 1965, A299, B539, A306, A307.
6.   L. W. Beck, 'Translator's Introduction' to Kant's *Critique of Practical Reason*, (Indianapolis: Bobbs-Merrill, 1956), p. XIV.
7.   Kant, op. cit., 1965, A297.
8.   Beck, op. cit., p. XV. Such claims would not be faith-claims but rather the claims of naive credulity. Such claims made upon insufficient evidence when evidence is potentially obtainable is simply intellectual dishonesty.
9.   It is important to note here that the second edition of the first *Critique* was published about the same time as the second *Critique* came off the press. We ought therefore to expect a good deal of overlap of the discussion in these two works and some change in the former due to the position taken up in the latter.
10. Kant, op. cit., 1965, BXXV.
11. Ibid., BXXV.
12. Ibid., BXXV.
13. Ibid., BXXVIa; my emphasis.
14. Ibid., BXXI.
15. Kant explicitly draws attention to the differences between mere hypotheses or assumptions and postulates in the *Critique of Practical Reason* (Indianapolis: Bobbs-Merrill, 1956). See especially pp. 142, 147.
16. Cf. Kant, *The Critique of Judgement*, (New York: Hafner, 1951), p. 321.
17. Kant, op. cit., 1965, BXXX.
18. This is the assessment of F. Ferré in his *Basic Modern Philosophy of Religion* (New York: Charles Scribner's Sons, 1967), p. 222 – an assessment which I shall criticize later in this chapter as slightly naïve.
19. Barth, op. cit., p. 161. H. J. de Vleeschauwer makes a similar claim in *The Development of Kantian Thought* (London: Nelson, 1962). He insists that 'for fifty years Kant dreamed and planned to establish that future of metaphysics, and for him to proclaim its downfall amounted to discrediting it temporarily in order to lay secure foundations for it. His complaints are directed against a particular metaphysics and a particular (philosophical) method.... To discover ultimately the correct philosophical method and by means of it to construct an eternal metaphysics were the aims cherished by Kant' (p. 2).
     A recent critique of Kant's argument by Peter Byrne – 'Kant's Moral Proof of the Existence of God', *Scottish Journal of Theology*, 32 (1979): 333–43 – I suggest fails to take this intention seriously and places an emphasis upon Kant's 'Critique of all Theology Based Upon Speculative Principles of Reason' that is not there in the original. I have more to say on this below.
20. Kant, op. cit., 1951, p. 324.
21. This is seemingly overlooked by J. Hick in his *Faith and Knowledge* (Ithaca, NY: Cornell University Press, 1966) in which he suggests that the reference to faith in Kant is 'tied' to the will rather than to reason (See especially p. 12).
22. Ferré, op. cit., p. 223.
23. Kant, op. cit., 1965, B499.
24. Kant, op. cit., 1965, B850.

25. Ibid., B850.
26. Kant, op. cit., 1951, p. 325.
27. Kant, op. cit., 1965, B851.
28. Ibid., B853.
29. Kant, op. cit., 1965, B855.
30. Ibid., B856.
31. Ibid., B662.
32. Kant, op. cit., 1965, B857.
33. Ferré, op. cit., p. 222.
34. W. H. Walsh, *Kant's Moral Theology* (London: Oxford University Press, 1963).
35. Ibid., p. 284.
36. Walsh, op. cit., p. 284. Byrne, op. cit. is similarly critical. Byrne, however, simply argues that Kant's position here is incoherent. The criticisms of Walsh set out here apply to Byrne with equal force.
37. Hick, op. cit., p. 4. On this point see also Ferré, op. cit., pp. 86–9.
38. John Baillie, *Our Knowledge of God* (Oxford University Press, 1939), p. 161.
39. Kant, op. cit., 1965, B833.
40. Kant, op. cit., 1956, p. 132.
41. Ibid., p. 132 (my emphasis).
42. Ibid., p. 134 (my emphasis).
43. Ibid., p. 133.
44. Kant, op. cit., 1956, p. 135.
45. Kant, op. cit., 1965, B859.
46. Kant, op. cit., 1956, pp. 5, 6 (my emphasis).
47. Kant, op. cit., 1956, p. 121. Space does not afford further discussion of this matter here. It must be pointed out, however, that Walsh's claim that Kant's pure moral theology is identical in essentials to the 'functional' view of theology expressed by R. B. Braithwaite in his *An Empiricist's View of the Nature of Religious Belief* (Cambridge: Cambridge University Press, 1955) is simply wrong, although it might apply, I think, to 'ecclesiastical' or 'doctrinal' faith as it is expressed in Kant's *Religion Within the Limits of Reason Alone*. (On this score it seems to me that G. E. Michalson, Jr. [in 'The Role of History in Kant's Religious Thought', in *Anglican Theological Review*, 59 (1977): 413–23] attributes too much value, so to speak, to doctrinal faith.) For a position somewhat similar to the one I adopt here see A. W. Wood, *Kant's Moral Religion* (Ithaca, NY: Cornell University Press, 1970).
48. Baillie, op. cit., p. 161.
49. Ibid. p. 161.
50. Baillie, it is obvious, had a profound sympathy for Kant's position but felt the change from traditional theology was not radical enough. Faith, Baillie wished to argue – particularly in his *The Sense of the Presence of God* (London: Oxford University Press, 1962) – is a direct, non-inferential but not non-mediated apprehension or awareness of God involving personal commitment. To see it as less, according to Baillie, would be to sell the 'revolution' short.

     For a similar understanding, see F. E. England, *The Validity of Religious Experience* (New York: Harper, 1938). I have discussed a similar thesis in my 'The Religious Experience Argument', *Sophia*, XIV (1975): 19–28.

51. Kant's preface to the second edition of the *Critique of Pure Reason* seems to state the matter in precisely this way; see especially BXXI and BXXII.

52. Byrne, op. cit., p. 334.

53. Ibid., p. 335.

54. Ibid., p. 335.

14 THE 'CENTRIPETAL THEOLOGY' OF *THE GREAT CODE*

1. Northrop Frye, *The Great Code: The Bible and Literature*, (Toronto: Academic Press Canada, 1982).

2. Ibid., p. xi. It might be noted here that the word 'theology' does not appear in the index of *The Great Code* even though it, and its cognates, appear on a variety of occasions in the text.

3. Ibid., p. xxi.

4. This assessment appears in the preface to the book and is elaborated by Frye in an interview with Andrew Kaufman, 'Northrop Frye on Literature' in *The Newspaper* (27 October 1982), p. 5. Frye suggests in the interview that had he written such a book in the sixteenth or seventeenth century he would have been 'burned alive'. In the eighteenth or nineteenth century, he claims, it 'would have raised a tremendous storm of irrelevant emotions' because the book sounds so uncommitted. I suspect, were his theological agenda a little less well hidden, it would do so even today.

5. Frye's assessment of the outcome in the conflict between traditional theology and science and analytical philosophy is obvious here. See, however, note 35 below.

6. Frye, op. cit., p. 77.

7. Ibid., p. xxviii.

8. Frye's structure here seems to retain a trace of Comte's famous stages of development in human thought – the theological, the metaphysical and the positive. It must be noted here, as well, that Frye also suggests that the Bible constitutes a fourth stage of language development, although his analysis of that stage is not at all clear or persuasive. The Bible is, he says, rhetorical but a peculiar form of rhetoric for which he uses the term *kerygma*. Its vehicle is myth and therefore it is not argument nor is it concerned with information. It is different from all three of the elements that emerge in the process of language development and yet contains all three elements – a statement that explains nothing. His justification for such empty characterization is that '[t]he Bible is far too deeply rooted in all the resources of language for any simplistic approach to its language to be adequate' (p. 29). And his description of that form of discourse, which I quote at length here for the reader, leaves one in little doubt that '*Kerygma*' does not contain

the demotic but rather stands over against it as an alien mode of thought:

> The linguistic idiom of the Bible does not really coincide with any of our three phases of language, important as those phases have been in the history of its influence. It is not metaphorical like poetry, though it is full of metaphor, and is as poetic as it can well be without actually being a work of literature. It does not use the transcendent language of abstraction and analogy, and its use of objective and descriptive language is incidental throughout. It is really a fourth form of expression, for which I adopt the now well established term *kerygma*, proclamation.... *Kerygma* is a mode of rhetoric [but] ... unlike practically all other forms of rhetoric, it is not argument disguised by figuration. (p. 29)

This is not the only problem, moreover, to emerge from Frye's discussion of the stages of language development. As my outline here will indicate, Frye at times seems to argue that there is a radical break between the metaphorical on the one hand and the metonymic and demotic on the other, while in other passages he maintains that the break comes between the metaphorical and metonymic over against the demotic. My discussion merely reveals that inconsistency without accounting for it, since, in either event, I argue that Frye holds there to be but two modes of thought that stand opposed to one another.

9. Frye, op. cit., p. 11.
10. Ibid., p. 16.
11. Ibid., p. 15.
12. Ibid., p. 21.
13. Ibid.
14. Ibid., pp. 15, 16.
15. Ibid., p. 6.
16. Ibid., p. 27.
17. Ibid., pp. 55, 174.
18. Ibid., pp. 29, 37, 41.
19. Ibid., pp. 81, 82.
20. Ibid., p. 37.
21. Ibid., 14.
22. Ibid., p. 61.
23. Ibid., p. 67.
24. Ibid.
25. Ibid., p. 76.
26. Ibid., p. 67.
27. Ibid., p. 229.
28. Ibid., p. 64.
29. Ibid., p. 218.
30. Ibid., p. 228.
31. Op. Cit., 'Northrop Frye on Literature', p. 5.
32. Ibid.
33. Ibid.

34. Eberhard Jüngel, *God as the Mystery of the World*, (Grand Rapids: Eerdmans, 1983), p. 3.

35. Frye's radical distinction between the demotic as concerned with information and knowledge and the metaphorical as concerned with meaning, as if two wholly different and mutually irrelevant language games were being played, is reminiscent of similar arguments regarding the nature of religious thought by philosophers under the influence of the 'later' Wittgenstein. Much of Frye's 'argument' seems to parallel the debate between the cognitivist traditional theologians and the so-called 'Wittgensteinian fideists' (i.e. noncognitivists), in the philosophical literature from the late 1940s to the present. His suggestion that one can play both 'games' – the metaphorical and the demotic – at the same time is however, not persuasive, for reasons I can only state but not elaborate here. It may be true that 'the metaphorical' is not scientific (epistemic or cognitive) in intention as is 'the demotic,' but it does, nevertheless, function as the only 'knowledge' the pre-scientific community had of the world in which they lived. To live in their metaphoric world would also have been to live in the only 'scientific' world they had. After the rise of 'the demotic', matters are considerably more complex for now 'the metaphoric' that 'doubled' as 'the scientific' has competition and it is not wholly clear that the 'metaphorical' can subsist alone. I presume Frye's appreciation of Paul Ricoeur's talk of 'the second naivete' becomes operative here, but, I think, to no avail. That argument cannot, however, be taken up here.

15 AN UNHOLY ALLIANCE? THE CREATIONISTS' QUEST FOR SCIENTIFIC LEGITIMATION

1. This is not a fault peculiar to evolutionary theory but characteristic of all scientific theory, as philosophers have often pointed out.

2. The terminology of counter-instances and anomalies is taken from T. S. Kuhn, *The Structure of Scientific Revolutions* (Chicago: Chicago University Press, 1962).

3. On this source see, for example, Dorothy Nelkin, *The Creation Controversy: Science or Scripture in the Schools* (New York: W.W. Norton, 1982); or P. Kitcher, *Abusing Science: The Case Against Creationism* (Cambridge, Mass.: MIT Press, 1982).

4. I have argued that matter in a recent essay, 'Religion Transcending Science Transcending Religion ...' in *The Dalhousie Review* 65 (1985): 196–202 (reprinted in this volume as Chapter 6), and so will not discuss it here.

5. Individuals have put up resistance and opposition to creationists for some time, but a collective consciousness has not, I think, until very recently, emerged. On this score, see the comments of scientists such as C. McGowan of the Royal Ontario Museum and the University of

Toronto interviewed by Jerry Amernic in 'The Creative Debate: God versus Darwin in the Classroom,' in *Quest* (April 1982): 23–8. A collective scientific consciousness, however, has emerged in recent years, as can be seen, for example, in the founding in 1980 of the journal *Creation/Evolution* edited by Frederick Edwords, an administrator of the American Humanist Association. As the editorial for the inaugural issue put it, the journal was designed to answer 'in simple but correct language all the significant arguments creationists usually put forth in their publications and debate' ('Editorial', *Quest* 1 [1980]). The group that publishes the new journal describes it as 'a non-profit publication dedicated to promoting evolutionary science'. (The situation with respect to the existence, or lack thereof, of a collective consciousness on the creation science problem depends to some extent on social context; there is far less of a collective consciousness in this regard, for example, in Canada than there is in the USA.)

6. See, for example, Kitcher, op. cit.; M. Ruse, *Darwinism Defended: A Guide to the Evolution Controversies* (London: Addison Wesley, 1982); and The Darwinian Revolution: Science Red in Tooth and Claw (Chicago: University of Chicago Press, 1979); C. McGowan, *In the Beginning: A Scientist Shows Why the Creationists are Wrong* (New York: W.W. Norton. 1983).

7. See Kitcher op. cit., and Ruse op. cit.

8. See, among others, Nelkin, and the material gathered by M. C. La Follette (ed.), *Creationism, Science and the Law: The Arkansas Case* (Cambridge, Mass.: MIT Press, 1983).

9. See here especially Kitcher, op. cit., and the essays in La Follette, op. cit.

10. See, for example, the essays in Roland M. Frye (ed.), *Is God a Creationist? The Religious Case Against Creation-Science* (New York: Charles Scribner's Sons, 1983); or Conrad Hyers, *The Meaning of Creation: Genesis and Modern Science* (Philadelphia: John Knox Press. 1984). See also, in some respects, A. R. Peacock's *Creation and the World of Science* (Oxford: Clarendon Press, 1979).

11. Sociologists usually talk of variant forms of rationalism. My hesitant use of the phrase 'deviant rationalism' is meant to point to two elements that characterize scientific-creationism as well as other neo-evangelical and fundamentalist groups. First, it is indicative of the deep concern such groups have for 'rationalist identity' and second, that that identity depends upon the maintenance of a fully consistent and coherent philosophical/religious framework of beliefs that is, however, built upon the adoption of assumptions and presuppositions that are very different from those found acceptable by the larger academic and intellectual community around them, of which they wish to be considered members in good standing.

12. The anxiety here referred to is a 'cognitive anxiety.' As already intimated in note 11 above, members of this kind of community wish to retain both rationalist and religious identity. Given the vast substantive differences between the two corresponding systems of belief, however, they attempt to retain both identities on a purely formal

basis, that is, by arguing that both rational and religious modes of thought have identical structures. Any apparent discrepancies of belief between the two systems, therefore, can, on formal grounds, be assumed to be merely apparent. (The circularity of this argument is obvious and needs no further comment. I have analysed its use in a particular historical religious context in my 'Philosophical Reflections on Twentieth-Century Mennonite Thought,' in H. Loewen [ed.], *Mennonite Images: Historical Cultural and Literary Essays Dealing with Mennonite Issues* [Winnipeg: Hyperion Press, 1980], pp. 149–64, reprinted in this volume as Chapter 11.)

13. For details, see La Follette, op. cit.

14. An example of this position, often taken up, is that of Bernard W. Anderson, 'The Earth is the Lord's: An Essay on the Biblical Doctrine of Creation,' in Frye, op. cit. Anderson writes: 'the biblical view of creation is not an effort at primitive science. It does not purport to deal primarily with the speculative question which lies properly in the domain of the science of nature' (p. 177). Anderson, however, does not appear to reject all cognitive significance of this mythic view and is not, therefore, a 'hard-line' poetic-creationist.

15. Conrad Hyers, for example, espouses a form of such poetic-creationism in his essay 'Biblical Literalism: Constructing the Cosmic Dance', in Frye, op. cit. However, see also Hyers op. cit., referred to in note 10 above.

16. Conrad Hyers writes: 'When one looks at the myths surrounding cultures, in fact, one senses that the current debate over creationism would have seemed very strange, if not unintelligible, to the writers and readers of Genesis. Scientific and historical issues in their modern forms were not issues at all. Science and natural history as we know them simply did not exist even though they owe a debt to the positive value given to space, time, matter and history by the biblical affirmation of creation' (Hyers, op. cit, p.100). A more general and less ambiguous statement about the non-cognitive character of all myth can be found in the work of Northrop Frye. On this score see my '"The Centripetal Theology" of *The Great Code*', *Toronto Journal of Theology* 1 (1985): 122–7, reprinted in this volume (Chapter 14).

17. This is, I think, the dominant position in Christian circles and is well represented in the work of Chicago theologian Langdon Gilkey and constitutes the dominant view of the religious objectors to the Arkansas bill on creation-science. See here, especially Gilkey's contribution, 'The Creationist Controversy: The Interrelation of Inquiry and Belief', in La Follette, op. cit., and his contribution 'Creationism: The Roots of the Conflict', in Frye, op. cit. (One might also read Gilkey's more comprehensive *Maker of Heaven and Earth: A Study of the Christian Doctrine of Creation* (Garden City: Doubleday, 1965.)

18. Gilkey, in La Follette, op. cit., p.135.

19. Ibid., p.134.

20. The religious/theological attractiveness of metaphysical-creationism, it seems to me, has given rise to a recent revisionist history of the relationship between the religious and scientific communities. The most

concerted effort in this respect is James R. Moore's *The Post Darwinian Controversies: A Study of the Protestant Struggle to Come to Terms with Darwin in Great Britain and America 1870–1900* (Cambridge: Cambridge University Press, 1979). (The position is already adumbrated in an earlier and brilliant bibliographical article: 'Evolutionary Theory and Christian Faith: A Bibliographic Guide to the Post-Darwin Controversies', in *Christian Scholar's Review* 4 [1975].) It seems that Moore takes the fact that some individuals hold both creation beliefs and evolutionary beliefs (whether argued or unargued does not seem to matter) simultaneously, as evidence of the compatibility of the two views; a psychological/historical fact, it seems, is mistaken for a logical truth.

N.C. Gillespie's *Charles Darwin and the Problem of Creation* (Chicago: University of Chicago Press, 1979), published in the same year as Moore's book, presents cogent arguments, which I make use of here, against the revisionist history of Moore and others. Moore has, elsewhere, recognized Gillespie's interpretation to be 'unimpeachable', but only from a positivist and Whiggish standpoint – see Moore's review of N. C. Gillespie's *Charles Darwin and the Problem of Creation*, (Chicago: University of Chicago Press, 1979) entitled 'Creation and the Problem of Charles Darwin', in the *British Journal for the History of Science* 14 (1981): 189–200. However, in a further note in his 'On Revolutionizing the Darwin Industry: A Centennial Retrospect', in *Radical Philosophy* 37 (1984), Moore has claimed, but not argued, that 'much can be said against Gillespie's larger interpretation' (p. 15). He simply remarks that it seems to him an odd conflation of Comte and Foucault and remarks, rather patronizingly, that his book will nevertheless 'remain a waymark in the historiography of Darwin's metaphysical beliefs' (p. 15, 16). Gillespie's book, however, is primarily a methodological one and its strength is the argument against the revisionists.

Langdon Gilkey (see note 17), and others such as R. P. Aulie ('Evolution and Special Creation: Historical Aspects of the Controversy', in the *Proceedings of the American Philosophical Society* 127 [1983]: 419–62), follow Moore in this, what appears to me, weakly argued judgement, quite uncritically. This concerns me, especially in light of a recent lecture delivered by Moore touching on this problem ('Engines of Empire, Energies of Extinction: Reflections on the Crisis of Faith', for a conference on the Victorian crisis of faith, at the University of Toronto, November 9–11 1984), although from a different perspective, that seemed to reverse the conclusions he came to in his 1979 study already referred to above (Moore, *The Post Darwinian Controversies*). And his argument in 'On Revolutionizing the Darwin Industry' seems to be the kind of justification needed for such a reversal – what he refers to as 'revolutionary historical practice' – that it seems (and here he quotes J. C. Greene, 'Reflections on the Progress of Darwin Studies', *Journal of the History of Biology* 8 [1975]: 243–73, and *Science, Ideology and World View: Essays on the History of Evolutionary Ideas* [Berkeley: University of California Press, 1981]) allow us 'to shape the past in light of some desired future'. Indeed, he insists that the historian's task cannot be merely this but rather that he or she must allow 'the present to set the agenda for constructing interpretations of the past that appear both more hopeful and more authentic than those by which historians flatter and condone the present' (p. 21).

For Moore, in fact, the future of humankind seems to depend on the success gained in this task – a somewhat ironic statement from one who criticizes Gillespie for adopting a Whiggish standpoint. (Moore's earlier work is perhaps more Whiggish than he perceived – see the telling critique of his thesis in the review of Moore's *The Post-Darwinian Controversies* by David B. Wilson in the *British Journal for the History of Science* 14 [1951]: 200–2.)

21. The titles of contemporary articles and books on the creation/ evolution question surely suggest warfare imagery, and with good reason. F. Edwords, in the inaugural editorial to *Creation/Evolution* (see note 5 above), is entirely 'on target' when he suggests that the new journal will assist evolutionists 'in this battle'.

22. See here my further argument on this score in the article referred to in note 4 above, as well as in my 'Being Faithful and Being Reasonable as Mutually Exclusive: A Comment on Shein's and Grean's Interpretation of Shestov', *Journal of Ultimate Reality and Meaning* 7 (1984): 166–9.

23. Gillespie, op. cit.

24. Ibid., p. 13.

25. On this topic see also Aulie, op. cit., p. 427.

26. See Gillespie, op. cit., chapters 7: 'Special Creation in the *Origin*: The Theological Attack', and 8: 'The Question of Darwin's Theism'; and also Aulie, op. cit., p. 435.

27. Gillespie, op. cit., chapter 7.

28. Ibid., p. 88.

29. Ibid., p. 125.

30. Ibid., p. 155.

31. This point is particularly important, it seems to me, in light of the use that Moore makes of A. Gray in his revisionist history of the nature of the relationship between the scientific and religious communities. See Moore, *The Post-Darwinian Controversies*.

32. Gillespie, op. cit., p. 108. It is important not to read back a twentieth-century logical positivism into Gillespie's use of the term 'positivist' in this quotation, or indeed, into his use of 'positivism' in the passage quoted on p. 153 (see note 34).

33. There is much debate over teleological explanations and the reductionism their rejection seems to involve that cannot be taken up here in the detail it deserves. In my comments here I have followed the position taken up by A. Rosenberg in his recent *The Structure of Biological Science* (Cambridge: Cambridge University Press, 1985). I have adapted that usage for another context (but which may be helpfully consulted by the reader here), in my 'The "Academic Naturalization" of Religious Studies: Intent or Pretence?' *Studies in Religion* 15 (1986): 197–203.

34. Gillespie, op. cit., p. 153.
35. Such metaphysical implications do require further analysis but that work must be left for another time. One might here, however, consult such diverse authors as, for example, T. A. Goudge, *The Ascent of Life* (Toronto: University of Toronto Press, 1961); H. Jonas, *The Phenomenon of Life: Toward a Philosophical Biology* (New York: Dell Publishing, 1968); G. C. Simpson, *Biology and Man* (London: Harcourt Brace Jovanovich, 1969); E. W. Sinnott, *The Biology of the Spirit* (New York: Viking Press, 1955) and also his *The Cell and Psyche: The Biology of Purpose* (New York: Harper & Row, 1961); and T. Dobzhansky, *The Biology of Ultimate Concern* (London: Fontana, 1971).
36. This is a phrase I have borrowed from N. Smart. See my 'Science and Religion: Is Compatibility Possible?', *Journal of the American Scientific Affiliation* 30 (1978): 169–76, reprinted in this volume (Chapter 5). (It must be noted here that the views expressed in this paper have been radically altered. I have expressed that 'altered position' in a paper entitled 'Incommensurable and Incompatible: Programmatic Comments on the Relations between Scientific and Religious Thought' [Read to the Triangle Club, Cambridge University, 6 March 1987.] Portions of this paper are found in 'Is Science Really an Implicit Religion?', *Studies in Religion*, 18 [1989]: 171–83, also reprinted in this volume [Chapter 7].)
37. For further argument to that effect, see Chapter 6: 'Religion Transcending Science ...'.
38. Lev Shestov, *Potestas Clavium* (New York: Henry Regnery, 1970), p. 64. See also my articles referred to in note 22 above. The point Shestov makes, and that I have argued here, is that perceived, although merely as a possibility, by D. Evans in his *The Logic of Self Involvement: A Philosophical Study of Everyday Language with Special Reference to the Christian Use of Language about God as Creator* (London: SCM Press, 1963). Evans is aware, that is, that if the cause of the universe does not bear some remote analogy to human intelligence, then creationist reasoning, of whatever variety, is not a possibility. He writes: 'We should realize ... that the teleological argument must be able to go this far, if there is to be any rational basis in nature for a biblical Creation onlook. If there is *no* reason at all for inferring a Designer from the order of the universe, there is no reason *apart from sheer biblical authority* for looking on natural phenomena as God's pledge or self-expression to man' (p. 263; emphasis is added).

Index